DEAR READER

DEAR READER

THE UNAUTHORIZED AUTOBIOGRAPHY OF
KIM JONG IL

MICHAEL MALICE

"When the word leader, or leadership, returns to current use, it connotes a relapse into barbarism. For a civilized people, it is the most ominous word in any language."

Isabel Paterson, 1943

Dear Reader: The Unauthorized Autobiography of Kim Jong Il
Michael Malice
Publisher information
Copyright information
Cataloging information
ISBN-10 1495283259
ISBN-13 978-1495283253

Table of Contents

Chapter 1

Korea is Lost

I remember the day that I was born perfectly.

Over the northernmost part of Korea towers Mt. Paektu. Its majesty has fascinated mankind for centuries. The mountains around Mt. Paektu are covered with whitish pumice stone, giving them a snow-capped appearance even in summer. Mt. Paektu itself is topped not by a peak but by Lake Chon, enormous and mysterious. Though many artists have captured Mt. Paektu's solemn and noble image, none have been able to communicate its soul. When the sun rises on Mt. Paektu, the entire expanse of Korea becomes full of vitality.

This ancestral mountain of the Korean people encompasses the entire nation's spirit—and it was also where I was born. Mt. Paektu is located at 42 degrees north latitude, and I was born in 1942. The mountain known as General Peak stands exactly 216 meters away, and I was born on 2/16. There are too many significant facts associated with my birth for them all to be a mere coincidence.

There was something mysterious about the weather on the day of my birth, like a wonder from heaven. Normally, violent snowstorms accompanied the mid-February temperature of around -40 degrees. But on the day that I was born, snowflakes began dancing like flowers on the summit of General Peak. The morning sun shone so strongly that the thick ice covering Lake Chon began to break. The cracking sound resounded through the mountains, as if the great fortune of Korea was gushing out from the bottom of the lake.

The greatest wonders of Mt. Paektu were at the base, where stood the secret base camp of the Korean revolution's central leadership. It was in that humble log cabin that I was born. My name came from my parents: The "Jong" is after my mother, anti-Japanese heroine Kim Jong Suk, while the "Il" came from my father. Father was not there to greet me on the day of my birth, for General Kim Il Sung was leading the Korean revolution. The labor that he was engaged in that day was part of a process far longer and more difficult. He was giving birth to a free, liberated Korea.

At the time of my birth, there was no "North Korea" or "South Korea." There was Korea and only Korea, and the idea of such a nation being split in half was an absurdity. Korea had been one unified nation for over 5,000 years. The ancient Koreans had lived on the same Korean peninsula since the Neolithic era. At the beginning of the third millennium B.C., the Korean state of Chosun was established by King Tangun in Pyongyang—the very city which remains the capital today. Indeed, Chosun was the first political state in the world.

Each state on earth has undergone a complicated formation process. Some were formed by merging two or more clans or races. Others were founded by a foreign conqueror. Still others were dominated and reigned over by foreign invaders, who were either repulsed or assimilated as history progressed. All of the other states in the world merged multiracial communities into one nation over a long period of time. Only Korea went through a course of steady growth as one single nation, maintaining her unity since the dawn of history.

The nation had a long and proud history under the Chosun dynasty, one of the longest-lived monarchies of all time. Not once in Korea's 5,000-year history did the Korean people commit aggression against any other country. Unfortunately, the same could not be said for her neighbors. Korea suffered innumerable acts of aggression from foreign forces over and over again throughout the centuries, with varying results.

As time went on, Korea's feudal government grew increasingly oppressive. The peasantry began to revolt by the end of the nineteenth century. Terrified, the authorities called in their Qing Chinese allies for assistance. Seeing an opportunity to strike, the Japanese invaded Korea under the pretext of "helping" and "protecting" the Korean people against the Chinese. They drove out the Chinese—but they never left.

In 1895, Japanese mercenaries raided the Royal Palace. There, they found Queen Min hiding in the corner of her bedroom. The Jap bastards slashed her repeatedly with their swords before burning her to death and taking King Min hostage. Now it was Russia, Japan's ardent enemy, who saw an opportunity. They rescued and reinstated King Min. The two states' growing conflict led to Japan unleashing the Russo-Japanese War in 1904, in an attempt to seize total control of both Korea and the northeast Chinese area of Manchuria.

The Japanese imperialists plundered Korea in the military's name. The Korean people were reduced to no more than slaves, forced to carry supplies and lay railways for the imperialist Japanese army. In the process, thousands upon thousands of Koreans were killed by Japanese soldiers. Those who weren't worked to death were instead shot at the slightest provocation.

The Jap devils successfully achieved their goal, driving out all the Chinese and Russian forces from the Korean peninsula. Japan then proclaimed a "treaty" with Korea in 1905. The king of Korea refused to sign the document, but there was nothing else that he could do. The Japs took control of Korea's internal affairs and imposed their own rule, depriving Korea of any diplomatic rights. Korea was no longer an independent nation, but instead a colony completely ruled by Japan.

The following decade was a period of ordeals, darkness and starvation for the Korean nation. The country was reduced to a huge prison, with a terrorist administration unseen since the medieval era. As the popular saying goes: "ruined people are little better than a dog in a house of grief." The people were forced into absolute submission and deprived of all their freedoms, including freedom of speech, assembly and association. The natural beauty of the Korean homeland was mercilessly downtrodden by the military jackboots and cannon wheels of Japan. Korea became a hell on earth.

Internationally, Korea was regarded as a weak nation and mocked as a backward feudal state. In 1907, for example, the world community held their second international peace conference in the Hague. The Korean envoy was refused the right to participate, which drove the man to commit suicide by disembowelment. If any salvation was going to come for Korea, it wouldn't be coming from abroad. It would have to come from the Korean people themselves.

The Korean people attempted to fight back under the auspices of the anti-Japanese Righteous Volunteers movement. The Righteous Volunteers successfully demonstrated that the patriotic spirit of the Korean nation still thrived. But they were unorganized and lacked weaponry, tactics and strategy. They couldn't withstand the Japanese offensives, and their struggle ended in failure.

Learning from such mistakes, my grandfather Kim Hyong Jik and several other independence campaigners organized the Korean National Association on March 23, 1917 in Pyongyang. This underground revolutionary organization drew its membership from people from all walks of life: workers, peasants, teachers, students, soldiers, merchants and artisans. In order to maintain secrecy, the KNA only admitted carefully selected and well-prepared patriots. Its documents were compiled in cipher, and they used code words for communications between its members. Yet despite all these precautions, the Japanese imperialists managed to conduct a crackdown on the secret organization in the autumn of 1917. More than 100 people were arrested, including my grandfather—and though he was only five years old, Father was there to witness the whole thing.

It seemed as if the Korean people were doomed to an eternity of torment. Later uprisings, like those of March 1, 1919 and June 10, 1926, were also brutally suppressed, with many Koreans bayoneted in the street. The Korean people couldn't win, because a mass of people without a leader is no more than a crowd. They desperately wished for an outstanding revolutionary leader to come, someone who could lead them to victory over the Jap bastards.

The answer to the Korean people's most heartfelt wish came in the form of my father: Kim Il Sung.

I didn't fall asleep to bedtime stories when I was a baby. No, I was raised on my mother telling me all about Father and his upbringing. These weren't mere family tales intended to increase bonds between father and son. What Mother wanted to do was to foster my conscious and purposeful loyalty to Father as a political leader. She taught me about the validity of the revolutionary cause and its inevitable victory. She described the glory and happiness of fighting for the cause. She inculcated in me a sense of devotion, a self-sacrificing spirit and a sense of responsibility, qualities necessary for the attainment of the cause. Most importantly, she wanted me to follow in Father's revolutionary footsteps when I grew up

"Your father was born as Kim Song Ju on April 15, 1912 in Mangyong-dae, Pyongyang," she told me. "One day, when he was a very little boy, he climbed an ash tree outside his house. Then he reached his arms out as far as he could so that he could catch the rainbow. That's how ambitious, good-hearted and virtuous the General was, even as a child only several years older than you."

It had always been clear to Grandfather that Father was not a regular child, for even in his youth he was full of revolutionary consciousness. Father honed his marksmanship skills by shooting Jap policemen in the eyes with a slingshot. Father despised the landlords who were oppressing the Korean people, and he resented the Christian missionaries who preached "turning the other cheek"—a surefire way for a nation to fall. Father always gave a hard time to the children of such types, never passing up an opportunity to shove them into the Daedong River.

When Grandfather was released from prison in 1918, he took Father with him to live in Manchuria, then the seat of revolutionary activity. After several years, it became clearer and clearer to Grandfather that a great destiny awaited his son. "The wealthy landowners are sending their sons abroad to study," he told Father in 1923. "They believe that the United States or Japan are the places where one should seek modern civilization and education. But I believe in Korea, and that a man of Korea should have a good knowledge of his nation. You must experience the misery that the Korean people are living. Go study in Korea from now on. Then you will know what you need to do."

Only eleven years of age, Father walked 1,000 *ri* (250 miles) back to Mangyongdae. This journey of learning taught him much about how the Korean people were being exploited. After two years of study, he heard that Grandfather had been arrested once again, and felt that enough was enough. Standing at the gate to his family home, Father took one last look at the place where he'd been born. "I won't return," he vowed, "until my country has been liberated from the Jap bastards!"

In early 1925, Father began a 1,000 *ri* journey for national liberation back to Manchuria. Much of his trip was through steep mountains, where wild beasts roamed freely even during the day. But though he was not yet thirteen years old, Father had no fear. Eventually he came to the

Amnok River that bordered Korea and Manchuria. Without a moment's hesitation, he crossed the river by walking on fallen leaves and officially began his quest to liberate his motherland. When Grandfather passed away in 1926, Father was more determined than ever to complete the mission that his own father had begun.

Once in Manchuria, Father discovered that the Korean revolution was under the command of the communists and the nationalists. To his dismay, both groups were more interested in trying to control a tiny movement than in uniting the people. Father knew that it was the masses who were the masters of the revolution, not some faction. For a revolution to work, revolutionaries needed to go into the masses to educate them, organize them and arouse them into revolutionary struggle. Mother always stressed this last point repeatedly. Some thought revolution was inevitable, but it was very clear that Mother felt otherwise. Without Father, she insisted, it would have been the same failed rebellions over and over again.

ON REVOLUTION

Dictators often use the word "revolution" to justify their acts. But suppressing and even murdering honest people cannot be justified by the term. Regardless of their form and character, any historical acts pervaded with a disregard for man can only be counter-revolutionary. Westerners don't like to speak of revolution, understanding it to mean overthrowing and destruction. Yet revolution isn't simply a violent struggle. It's a historical movement designed for the love of the popular masses, a process of constant reform on their behalf.

On June 30, 1930, after years of organizing, Father was finally ready to set out his strategy for reclaiming Korea from the evil Japanese. He convened a meeting of leading cadres in Kalun and mapped out what he foresaw as the precise course of the Korean revolution. Father emphasized that the revolution had to be carried out on one's own responsibility and with one's own conviction, without asking for approval or directives from others. To suit the Korean situation, the Korean revolution needed to be carried out by Koreans themselves at all times. This was a great idea, and it was an unprecedented idea.

It was the Juche idea.

"Korea has been conquered through Japan's force of arms," Father went on, "and that is how she will be freed. Rioting and demonstrations are all well and good, but the Japanese oppression calls for armed struggle. Violence should be countered with violence, and arms should be countered with arms."

Many of the cadres were concerned. The Japs had far more men and far greater technology. They pointed out that armed struggle seemed like suicide—and they were right. Direct armed struggle *would* have been suicide. Yet there was one method by which a small number of men could defeat a larger, more powerful foe: guerrilla warfare.

In 1932, at the age of twenty, Father organized what would become the Korean People's Revolutionary Army. At that time, there was no liberated zone anywhere in Korea, nor was there any foreign assistance. No rich man offered war funds. Not a single missionary provided support. Yet none of that mattered. Father believed in the Korean people, and so he and his guerrillas organized the masses themselves. They helped farmers, sweeping their backyards and splitting firewood. They worked on the farms, conducting political education in plain words. Activists carried mimeograph machines on their backs, printing publications. Wherever they went, the guerrillas actively developed political work among the people. And whenever they could, they fought the Jap bastards.

Under Father's leadership, the KPRA became a powerful force in a few short years. His brilliant knowledge and indomitable iron will were unprecedented in the history of world military affairs. His Juche-oriented strategy and superb command were wholly original, with nothing like them to be found in any book on military science anywhere in any era. The guerrillas wrested weapons from the enemy and armed themselves with them. Making the most of their familiar terrain, the KPRA frustrated the Japanese imperialists at every turn. Father's men grew so fond of him that they renamed him "Kim Il Sung," meaning "the sun to come." His new name reflected the people's desire that he become Korea's savior, shining across the entire peninsula.

In 1936, General Kim Il Sung and the KPRA built their secret headquarters at the foot of Mt. Paektu. Now they had a base from which to launch attacks, which they constantly did. On a localized level, such successful skirmishes destroyed the myth of Japanese invincibility—which was replaced by the myth of General Kim Il Sung. The people began to say that he was gifted with second sight, that he applied a magical method of contracting space, that he was a commander sent from heaven to liberate Korea. But due to the strict news blackout imposed by the Japs, his military successes were never established as the truth. In fact, the Japanese censorship was so successful and pervasive that no contemporary accounts of General Kim Il Sung's activities exist.

Though the people believed in General Kim Il Sung and desperately wanted the KPRA to win, after three decades of Japanese rule many still believed that victory was impossible. The Japanese were simply too strong. The guerrillas needed to demonstrate that they could actually accomplish what they had set out to.

Then came Pochonbo.

Whenever Mother mentioned the town's name, her entire body tensed with excitement. To hear her discuss the battle was to actually be there on that historic day. On June 3, 1937 the main KPRA unit broke through the enemy's border guards outside Pochonbo. They organized and planned and waited, watching the town from atop a hill. The following night, at precisely 10 p.m., General Kim Il Sung fired his pistol into the air. The gunshot was a greeting to the Korean motherland—and a challenge to the Japanese imperialists who were about to be punished.

At the sound of his signal, the KPRA soldiers started their attack. In an instant, the police substation was destroyed and set ablaze. The raging fire quickly spread, consuming the Japanese edifices of oppression one after another. The subcounty office fell first, followed by the forest protection office, the fire station and the post office. Soon Pochonbo was a sea of flames.

The Pochonbo victory shook the colonial ruling system to its very foundation. Prior to that night, the Japanese imperialists had bragged that there wouldn't be any more "disturbances" in Korea. They believed that they had everything under complete and utter control—until the large KPRA force brazenly swept away the enemy's ruling machinery. The haystack that the Japs had been carefully building for decades went up in flames in a single instant. The light it gave off—the light of national liberation—blazed over the Korean peninsula.

After Pochonbo, everyone in Korea knew that General Kim Il Sung and his army had come to set the nation free. The people looked up to him with unbounded respect and reverence, while the Jap imperialists trembled with uneasiness at the mention of his name. The Korean revolution was no longer a mere guerrilla struggle. This was war, and it was the first national-liberation war in colonial countries in world history. Publicly humiliated and running scared, the Japs responded with ever-increasing brutality. A bounty was placed on General Kim Il Sung's head, one that grew larger and larger as the Japanese desperation grew.

Then the crafty Jap bastards changed their plan. It was no longer enough for them to simply rule, exploit and enslave the Korean people. Now they tried to destroy the very idea of Korea itself. Korea has always been a homogenous nation that hated assimilation with alien countries and took pride in her pure blood. The Jap propagandists began to spread the lie that Koreans shared the same ancient progenitor and bloodline as the Japanese themselves. They claimed that both peoples belonged to one "imperial" race. Their dominant slogan was "Japan and Korea as one body!" The Japs forced every Korean to take a Japanese name, and introduced the alien religion of Shinto into the Korean nation.

In a final humiliating attempt at domination, the Japs even outlawed the Korean language itself. Schools became taught exclusively in Japanese, and a nationwide campaign was launched to "encourage" the Korean people to abandon their language of thousands of years. Korean news-papers were outlawed. Mass media, literary works and music: all were subverted for the purpose of disseminating Japanese. Those who studied Korean were arrested, imprisoned or killed. The Japs' scheme to exter-minate the language was an unprecedented threat to the Korean culture.

Sensing a final victory in their grasp, in late 1938 the Japanese sent an unprecedented number of their men to find General Kim Il Sung and the KPRA—and to exterminate them once and for all. As the Japs threw everything they had against the guerillas, the men began an Arduous March to safety. During this hard trek, the guerillas fought tight battles against the enemy almost every day, sometimes more than twenty battles a day. Worse, an unusually heavy snowfall completely covered the moun-tains and made travel near-impossible. In some places the soldiers rolled on the ground to make a path; in others, they had to tunnel through. The guerrillas' boots grew so worn that the soles began to come off. Their torn uniforms exposed their bodies to temperatures that often hit -40 degrees. Yet the KPRA could not stop even for an instant, or else they would be set upon and killed on the spot.

As the march progressed, General Kim Il Sung employed a variety of tactics suited to the rising challenges. He combined large-unit action with small-unit operation. He concentrated and dispersed forces, using both zigzag and telescope tactics. As the KPRA battled the elements and the demon Japs, another foe emerged: hunger. Marching through deep forest, the guerrillas' meals consisted of handfuls of corn or a few spoonfuls of parched-rice flour. When those reserves were consumed, they choked down grass roots and the bark of trees. Soon even those were not available; there was only snow to allay their hunger. The men collapsed one after another, exhausted from fighting ceaseless battles without food or rest.

General Kim Il Sung did what he could to inspire his men onward. "Please think of the homeland at every step!" he implored. "Never forget that you bear the destiny of the country on your shoulders. Brace up, a little more. Just a little more!" His warm care gave the soldiers the conviction and strong will they required to overcome this most severe trial.

After one hundred days, the men finally broke through to safety. The Arduous March was over, and victory was on the horizon. Rather than regarding the Japanese as invincible, now it became clear that it was the guerrillas who could not be stopped. It was no longer a boast that the KPRA could handle everything that the Japanese had. Each of the men had personally handled it—and they had survived. This filled them with great morale and a firm conviction to see the revolution through to the end.

Though the worst was over, there was never a moment where danger was eliminated; it only differed in degree. No one felt this danger more than General Kim Il Sung, for the Japs and their lackeys knew that defeating him would end the revolution and crush the spirits of the Korean people, possibly for good. During one skirmish, the General suddenly found himself tackled by one of his own men. Then, a shot was fired in the direction behind where he'd been standing. General Kim Il Sung was stunned, for he knew that he'd been seconds away from death. He moved to thank the soldier and compliment him on his marksmanship.

Yet when General Kim Il Sung turned around, he saw not a rugged guerrilla but a beautiful woman. "Are you all right, General?" she asked, scanning the trees for any other snipers.

"I'm fine," he said. "Thank you, Comrade Jong Suk."

Mother always claimed that she took no particular pride in saving General Kim Il Sung's life, but the fact that she repeated this same story so frequently and in such an animated fashion told me otherwise. In fact, it was probably the story about herself that she told the most. She was always far more interested in telling me about the General than in discussing her own upbringing.

In her own childhood, I learned, Mother had lost both her parents to the hands of the enemy. She soon joined the revolution, and venerated General Kim Il Sung as did all the other guerrillas. On the one hand, Mother was extremely traditional and deferred to Father in everything. She used to cut her hair, for example, and line Father's shoes with it. Another time, she washed his clothes and found it far too cold for them to dry outside—so she put them on herself and walked around in an effort to dry them out.

Mother insisted such behavior was a revolutionary following her leader, not a wife simply obeying her husband. She wasn't the weak submissive type that a stereotypical "dutiful wife" brings to mind. Known for her marksmanship, Mother was as comfortable holding a pistol as she was cradling a baby. She was just as much of a guerrilla fighter as any of the men in the KPRA.

Mother always discussed her relationship with the General in terms of revolution, not romance. But sometimes she couldn't help herself and the truth came out. The two were married in 1941, at the height of the revolution. Most newlyweds look forward to a peaceful beginning to the rest of their lives. But by the time they said their vows in the Paektusan Secret Camp, the war in Korea had spread to engulf the entire world. The Nazis and the Italian fascists were battling in Europe. In Asia, Mao's revolutionaries were marching against both the nationalist Chinese and the Japanese forces. Russia and the United States were in the mix as well. It was truly a world at war—and this is the world into which I was born.

On February 16, 1942 the cry of a newborn was heard from the log cabin at the Paektusan Secret Camp, like a baby giant's yell piercing through the ancient stillness of the mountains. That night, a new star emerged in the sky over Mt. Paektu. This lodestar was special in its significance. When a beam of light from that star passed by a place, the land turned out to be fertile. If the beam shined over a region, all kinds of treasures gushed out from beneath the soil in torrents. The scene into which I was born has never been told in any of the myths of any hero in history, both on this earth or elsewhere.

The guerrillas at the camp swiftly exchanged the news of my birth. They'd been wishing from the bottoms of their hearts that another hero of the nation would be born, someone who would embody the General's character, genius and virtues. As if by mutual consent, the guerrillas gathered around the revolutionary flag and pledged once more to fight for the speedy liberation of our fatherland.

The news of my birth spread rapidly, like a legendary tale. Political workers throughout Korea grew so overjoyed that they inscribed messages on trees everywhere they went. This didn't make the Japs happy, to say the least. The idea of a heaven-sent boy destined to bring independence to Korea gave lie to their myth of "one nation" unified forever under "one blood."

Several months after my birth, in June 1942, I was finally able to see General Kim Il Sung for the first time. The soldiers at the camp welcomed him in

> **BIRTH ANNOUNCEMENT, KPRA STYLE**
>
> "Twenty million fellow countrymen, the lodestar has arisen above Mt. Paektu, an auspicious sign for Korea's independence!"

delight, as he updated them on recent small-unit actions. Then he came up to Mother, cradling me against her bosom. The General took me in his strong arms, holding me close to his heart and gazing into my lovable face.

"We shall bring him up to be an heir to the revolution," he told Mother. "I want to see my son carry forward Mt. Paektu's red flag."

Mother couldn't agree more, and raised me accordingly. The battlefield that was Mt. Paektu had no blankets with which to wrap up a newborn. Instead, it had camaraderie. The KPRA women tore cotton out of their uniforms, each contributing a piece of cloth to make me a patchwork quilt. When Mother had duties, she handed me over to other women in the camp for safekeeping. I was even breastfed by other guerrillas on many occasions.

Some children spend their boyhood days pampered, living in an environment that nurtures in them a vague, poetic yearning for an unknown world. I grew up in an era of violent upheavals unparalleled in the thousands of years of Korea's history. Due to the revolution, my childhood was replete with ordeals. My young mind was dominated by the stark and solemn reality of war, destruction and violence. Day in and day out, fierce battles raged on. Any breaks in combat were filled with military and political training sessions. Everybody had to tighten their belts because of the training camp's supply shortages. Though the soldiers tried their best to obtain food for me, I often had to eat army rations or even flour-gruel as I got older.

The image I grew most familiar with was that of Mother in her military uniform, and the sounds I grew most accustomed to were raging blizzards and ceaseless gunshots. My childhood friends were battle-hardened guerrillas, my nursery a secret military camp deep in a primeval forest. My playthings were ammunition belts and rifle magazines, and my clothes were always impregnated with powder smoke. In those days, suffocating hot winds, biting snowstorms and strong rainstorms were more frequent than clear skies and warm spring breezes. I grew up amidst cold, hard reality: the reality of a fatherland which could be rebuilt only through struggle.

The world knew no one like me, bred on the field of fierce and grim battle, with so many family members devoted to the cause of the motherland and the revolution. I couldn't have grown up otherwise, being born on patriotic and revolutionary soil without parallel in the world. Can't we call this the will of history?

From my very infancy I was precocious and full of guts. In part, I was fortunate enough to be endowed with such qualities. More importantly, I learned the truth of life from fighters who had the strongest sense of justice in the entire world. The guerrillas' noble feelings became rich nourishment for my young mind; their mettle, as soaring as the height of Mt. Paektu, added flesh and blood to my manly personality. These brave men and women were the greatest that mankind had to offer—the precise opposite of the craven Jap bastards.

THE NAZIS OF THE ORIENT

Wherever they went, the Japanese troops engaged in murder, plunder and destruction. The Japanese committed every atrocity and every crime against humanity that their German counterparts did. Like their Nazi brethren, the Japs also experimented on live, human subjects. The notorious 731st Unit conducted such work in secret, tying prisoners to surgical tables and quartering their bodies without anesthesia. Those who weren't dismembered were subjected to germ-warfare experiments—once again, exactly as the Nazis did.

Yet the Japanese managed to do the Nazis one better. At first, Japan's soldiers raped or gang-raped women in occupied areas, often killing them brutally as well. The Japanese officers insisted that it was good for morale, claiming that "one must be able to rape in order to be a strong soldier." This attitude gave rise to strong anti-Japanese sentiment. Caring more about their reputation than the innocent women that they defiled, the Jap devils decided to draft women into becoming sex slaves—the first and only people to do so in history. Their victims of choice were the daughters of Korea, who made up of 90% of the total number of these "comfort girls."

The young men of Korea didn't have an easy time of it either. Japan did not let any "resource" go to waste in prosecuting the war. Nearly 8.5 million young Koreans—virtually the entire young labor force, a huge percentage of the 20 million total Korean population— were taken away to Japan, Manchuria and overseas areas occupied by the Japanese. The Japs detained such requisitioned Koreans in Nazi-style concentration camps. The Japanese worked the Koreans hard, with little rest, and without feeding or clothing them properly. Once a person was put in such a camp he would never come out.

> Sometimes the Korean workers tried to run away, unable to stand the harsh slave labor. If they were caught, they were subjected to unimaginably horrifying tortures. If they became disabled and thereby lost their value as laborers, they were buried alive or burned to ashes. But for General Kim Il Sung and the KPRA, Korea's entire young generation would unquestionably have been destroyed.

One day in August of 1945, I was surprised to hear the guerrillas cheering with excitement outside the cabin. Mother swept me up and put me over her shoulder, dancing around with her comrades. "Jong Il," she said, "the best possible thing has happened today!"

I didn't dare say the words. I couldn't believe what she was telling me. "Can this be?"

"Yes! Korea is free! The day we have been fighting for has arrived at last!"

With the destruction of fascist Germany and Japan's repeated defeats on all fronts, the conditions had finally become right for one last national Korean offensive. The KPRA's all-out attack began on August 9, simultaneous with the Soviet Union's declaration of war against Japan. General Kim Il Sung led his army in a concerted push through the enemy's border strongholds, at the same time ordering secret fighting units to rise up across the peninsula.

The KPRA units advanced like surging waves, working in close contact with the Soviet forces. Due to the fierce attack of the KPRA units and the all-people resistance, the Japanese imperialist troops were annihilated. One week later, on August 15, Japan hastily declared an unconditional surrender. Cheers of joy shook the entire nation. As the victorious KPRA advanced southward, people rushed from their homes to greet General Kim Il Sung. Forty years after its loss of sovereignty, Korea had put an end to her long dark night of stifling slavery.

Father was so busy attending to his great victory that he sent word for us to meet up with him in Pyongyang. It took two more months until Mother and I were able to make our way there, since so many of the travel routes were fraught with confusion. Finally, we ended up taking a freight car with the other KPRA women. After the hardships of the Paektusan Secret Camp, the lowly freight car still felt like quite a luxury to me. I wasn't sure where to look next as the train travelled through our beautiful motherland. I wanted to see every farm, every tree, every brave Korean that we went past. The villages put a bright smile on my face and filled my heart with joy. It was like I was living inside a fairy tale.

But inside the train car it was a different story. The proud KPRA women seemed more intense than delighted. "Why do they look so sad?" I eventually asked Mother.

She let out a deep sigh. "They're thinking of all our comrades who didn't live to see the homeland liberated. How nice it would have been if they were returning with us to the beautiful nation that the General has won back!"

As we approached Pyongyang the train sounded long, shrill whistles, as if it were to unable to hide its own excitement. When I caught my first sight of the city, I saw both the damage it had suffered—and the potential General Kim Il Sung always said that it had. But I was still a little boy, and seeing Pyongyang couldn't compare to seeing my father again. When we were finally reunited, I sat very quietly on his knee while my parents discussed all the work that had transpired.

"You know," Father said, "I've been meeting with important figures from Korea and abroad. I've been coordinating the transition to a free Korea, but the work has been very difficult. I almost found time to return to Mangyongdae to see my grandparents. I stood there at a fork in the road, wanting to go back, but I knew that my schedule wouldn't allow it. Family could wait, but visiting the Pyongyang Cornstarch Factory could not. The people must always come first."

"General, they surely know that you're back by now," Mother said.

My parents both laughed at this. "I suppose so," Father said.

"Why are you laughing?" I asked.

"I'd held off announcing my return to Pyongyang," explained Father. "But due to word of mouth, I couldn't delay the people's desire to see me in the flesh any longer."

The day prior, the General had attended an enormous welcoming rally. As he mounted the platform, the audience had cheered, "Long live General Kim Il Sung!" The entire crowd had been so moved when they saw their adored hero that every single one of them shed silent tears.

Then he had come up to the microphone. "The time has come," the General said, "when we Korean people must unite our strength to build a new, democratic Korea. People from all strata should display patriotic enthusiasm and turn out to build a new Korea. Let those with strength give strength; let those with knowledge give knowledge; let those with money give money. All people who truly love their country, their nation and democracy must unite closely and build an independent and sovereign democratic state."

"Manse Chosun!" they had replied. *Long live Korea!*

"Now we can go to Mangyongdae," Father explained. "You can see where I grew up."

All three of us got into a car and returned to the family home. As we passed the brushwood gate, I could not help but pause to touch it. Here was the same exact gate where Father had vowed to return only once Korea has been liberated—a vow that he had now fulfilled, twenty years later. The modest gate had been transformed from one of tears, expectation and waiting into a glorious arch of triumph.

My great-grandparents greeted us in their humble peasant home. thrilled to be reunited as a family. We all sat on the floor around the table as Mother filled the men's cups with sake, everyone trying to speak at once. "I've been fully rewarded for the hardships I had to undergo," my great-grandfather said, tears streaking down his cheeks. "I can meet my grandson again, who has returned as a general. I can meet his wife, who is fine like a moon. I can hold in my arms my great-grandson, who shines like the first star of the evening and brightens this house. Thank you so much! Those who have gone before me would be happy in their graves."

As my family began to reminisce, my thoughts turned to when Father had been my age in the very place where I was sitting. I imagined him walking to school, picking fights with the children of the landlords. I imagined him helping around the home. And I imagined his mind brimming with Marxist revolutionary consciousness, visualizing a free Korea.

"General," I said, "do you remember when you climbed the ash tree to catch the rainbow?"

Father laughed, and then so did everyone else. "Of course. I was younger then. It was a foolish thing."

"Is that tree still there?"

He thought for a moment. "I don't see why not," he replied.

"There's no need to speculate," my great-grandfather told me. "The tree, the house, the family: we are all here, just as when your father left us. We are all a little older, but still our roots remain in the same ground."

I stood up and pounded my chest, mustering as much pride as any three-year-old could. "I want to be like General Kim Il Sung!" I announced. "I am going to climb that ash tree myself!"

Everyone in the family applauded. "Go catch us a rainbow," Mother said with a big smile.

With a salute, I left the house and walked down the path outside. Only then did I realize that I'd made a mistake. There were trees in every direction, and I had no idea which one of them was an ash tree. I wandered up and down the lanes, trying to figure it out for myself. Then I came across a bunch of village children playing around a tree that seemed a little different from the others. "Hullo boys!" I said. "That's an ash tree, isn't it?"

"You're right," they answered. "It's an ash tree."

I walked over and quickly climbed to a lower bough. "When my father was a boy," I explained, "he climbed this ash tree to catch the rainbow."

I climbed as high as I could as the children looked on. Then I shaded my eyes with my hand and scrutinized the skies. If I couldn't catch the rainbow, surely I'd at least be able to spot it. But, try as I might, I couldn't see it anywhere. All I saw were dark, ominous shapes.

I scrambled down the tree—almost scraping my knee in the process— and ran back to the house. The children called out after me, wondering what was wrong. But I wanted to be with my family. I needed to feel safe.

As I ran into the house, I hugged General Kim Il Sung as hard as I could and buried my head in his strong, manly chest. "Did you catch the rainbow?" he asked me.

"No," I replied, shaking my head.

"Did you see it, at least?"

"There wasn't any rainbow to be found," I admitted.

"It's all right," Mother said, stroking my hair. "The rainbow isn't always there. You'll see it another time, I promise."

"There wasn't a rainbow," I repeated, "but there were stormclouds upon stormclouds upon stormclouds."

"Where did you see so many stormclouds?" the General said.

I pointed my little finger to where they'd been. "That way," I told him. "They're coming from the south."

Chapter 2

Korea is Won

The first American assault on Korea took place in 1866. In August of that year, the scout ship *General Sherman* sailed up the Taedong River. The Yankee bastards committed many random predatory and murderous acts as they made their way to Pyongyang. There, they met with the Pyongyangites—and their doom. Led by my great-great-grandfather, Kim Ung U, the Koreans used fire-attack tactics to send the ship to the bottom of the river, killing every American aboard. The *General Sherman* incident showed the Yanks that it would be far easier to engage Korea politically than to attempt to conquer her.

Because the United States was so interested in Korea, in 1882 the US became the first Western state to establish diplomatic relations with the feudal Korean kingdom. The Korea-US Treaty stipulated that the two parties would assist one another if necessary, including each assuming the role of mediator should some third nation commit aggression against one of the signatories. What the Korean people didn't realize is how easily the Yankee bastards threw their treaties in the rubbish bin when the matter suited them.

In 1898 the Yanks launched the Spanish-American war. As a result of their imperialism, the United States acquired Spain's control of the Philippines. With this, the US imperialists finally got their long-sought foothold into Asia. In 1905 the Yankees secretly met with the Jap bastards and produced the Taft-Katsura Agreement. Just as the Japanese and the Nazis would later plan to divide the world in half, this agreement kept the two imperialist nations' colonies safe from one other. Seven years later, in a blatant repudiation of the Korea-US treaty, the Yanks agreed to recognize Japan's claim to Korea. In turn, Japan would leave the Philippines alone.

With the Pacific War, America now turned its back on Japan. Though painted by the Yanks as an American victory, in actuality the Soviet Union sacrificed twenty times as many men as the United States did. For the Americans, the Pacific War was one of profits and not sacrifices. Of all the combatants, only the United States rapidly expanded its economy, on the only continent free from fighting, as the only nation to gain huge wartime gains while suffering minimal losses. The US imperialists then arrogantly proclaimed that this was "the American century." They did not merely want to dominate the world, but an era of time itself.

In the last year of the Pacific War, Japan had restructured its command system and divided Korea administratively across 38 degrees north latitude. Troops stationed to the north of the line were placed under the command of the Japanese Kwantung Army, while those to the south came under the command of the 17th Corps. This system formed the blueprint under which the Americans and the Soviets accepted the Japanese surrender. Any Japanese forces stationed in Manchuria, the island of Sakhalin, and Korea north of the 38th parallel had to offer surrender to the commander of the Soviet Far East Army. Those in Japan proper, the Philippines, and Korea south of the 38th parallel surrendered to the commander of the US Far East forces.

On September 7, 1945—a mere 23 days after Korea has been liberated—advance contingents of the US forces landed at Inchon, just south of the 38th parallel. The next day, 45,000 soldiers landed in Pusan, entering Seoul on the 9th. The US troops proceeded to occupy the entirety of Korea south of the 38th parallel, supposedly to disarm the Japs—implying that they would leave once the Japanese army was disarmed.

Korea was not divided when she won back her freedom in 1945. Nor was there ideological antagonism within the country upon which to base such a division. If any nation were to be divided, it should have been the vanquished Japan (just as her close ally Nazi Germany was). Two competing proposals for establishing a Korean national government thereby emerged. The Soviet Union, recognizing the ability of General Kim Il Sung, suggested establishing a national government first and then assisting it by trusteeship. The United States, on the other hand, envisaged a military government enforced by the occupation army, with a national government to follow "in due course." What "in due course" meant, when it would end and who would determine it were all questions that had no objective answer. Clearly, the actual answer was "whatever the United States decides." The United States wanted to dominate Korea while the Soviet Union intended to assist her.

Each side proceeded according to their own per-

THE JEWISH QUESTION

In the case of Nazi Germany, the object of its persecution was the Jews. Then and now, the Jews exerted a great influence in many spheres in Europe and the United States: politically, economically, academically and journalistically. The Jews made sure that their holocaust was not ignored, forcing Germany to apologize and pay indemnities for its crimes.

On the other hand, Japan's Asian holocaust did not attract international concern, and the Japanese government was not subjected to the same severe criticism. Its war crimes weren't dealt with as they should have been at the International Military Tribunal for the Far East. The Korean people, subject to discrimination as an inferior race, were not in a position to exercise any influence.

spective. In the south, America was desperate to maintain its foothold on Korea. If its air forces could take off from the Korean peninsula, then the radius of their action would include the entire Far East—a region of crucial world interest. Ignored the wishes of the Korean people, the US imperialists swiftly installed a military "government" in the south. This colonial regime, devoid of any political sovereignty or economic independence, was simply a tool serving the Yankees.

The US imperialists immediately began to turn the south of Korea into their private Asian military headquarters. They drafted "agreements" to build military bases and began to organize a puppet army. Their forces came from those who'd served in the Japanese Imperial Army in the past, men who had committed monstrous crimes against the Korean nation. Even non-commissioned officers were recruited from among such human dregs.

Finally, the US imperialists pulled one of their favorite tricks, one that they continue to use until this day. Whenever they conquered a nation and brought it into their empire, the Yanks installed some native figure as a strongman, presenting a facade of democracy and independence. This puppet would be exhibited as the duly chosen representative of his country, while at the same time being utterly and completely beholden to his American masters. In south Korea, that man was Syngman Rhee.

English-speaking, with degrees from Harvard and Princeton, Rhee flew into Korea on an American military plane. He advanced economic proposals notorious for their absurdly pro-American nature, and conceived of the Korean economy as an appendage of America's. He was considerably isolated from the Korean people for his reckless and incoherent political views.

Rhee was not selected because he had a huge base of support in Korea; he did not. Rhee was not selected because he was known for his leadership skills; he was not. Rhee was not selected because he had a strong sense of loyalty and attachment to Korea; he had none. He was selected for one reason and one reason alone: He was the one man in all of Korea who would publicly proclaim, "We contemplate a political regime like that of the United States."

In the north, however, things proceeded very differently after Japan's surrender. General Kim Il Sung formed people's committees, setting up the Provisional People's Committee of North Korea on February 8, 1946. The fundamental question in the anti-imperialist, anti-feudal democratic revolution—the question of power—was thus solved successfully in north Korea. During this period, the Soviet army had some troops garrisoned in north Korea to assist the nation's transition from a Japanese colonial hell to a people's republic. Since General Kim Il Sung and the people of the Soviet Union both took inspiration from Marxism-Leninism, there was a natural kinship.

One morning during the transition, I saw Mother pacing outside the house. Not understanding what she was doing, I immediately ran to investigate. "Why are you walking around like that?" I asked her.

"Hush!" she said, gesturing for me to come close. I saw that she was by the General's bedroom window, and she had a large stick with her.

"Is everything all right?" I said, quietly walking over to her.

"You know how hard the General is working for the people," she whispered. "He only manages to get to bed just before daybreak, and then soon he must be up again. Well, all these sparrows are a real nuisance. They seem to enjoy making as much noise as possible, and the more noise they make the more trouble they bring. If I drive them off, the General will have a sound sleep. Remember: It's important to do everything you can to assist General Kim Il Sung in rebuilding the nation."

"I understand," I said, taking her words to heart.

As the days went by, my faithfulness to the General only increased. Seeing that he relished clams, Mother and I gathered some from the Taedong River and brought them home in a handkerchief. We spread sand on the road which was used by the General's car, and burned wormwood under the windows of his bedroom to chase away mosquitoes. I picked wild grapes, northern kiwifruit and hazelnuts in thick bushes so I could put them on his desk.

But I didn't just want to help General Kim Il Sung. I desperately wanted to live up to his military legacy. So I began taking my wooden toy gun, and I dutifully brandishing it outside the General's office. As Mother passed by me one afternoon she did a double-take. "Why are you standing there like his bodyguard?" she asked.

"I'm also a bodyguard!" I insisted.

She came over and patted me on the head for a long time. Well, that was all the encouragement I needed. I thought I was a real, live bodyguard and took my role extremely seriously. Whenever I was in General Kim Il Sung's office, I always kept an eye open to make sure that there wasn't any trouble. So it was that I was with him one cold day while he ate a modest lunch—working the entire time, of course. After he finished eating, he stretched out his arms and yawned. "I'm going to my room to take a nap," he told me. "Will you be all right in here?"

"Yes, General," I said. Then I stood up and saluted. The General smiled in return, then went to his side room and closed the door behind him.

Soon after, a foreign military official entered the General's office. The man had many military ribbons pinned to his chest and was clearly an important and distinguished personage—but that didn't matter. I was still a bodyguard, and I had to do my job. I immediately stood in front of the door where General Kim Il Sung was napping, blocking the foreigner's way.

The man stopped short, confused. "Little boy," he said, "get out of my way. I need to speak with General Kim Il Sung."

"The General has just finished lunch and is taking a nap," I informed him. "You can't speak with him at the moment."

"Oh? And who might you be?" he said, with a stern look.

"I am Kim Jong Il," I replied, in a firm voice. "And no one is allowed to enter the General's room. Come with me, please." Dumbfounded, the foreign official followed me to a waiting room. "It's cold outside, so please wait here. It will only be a little while." I left him sitting there, and returned to my "post" outside the General's room.

Not long after, General Kim Il Sung got out of bed and opened his door. "I almost tripping over you there!" he told me. "Were you standing here this entire time?"

"Yes, General. This is where your bodyguard belongs, isn't it?"

"I suppose so," he chuckled.

"There's a man here to see you," I said, in my best childhood impression of professionalism.

"What man? Where is he?"

"I don't know his name, but I told him to wait for you."

The General followed me down the hall, finding the official sitting there just as I'd left him. The two saluted each other and broke into big smiles. "I see you've met my son."

"I have," the man said.

"Comrade Jong Il, this is General Shtykov. He's the commander of the Soviet army that is stationed in Korea."

"Thank you for your patience," I said. "It is a pleasure to meet you."

"Likewise," the man replied. "You have a fearless, bold and dignified attitude—just like your father. You are truly a boy general."

I looked up at General Kim Il Sung, and he was beaming with pride.

"My son is very special," he said. It wasn't merely a father boasting about his son; it was quite simply the truth. From infancy, I had learned words earlier than most children. I displayed powers of keen observation and clear analysis from my earliest years. I was also sensitive to nuance, grasped ideas clearly and was able to express my thoughts accurately. Since language is a means of thought, being precocious in language highly accelerated the development of my thinking.

Due to my faculty for creative thought, I regarded every problem with an innovative eye and exhibited an extraordinary perspicacity with regards to things and phenomena. I remembered everything I saw and perceived ten things when I heard one. I was so profound that all my utterances were original, novel and inventive. Once I began some difficult task, I was able to carry it to completion by my own efforts. Courageous and ambitious, I did everything in a big way due to my strong and daring character. Possessed of warm human love and broadmindedness, I was always generous, unceremonious and warm-hearted among people.

QUALITIES I DEVELOPED

Curiosity
Creative thinking
Manliness
Magnanimity
Audacity
Courage
Confidence
Willpower
Frugality
Simplicity
Modesty

I dreamed of growing up and one day providing the masses with a plentiful and cultured life, just as General Kim Il Sung was doing. Vast expanses of fields were now full of golden waves of crops, while factory chimneys belched smoke, towering high into the blue sky. The children of workers and peasants streamed into schools, with satchels dangling from their shoulders. In the evening every home overflowed with merry laughter. Young people competed with each other to join the glorious Korean People's Revolutionary Army, solemnly pledging themselves to prevent the enemy from depriving them of such happiness. The resourceful working people performed their assignments in high spirits, following the national economic policy. The new Korea was prospering, moving dynamically towards a bright future in accordance with the magnificent plan unfolded by the General.

Proud of what was being done in Korea, Mother often took me along with her when she visited new facilities. One day when I was four, she brought me to a farming district in Taedong County. We were walking along a footpath between rice fields when I saw farmers at work in the distance. I could hear them singing "The Song of Farmers" as they performed their tasks.

"Do you like that song?" Mother asked me. "They're happy because they're working their own lands for the first time in their lives, thanks to the General."

THE AGRICULTURAL REVOLUTION

General Kim Il Sung had wasted no time in implementing reforms. His first goal was to eliminate the economic foundations of the reactionary classes, beginning with the landlords who he had so despised since he'd been a child. Accordingly, he proclaimed the agrarian reform law on March 5, 1946. Any land that wasn't considered proper for distribution—things like orchards, irrigation facilities, and forests—would be controlled by the government. Any land owned by Japan, Japs, Jap supporters or other such class enemies was confiscated and distributed to the peasants. All debts owed to landlords were voided, and their land and property was also confiscated and distributed to the people.

The entire reform was carried out in under a month, a miracle. The General followed this up with measures such as the labor law, the law on the nationalization of key industries, the law on sex equality and measures for the democratization of judicial administration and education. Just like that, the anti-imperialist, anti-feudal people's democratic system was established in a very short time.

I didn't know much about the legal system and the changes that had been made. All I knew was that the farmers were singing and seemed happy. Still, they were sweating quite heavily as they hauled up water in the scorching sun. "Is there any easier way to raise crops?" I asked Mother. "Transporting so much water seems exhausting."

"For now, no," she admitted. "But I'm proud that you're thinking along such lines."

"When I grow up," I promised, "I'll free the workers from such toilsome labor." I knew that this wouldn't be an easy promise to keep. The situation was the same everywhere. When I visited the Pyongyang Silk Mill with Mother the following week, for example, I was struck by how terribly strenuous that work seemed as well. Eliminating such hardships would truly take a revolution.

After we visited the mill, Mother and I climbed up a hill and gazed down on Pyongyang. "Look how wonderful it is!" she said with a sigh. "Koreans used to live in single-story shacks. Now, thanks to the General's leadership, a city of tall buildings is taking shape. Son, you must build tall buildings for the people one day, buildings of 30 or even 40 stories."

"Mother," I replied, "I will build for the people houses 100 stories high!"

"I know you will," she said. "I know you will."

As quickly as Korea was changing, so too was our family. As the weeks passed, General Kim Il Sung began to have ever more issues to manage. His task of building a regular armed force, for example, made steady headway: the Korean People's Revolutionary Army developed into the Korean People's Army. And when my sister, Kim Kyong Hui, was born in 1946, Mother had to divide her time between the baby and her duties to the General. As for me, it became time to enroll in school.

I always went to class in simple clothes and rubber shoes, carrying my books in a wrapper just like all the other pupils. If I was ever offered boots or a satchel, I declined. "I like living like the others," I insisted. Even though I was only in kindergarten, I was already reading newspapers and magazines. I was also so extraordinarily talented in math that I was able to solve three-digit arithmetic problems very easily.

Like most gifted children, I had an enormous sense of curiosity. Once a question crossed my mind, I delved deep into its core and made the answer clear at any cost. I sought the help of my teacher in the rare cases where I couldn't work out a solution by myself. It seemed I was constantly asking her about something or other. "Why aren't there any black flowers?" I wondered during one lesson.

"Because it's harder for the bees to see them," she said.

"How do day and night and the different seasons come about? Why is the moon full sometimes but half at other times?"

"I can recommend a book to help you understand."

"Why does the wind blow, and why does it snow or rain? Why does the river flow? And does the sea flow, too? How do fishes keep their eyes open and breathe in water? Why do stones fall to the ground but balloons go up into the sky?"

She sighed. "Let's go to the library after class. I'm sure I can answer all your questions about the natural world then."

I smiled and then considered what she'd said. I decided to avoid questions about nature, so asked about politics instead. "When did man come into being, and how did society develop? How do landlords and capitalists exploit peasants and workers? Which is worth more: man or money? Why did the Americans come to south Korea?"

"Maybe you should ask your parents when you get home," she sighed.

It was the smartest thing that she could have said. My parents never faltered with any of my questions. Even though they were busy, they took the time to explain answers in detail so that I could get a correct understanding of complex natural and social phenomena. "If you have any more questions," Mother said that evening, after a very long talk, "don't exasperate the teacher. Just wait until you come home. Do you promise?"

"I promise."

The next day, I did my best to keep all my inquiries to myself. I kept quiet during reading, and I kept quiet during drawing. Then it came time for counting. "Class," the teacher said, "if I have an apple and I add another apple, how many apples will I have?"

"Two!" the other kindergarteners yelled out.

"And if I have a cake and then I bake two more cakes, how many cakes will I have?"

"Three!"

And so it went on, the children adding guns and chairs and anything else that they were familiar with. The math was far too simple for me, so my mind began to wander. I did my best to hold my tongue, but when the teacher went to move on to another subject I couldn't help myself. "Wait!" I said, rising abruptly. "There are cases when one and one do not make two, but make one."

It was so unexpected that the teacher couldn't quite follow what I was saying. "Um...when do one and one not make two?"

"When my lump of clay is added to my sister's, it makes a large one.

A large *one*. When I water the flowers, one drop of water on a petal joins another drop to make a large *one*. And if many drops join together, they make a still larger drop."

I was so exceptionally clever and bright that I had often surprised the teacher. But this was truly amazing. Here I was, a kindergarten student, seeing cases which contradicted and challenged such a self-evident truth as "one and one make two." This was something entirely beyond ordinary people.

The teacher hesitated for a while, not knowing how to respond. "Today," she said, "I have taught you the *fact* that one and one make two. And that is the end of the matter."

I was not at all satisfied by that answer. I sat quietly and patiently like a good pupil, but as soon as school let out I headed home as fast as I could. When I found Mother I told her what had happened. "So which one of us is right?" I said. "Me, or my teacher?"

Mother was moved with great surprise at my amazing question. "Both your thought and the teacher's answer are correct," Mother explained. "On the surface, your teacher explained a simple fact. But you have hinted at a deeper understanding. Sometimes, small things make one large thing when they are put together. Take the example of people's minds: When the minds of the many people who support the General are put together, they become a united force. And if all the minds in Korea were put together in such a way, it would become the greatest and most formidable power in the world. Do you see?"

I did see. Not only did I see the mathematical fact, but I also saw the sociopolitical implications behind it. It made me realize how important education was in shaping the minds of the people. Even a simple kindergarten math class could have profound ideological implications—for the better or the worse.

Yet I wasn't the only one receiving an education. All of Korea was being schooled in the nation's new communist ideology. Public discussions were held by Workers' Party (WPK) organizations, government bodies and rural communities. The masses' political awareness, patriotic enthusiasm and positiveness rose high. Selfishness, hedonism, immorality, laziness, bureaucracy, irresponsibility, mercurial spirit and other surviving traits of outdated ideas were exposed and overcome. Hostile elements, position-seekers and loafers were discovered and then purged. It was a time of celebration.

This pervasive sense of hope took hold at school as well. All the students decided to put on a play for our families. My class was chosen to perform a song-and-dance number called "I'll Become, I'll Become." One by one, we would sing what we would become when we grew up, ranging from teachers, doctors and scientists, all the way to musicians, workers and, finally, soldiers.

"You are the brightest student in the class," the teacher told me. "You should enter the stage first, singing the verse about becoming an educationist."

Something about that didn't sit quite right, but I agreed to do as I'd been asked. As the rehearsal went on that day, I grew increasingly upset. Then I realized what was the matter. "I won't participate in this play!" I announced.

The students looked at one another. It was grossly out of character for me to refuse to participate in any activity. "What? Why not?" the teacher said.

"I don't want to become an educator. I want to become a soldier of the Korean People's Army!"

"But that would mean entering the stage last," she explained. "Don't you want to enter the stage first?"

"What I want is for the soldier to enter first. Why should the soldier, who has the best profession, enter last?"

The teacher had learned how insightful my suggestions were, so she carefully considered what I had said. "You're right," she said, with a sigh of appreciation. "You're always right."

The order of the performance was changed beginning with the next rehearsal, with the soldier's verse now receiving top priority. The change in sequence emphasized my idea that the KPA is number one, but it also improved the harmonious flow of all the songs and dances. There was no contradiction between strong art and a strong message—especially when such things praised the military.

While we students were singing what we would become in the future, Korea herself was making the very same decision. What kind of nation should Korea become? Under the auspices of the General, the first democratic elections in Korean history were carried out in 1946, with ballots cast for all the provincial, city and county people's committees. No one was prouder and happier to cast her ballot than Mother. This is what she'd been fighting for all her life.

Over the following months, it became increasingly clear to all parties—the US, the Soviet Union, the United Nations and Korea—that elections needed to be held nationwide. Terrified of losing his unelected grip on power, in early 1948 Syngman Rhee asked the United States to hold a separate election in south Korea alone so as to consolidate his position. The US imperialists, delighted to abort their ongoing negotiations with the USSR, decided to push through Rhee's regional election by means of force. For the first time since the dawn of mankind, Korea was threatened with permanent national division. In response, General Kim Il Sung called for a general election across the whole of Korea, to be held by secret ballot on the principles of universal, direct and equal vote. He also called for the withdrawal of both the American and Soviet armies.

A fierce struggle arose, particularly in occupied south Korea. The US imperialists dissolved the local autonomous bodies of south Korea and the people's committees at all levels by coercive methods. They forced democratic parties and organizations underground. Loyal anti-imperialist Koreans were arrested, imprisoned, tortured and murdered. A general strike was staged by two million workers, and a revolt on Jeju Island in April 1948 brought out 250,000 people.

As a result of such unrest, the south's May 10, 1948 elections ended in failure. It was a "national" election only open to certain segments of the population living in the lower half of Korea. The Yankees only believed in democracy when the democratic process delivered a result that they approved of. In order to maintain their grip, the United States simply faked the election results to validate Syngman Rhee's puppet regime.

Faced with the danger of the country's division, General Kim Il Sung convened a conference in Pyongyang on June 29. There, a decision was adopted to hold a general election on August 25 in both north and south Korea. Frantic to cut off this democratic action, President Truman recognized Rhee's "government" as the Republic of Korea on August 12.

Despite Truman's assault on Korean sovereignty, the historic north-south general election was held anyway. In the north, deputies to the Supreme People's Assembly were elected openly by direct and democratic suffrage. In south Korea, for fear of American reprisal, the people's representatives were first elected in secret by the indirect method of collecting the signatures of voters. Then, the elected assembled in Haeju and held a conference to choose the deputies to the Supreme People's Assembly.

On the basis of this brilliant north-south general election, the historic First Session of the Supreme People's Assembly was held in Pyongyang in September 1948. The session proclaimed before the whole world the founding of the Democratic People's Republic of Korea, the only legitimate government for the whole nation. The DPRK Constitution was adopted and General Kim Il Sung was unanimously appointed Head of State, reflecting the will of the entire Korean people. It was a shining victory won in the struggle to build a unified, sovereign and independent state.

By the end of 1948, the Korean nation—which had lived on the same territory with the same blood from ancient times—had been divided into two. Though there were two competing governments, only one bore any claim to legitimacy: the government led by the new Prime Minister, General Kim Il Sung. He spent many nights worrying about the situation in the south, and Mother and I did all we could to support him. No one knew what the future would hold, but it increasingly looked problematic.

One September morning in 1949, Mother and I saw the General off as he went to deliver guidance at a factory. As she helped me shoulder my bag for school, I noticed that she looked very pale. "Are you feeling well?" I asked her.

"I'll be fine," she said, wincing in pain.

"I'll stay home from school today. You're ill. Let me help take care of you."

"Nonsense," she said. "I'll get better if you learn your lessons well. Now off you go."

"Why would that make you better?" I asked. "Promise me you'll go to the hospital."

"Fine, I promise. I'll see you when you come home, and you'll feel silly for worrying so much."

Holding back tears, I reluctantly left Mother and went to school as she'd requested. I couldn't concentrate the entire day. I was so worried about her that I rushed home the instant when class was over. I ran to her room to check up on her—but she wasn't there. That meant one thing:

she had gone to the hospital as she'd promised. Just because she hadn't returned home yet wasn't a cause for concern, I told myself. I resolved to stay brave, just as Mother would have.

My little sister Kyong Hui came into the room soon after. "Where's Mother?" she asked. "I want Mother!"

"She'll be home shortly," I promised her.

"But I want to see her *now!*"

I did my best to calm Kyong Hui. I played some games with her and read to her, and even managed to get her to fall asleep when it came time for bed. I knew that trying to sleep would be pointless for me, however. I stared out the window as time went on, expecting Mother to return home at any moment. In the middle of the night—I have no idea what time—I finally saw a car come in at the gate. I ran into Kyong Hui's room and shook her awake. "Mother is coming! Get up quickly!" I ran out to the porch, pulling my drowsy sister behind me.

My heart froze in my chest when I saw that it wasn't Mother who got out of the car, but one of her revolutionary comrades. The woman saw Kyong Hui and I standing there, and gave us a nod of acknowledgment. Then she walked past us to the sitting room. I followed her inside and watched as she took out Mother's best uniform. "Why are you taking those clothes?" I asked her. "Where's Mother? When is she coming home?"

The brave woman guerrilla wouldn't look me in the eye. "She'll come back when the day dawns," she said. "Just wait here for her."

"I'll be very patient." I sat there and waited with Kyong Hui, who soon fell asleep on my shoulder. Yet Mother still hadn't returned home by the time that the sun rose. I couldn't bear sitting around anymore. If Mother was too ill to come home, I'd simply take Kyong Hui and go see her myself. As I resolved to leave, I saw that many woman fighters and distant relatives of mine had started to gather in the house.

That's when I realized that Mother was never going to come home.

I looked in the direction of the hospital, unable to believe what was happening. Since the day that I'd been born, Mother had always been there for me and for the General. She came out to greet me with a smile whenever she heard my footsteps coming home. She could look at my face and know what I was thinking. "Mother!" I yelled, hoping there was some misunderstanding. "Mother, Mother, Mother! Come back!"

I was so upset that I began to stamp my feet in agony, loud enough that several mourners lost their composure. Seconds later, the entire household was in tears. The soldiers looked around at one another. Finally one of them came over and put her hand on my shoulder. "She's not coming, comrade."

"Why?" I snapped. "Why isn't she coming? She left Kyong Hui crying all night. Ask her to come back. She'll come back if you ask her, you'll see. My mother can do anything."

But the woman just shook her head. "That is one thing that she can't do, not anymore."

"How could she be so cruel?" I said.

"This is what it means to be a revolutionary," the woman explained. "Some give their all so that others may go on. That's how Comrade Jong Suk lived—and it's how she died, as well."

I hugged the woman and buried my head in her side, crying my eyes out. The following days were a blur. General Kim Il Sung rushed home, and the next thing I knew I was going with him to the assembly hall of the Party Central Committee. People came from all parts of the country to offer their condolences. But all I noticed was Mother lying in her coffin, dressed in her best military uniform and surrounded by flowers.

I watched the General stare at the display for quite a while. "Can someone bring me her watch?" he finally demanded. I could tell from his hoarse voice that he's been crying as much as I had. A woman guerrilla quickly brought over the watch to General Kim Il Sung. He took it into his hands and very carefully wound it up. "Comrade Kim Jong Suk had dedicated her whole life to the revolution," he told the woman. "I gave her this watch as a gift because she'd been so loyal to me during the anti-Japanese struggle. Let us send her off with it."

The guerrilla took back the watch and placed it on Mother's wrist. For a second it was as if she were asleep, raising her hand to be helped out of bed. I couldn't contain myself for another moment. I ran forward and wrapped my arms around the coffin. The woman gently tried to pull me away. "Come now," she said. "Be strong for your mother."

"Leave him alone," the General hissed. "Tomorrow he won't have any mother to wrap his arms around. And I won't have a wife." Very calmly, he took his handkerchief from his pocket. Only then could I actually see that he was wiping away tears.

After a dirge was played, the General took to the podium and spoke a few words. "Comrade Kim Jong Suk was most faithful to me," he said. "Everything she did was for the sake of her comrades, and she did nothing for her own self. I would say nothing if she'd lived in comfort, eating and dressing well even for a single day. What grieves me most is the fact that she passed away after suffering hardships all of her life."

After a few other speeches, everyone began to file out of the assembly hall. For a moment I turned to look back, but the General pushed me forward. Past the doorway I saw murky clouds covering the sky outside. Even the heavens were dark with sorrow, even the earth was soaked in tears, for Mother's untimely departure. She had only been thirty-one years old.

Hundreds of thousands of people filled the square in Pyongyang, gathering to bid farewell to the greatest revolutionary fighter, revolutionary soldier and revolutionary mother that Korea had ever known. The masses lined the entire route of the funeral procession, but I couldn't look at their faces as we rode home.

Eventually we came around the foot of Mt. Haebang and paused before our house. Then the soldiers who were lined up around the residence fired a 20-gun salute, after which the General gently ushered me out of the hearse. "Go look after your sister," he told me. "She's still very young and doesn't understand what's going on. I'll be back from the cemetery soon enough."

With a nod, I turned on my heels and walked into the house. Kyong Hui was crying when I walked inside. In truth, it felt as if she hadn't stopped even for an instant. "Brother, where's Mother?" she asked me. "Where has she gone?"

I hugged my sister and tightened my arms around her. "If you cry for Mother," I told Kyong Hui, "you will hurt the General and make him unable to work. If you miss her, don't go in tears to the General. Come to me from now on. I'll show you her photo and we can remember her together." Kyong Hui snuggled into my chest. My sense of loyalty to the General became maternal love, flowing into my sister's heart. To Kyong Hui, my embrace now felt just like Mother's had.

After I calmed my sister down, I went up to Mother's room for one final look. On her nightstand was a small pistol, perhaps the very same one she used to save the General from death. I picked it up and held it close to my chest. Mother had been faithful to General Kim Il Sung at all times, doing everything for the man with the heavy burden of building a new country. Now, it had fallen unto me to complete whatever she'd left unfinished.

A few mornings after the funeral, I was the one pacing with a stick outside the General's window. After about an hour of chasing away the sparrows, I turned my head and saw that he'd been watching me with great interest. "What's going on here?" he asked.

"Did the sparrows bother you?" I said.

"No. It was the fact that I couldn't hear them that woke me up. It sounded very strange. What are you doing with that stick?"

"Mother used it to chase them away in the morning so that you could rest."

"Then why do you have it?"

"Because Mother isn't here to chase them away anymore, General."

"Come over here," he said. I did as he asked. The General crouched down so that we were eye to eye. "You might still be small in stature, but you act like a full-grown person. I'll need your help in these coming days. Will you help me?"

"Of course." Then and there, I made a vow to hold the General in high esteem and devote everything for his sake, just as anti-Japanese heroine Kim Jong Suk would have wanted. Mother had died, but she wasn't really gone.

I was Mother now.

Chapter 3

Korea is One

On June 25, 1950, I woke up to a smell that I was very familiar with: the burnt bitter scent of war. I looked out the window and saw black clouds covering the clear, blue sky of the motherland. It had finally happened: the US imperialists had launched war upon Korea. My first thought was with the General. I hopped out of bed, only to discover that he was long gone. It made sense, of course. He would need to lead the war effort to victory. As agonizing as it was, all I could do was try to keep safe.

I kept listening to the radio in hopes of understanding what had happened. The news reports were contradictory and incomplete. That entire first day I was an anxious mess. I wanted to call the General and offer my help, but I knew I wouldn't be able to reach him. So I paced and kept looking out the window, waiting for the Yanks to rain death upon Pyongyang.

The following day, General Kim Il Sung addressed the entire nation. "Last night," he informed us, "the Yankees and their stooges launched a cowardly surprise attack while the people were still asleep. 100,000 soldiers penetrated two kilometers into the northern part of the nation."

It was a nightmare of nightmares. The Yankees hadn't lost a single battle in over one hundred aggressive wars. Many regarded the US as a dreadful and invincible being, a horned monster which made small children tremble. Yet there was one small child who refused to tremble at their name: Kim Jong Il. I knew how strong and heroic the Korean people were. Though it had only been five years since Korea's liberation from Japan, I was sure that we'd rise as one in the struggle against the US imperialists. We had a weapon far greater than anything America had to offer: the leadership of General Kim Il Sung.

"I lost no time in convening a meeting of the DPRK Cabinet," the General assured us. "I immediately issued an order to mount a counteroffensive to wipe out the invaders. The Military Commission of the DPRK has been organized as the supreme national leadership, with myself elected as its chairman."

To my great delight, all the news that I heard over the following days was entirely positive. The KPA had successfully frustrated the enemy's surprise attack, and began advancing rapidly on a counteroffensive. Within three days, Seoul had been liberated. Large numbers of students and other young people heeded the call to arms and volunteered to fight. Workers' regiments were organized in the major industrial districts and sent to the front. In a matter of weeks, the Yankees were driven to the very southeast corner of Korea to make their final stand.

I was so convinced of the General's brilliance that I thought that the war would be concluded there at Pusan. Finally, once and for all, Korea would be completely free of imperialism. But I was wrong. It wasn't that I overestimated General Kim Il Sung's skills. It was that I underestimated just how tenaciously the US imperialists were prepared to defend their war bounty of south Korea.

President Harry Truman then called upon the United Nations for assistance, blaming the conflict on General Kim Il Sung himself. To my horror, fifteen nations answered Truman's call. Now the KPA would have to fight against the land, sea and air forces of the United States—said to be the mightiest in the world—as well as the armies of its fifteen satellite countries and the puppet army of south Korea. Try as I might, I could not even imagine an easy, peaceful outcome.

On September 15, 1950 the Americans and their puppets succeeded in making a landing behind the KPA and thereby cutting off its supply route. An army can be the bravest in the world, but it's still helpless without access to weaponry and munitions. Despite having liberated 90% of south Korea, the heroic People's Army was forced to beat a temporary strategic retreat to delay the enemy as much as possible. Soon the Yankees penetrated into the northern part of the Republic.

As they occupied areas of northern Korea, the Yankees perpetrated the most brutal, largest-scale slaughter of people ever known in human history. As General Kim Il Sung put it, "Engels once called the British army the most brutal army. During World War II, the German fascist army outdid the British army in its savagery. The human brain could not imagine more diabolical and horrible barbarities than those committed by the Hitlerite villains. But in Korea, the Yankees surpassed the Hitlerites by far."

AMERICAN ATROCITIES

Scooping out eyeballs

Cutting off lips, ears, noses, tongues, breasts and/or faces

Sawing off faces

Skinning bodies

Sawing bodies to pieces

Suffocating by poisonous gas

Burning alive

Boiling alive

Burying alive

Disemboweling the pregnant

Trampling infants

Crushing with tanks

THE SINCHON MASSACRE

The US imperialists seized the city of Sinchon on October 17, 1950. On the very first day, Lieutenant Harrison, commander of the occupying troops, assembled all the overthrown landlords, wicked religious men, usurers, scamps and other human scum that were there. He issued them a declaration: "My orders are the law, and whoever violates them shall be shot unconditionally. Kill everyone mercilessly, old or young. Your hands should not tremble!"

Sinchon was turned into a hell on earth.

The methods of murder were so cruel as to make even beasts turn away from the sight. The villains pushed hundreds of civilians into an air-raid shelter and then set fire to it. They loaded Koreans into military trucks and drowned them in the reservoirs. In addition to the mass murder, the American aggressors also reveled in killing people individually. They nailed a model peasant's letter of commendation to his forehead and pierced his hands through with bayonets. Then they ran wire through his nose and ears and dragged him around the village for everyone to see. The American murderers did not hesitate to skin the heads of patriots and, following the examples of their Yankee ancestors, took the scalps away as "souvenirs."

Later that month, hearing of the American advance, the Chinese people organized volunteers and sent them to the Korean front. The KPA teamed with the Chinese units and began to launch counteroffensives. These units dealt a terrible blow to the enemy, making raids by relying on tunnels and applying many adroit Juche military tactics.

As the US imperialists were forced to abandon Sinchon, they committed one final atrocity. The troops gathered all the mothers of the village with their children. "It is too happy for the families to be together," Lt. Harrison proclaimed. "Tear the kids off at once and lock them separately. Let the mothers die in their anxiety about their children, and let the children die while crying for their mothers! Ha, ha! Ha, ha, ha!"

The American mercenary troops tore the babies away without any hesitation. The hills of Sinchon reverberated with their cries, and with the screams of mothers calling out for their darlings. The children and their mothers were locked in separate storehouses. The Americans threw rice straw on their heads, poured gasoline over them and set them alight. Then, to ensure that everyone was dead, the troops threw grenades inside. All that remained of the victims were their fingernails—embedded in the walls as they tried to scratch their way out—and the messages that they scribbled: *Avenge our death! The Americans are our enemies!*

With the assistance of the Chinese forces, the tide once again began to turn against the US imperialists. This filled me with enormous joy. Now, I thought, it was only a matter of time before they'd surrender. I was filled a certain sense of glee—but it was premature. One evening I was walking down the street when I heard some old men discussing the situation. They were terrified that President Truman, architect of Korea's destruction, was going to use nuclear weapons against our nation. I wanted to dismiss their fears as the prattling of elderly fools. Then Truman himself publicly threatened as much. "The use of any kind of weapons—including atomic bombs—on Korea is under consideration," he said.

It was a terrible prospect, to say the least. I knew this wasn't a bluff, since Truman was the only person in history to use nuclear weapons—and against a civilian population to boot. But what could I possibly do? I never had any contact with General Kim Il Sung, who was practically living at Supreme Headquarters. One day, finally, I managed to get the General on the phone. I knew I only had seconds of his precious time, so I asked the most important question at hand: "How can I help the war effort?"

"That's the easiest question that I've been asked all day," said General

Kim Il Sung. "The first and foremost task of a revolutionary is to study. You should wreak vengeance on the enemy by getting A's in school. Let your grades be your weaponry."

If that's what he thought, then I knew it was the truth. I studied harder than ever, not only for myself but for my country and for the General. Yet there was only so much I could do. At the time the educational system—like everything else in Korea—was being strained to the limit by the ongoing war. As the number of teachers available were stretched thin, common people often volunteered their talents in their stead.

One day, my class had a lesson on art from a local painter. The man pulled out a poster and put it on the wall in front of the room. "This is the *Mona Lisa*," he explained. "It was painted by Leonardo da Vinci, a renowned Italian artist active in the fifteenth and sixteenth centuries. Da Vinci made up his mind to paint the portrait of an ideal woman who had been haunting him. For a long time he travelled all over his country, crossing mountains and rivers, searching for a real woman who resembled his visionary idol. Finally, he found her."

The artist was so well-versed in the *Mona Lisa* that he discussed it at length without notes, passionately groping at the air as he spoke. I watched the students nodding their heads in delight, as if nothing he was saying was wrong. The entire horrible scene made me sick to my stomach.

"Da Vinci told the woman of his motive," the man continued, "and asked her to go with him. Moved by his passion, she complied with his request. She sat in his studio as he painted her portrait with zeal. He even invited a famous band to play music while he was painting. At last, after four years, the picture was completed. When the picture was opened to public view it caused a worldwide sensation. Depending on how you viewed it, the woman in the painting either looked melancholy or joyous. This is what made the *Mona Lisa* such a deathless masterpiece. It became a cultural relic of humanity which will be handed down to posterity."

The lesson finished, the artist left. The students remained behind in the classroom, waiting for our next speaker. All the children besides myself were so excited about the painting that the room became one loud discussion. "She must have been lonely because she was away from home for four years," one boy guessed.

"Being painted while listening to music?" a girl replied. "She must have been in rapture!"

"What we can agree on," the boy said, "is that a painting can't be comprehended by ordinary people if it is to be called a masterpiece."

I remained silent tor a while, waiting for someone to correct him. But no one seemed to have a problem with his claim. I couldn't believe it. "An enigmatic picture which changes appearance might have been a masterpiece at that time," I barked, "but in this era it can't be praised as such! If people who see a painting can't grasp its meaning, they can't say it's a good picture—no matter how talented the artist who may have painted it. A picture must be painted in such a way that the viewer can understand its meaning."

Hushed silence fell over the classroom. The pupils' eyes were all wide open. Here I was, condemning what was handed down in history as a first-rate artistic masterpiece. How could such a thing be possible? I was still a child!

"Just think," I continued. "If a student said that a mountain can be either high or low, the teacher will regard him as an idiot instead of giving him good marks. The same principle applies to pictures. How can a picture which seems to be either this or that be called a 'masterpiece'? A master-piece greatly moves and instructs the viewer. It makes sense to *everyone*."

Though they'd been hesitant to accept what I said, no one could argue with my points. By the end of the day, the fact that I'd criticized the

Mona Lisa spread throughout the school. Even the faculty pondered the matter. Finally, everyone came to realize that my evaluation was correct beyond dispute.

I was shocked that no one in the school—not even a painter himself!—had any inkling about the truth of the *Mona Lisa*. Worse, they'd subordinated their Korean natures to the values of a far-off country and its centuries-old tradition. That was when I realized how serious the war effort really was. We had to liberate, not simply the Korean peninsula, but the hearts and minds of the Korean people themselves. Liberating the peninsula would be the easy part—though that of course was hardly "easy." We weren't simply engaged in a war for Korean land or Korean territory. We were engaged in a Fatherland Liberation War.

In keeping with the requirements of modern warfare, General Kim Il Sung constantly developed new tactics by taking into account both Korea's geographical features and advances in weaponry. As a result, the "UN" Forces and the Syngman Rhee puppet army were successfully driven out of the northern half of Korea. The General then decided to ensure that no American soldier would ever step foot in north Korea again. The KPA built strong tunnel positions along the foremost line and on both coasts, and then used the tunnels to make raids on the Yankees. By June 1951, the front settled approximately along the 38th parallel. Not one inch had been ceded to the Yank bastards.

Bewildered by their string of defeats, the US imperialists racked their brains for a loophole. Unfortunately for them but luckily for Korea, they did not have the mind of General Kim Il Sung to call on. Stuck with the psychotic ravings of Harry Truman, war maniac, they were compelled to propose ceasefire negotiations.

The negotiations were a farce. The Yankee bastards were simply attempt to accomplish through 'diplomacy' what they were unable to achieve by force. Failing to achieve their duplicitous aim, the US imperial-ists broke off negotiations and launched what they called "strangulation" operations. This was their attempt to "strangle" the KPA by bombing north of the 38th parallel and cutting off the line of reinforcements.

Beginning that summer, I constantly heard the sounds of bombs dropping. I was on edge every second of every day. I never stopped wondering if today was the day when some American pilot would press the button that would kill me or one of my friends. Though none of my classmates said as much, I could tell that they all felt the same way. The way they sat in class, gripping their pencils and their books with all their strength, spoke to their tension. But rather than hiding like some of the other children, I always made it a point to watch as the planes dropped bombs in the distance. I wanted to never forget the sight of the Yank devils raining murder upon the brave Korean people.

One day after school, I saw an enemy plane get shot down by a KPA antiaircraft gun. My jaw dropped. I could clearly make out the Yankee airman parachuting down. I watched him fall towards a ravine, one that wasn't too far from my house. I ran outside and headed to where he was landing. I wanted to get a good look at this monster who was saving his own life after heartlessly killing who knew how many innocent Koreans.

Many others had the same thought, and I had to push my way through a huge crowd to see the villain. I watched as the KPA men restrained the enemy flier. Even though the Yanks had been the Korean people's sworn enemy for close to a century, it was the first time that I saw one face-to-face. He didn't look like a man—at least none that I'd ever seen. If anything, he looked like a cornered wolf, goggling his deep-set eyes and trembling with fear.

I could sense the tide of rising indignation from the crowd. They picked up pebbles and closed in on the Yankee bastard. "Look at him!"

I said. "Look how frightened he is! No matter how many of these brutes attack us, we have no need to fear them. We should beat them with a stick, and without mercy. Get him out of my sight!"

As the men took the murderer away, I realized what a victory the General was inaugurating for freedom-loving peoples everywhere. The Americans' plan for world domination was heavily based on their image of invincibility. They often boasted that they could conquer any nation they desired at any time, so any resistance would be pointless. Now, less than a decade after "winning" World War II and inaugurating an "American century," the US imperialists were very publicly facing defeat in the small Korean peninsula. American invincibility was being exposed for what it was: Propaganda. A myth. A lie.

As 1951 drew to a close, the US imperialists increasingly realized that north Korea had grown beyond their grasp forever and accordingly implemented a change of plans. The so-called "best army in the world" decided to do the one thing that it actually was best at: killing as many people as possible. Omar Bradley, America's very first Chairman of the Joint Chiefs of Staff, said it clearly: "The goal in Korea is to produce the maximum casualties."

Echoing the Axis of World War II, the Yankees now aligned with the Japs to draw up a barbarous war plan. Japan was changed from a vanquished nation into a supply base for germ warfare, as the Japanese delivered their biological weapons research to the Americans. Korea was no longer a battleground—she was now a testing ground, a chance for the US imperialists to perform military experiments on actual human beings.

I heard the news, and even I could scarcely believe it. Despite all that the Americans had done, despite seeing one of the beasts in the flesh, I still didn't think them capable of such depravity. But not only were they *capable*, they *excelled* at it. Beginning in November 1951, the Americans began to visit plagues upon Korea. During the night, germ bombs were dropped by B-29s over the northeast and northwest areas of Korea. These bombs were filled to the limit with insects: flies, fleas, bedbugs, mosquitoes, lice, beetles and grasshoppers. The insects themselves were infected with such diseases as cholera, typhus and the bubonic plague. Terrible epidemics spread. People developed fevers which led to severe pains and then, inevitably, death.

Germ warfare affects everyone indiscriminately, which is why it is so strictly forbidden by international law. Every single person in the north now had no option but to take part in the war. A powerful mass movement was launched to cope with the germ warfare. Newly-erected observation posts discovered the toxic bombs as they fell, which were then quickly destroyed. The illnesses were soon kept to a minimum, and the Americans were foiled once more.

The Americans next resorted to saturation bombing in a final attempt to wipe Korea off the map. The heinous American murderers destroyed factories, schools, theatres and houses at random. Helpless, I watched streets being reduced to heaps of ashes. The Yankees were trying their hardest to completely level the mountainous land that was north Korea. "When I grow up," I shouted at the planes, "I will make you pay a thousand times more for the blood shed by our people!"

Once again, General Kim Il Sung's brilliant command saved the day. The very same B-29s which had bombed Japan were shot down one after another in Korea by Koreans using Korean tactics. American planes were shot down, not by Soviet-supplied guns, but by Korean antiaircraft guns made up of rifles installed on cart wheels. American warships were sunk, not by Chinese naval vessels, but by the small torpedo-boats of the KPA. The Korean people were protected from artillery attacks, not by hi-tech foreign weapons, but by bombproof shelters and tunnels—in other words, by the Korean land itself. It was Juche tactics that pushed back the unprecedented assault, and it was only Juche tactics that could have done so.

All anyone could talk about was the future of Korea, whether there'd be anything to salvage even if victory was declared. Even though I was only ten years old, I realized that there was something extremely crucial that no one was giving enough thought to: the health and well-being of General Kim Il Sung. I knew he must have been barely sleeping. I knew that every single lost Korean life was like losing a child for him. I knew I had to step into Mother's footsteps, to go see him and take care of him—but I simply couldn't.

In early 1952, I realized that the General's fortieth birthday would be coming up, on April 15. Even though we'd been separated for almost two years at that point, I knew he wouldn't be thinking of himself on that day. What should have been a major national holiday would pass by under the clouds of war. I assembled my school's art circle and convinced them that we should put together a colorful performance to celebrate the blessed day. Despite the trying circumstances facing our nation, the other students also wanted to greet the event as best they could. They wanted to sing songs and to dance, not hear bombs explode and hide from danger.

We began rehearsals immediately, different groups practicing their parts wherever and whenever they had time. One afternoon, I was walking past a classroom when I heard a girl rehearsing her poem inside. I knew the poem well, as it was popular at the time. "Where Are You, My Dear?" was about a mother yearning for her daughter who was fighting, somewhere, at the front. The title referred to the mother calling out in grief for her daughter to return home safe and sound.

I stopped dead in my tracks, my fists shaking. I barged into the room, startling the girl. "Which Korean mother is tearing at her chest, crying for her daughter who has gone to the front?" I yelled.

"What?" the girl said. She didn't have any idea what I was talking about.

"Our mothers have sent their sons and daughters to war to vanquish the enemy. They tell their children to crush the Yanks and to come back home as heroes. The mothers of the fighting Koreans aren't feeble-hearted with worry. Do you know where I first heard this poem?"

"I don't," the girl admitted, bowing her head.

"Last New Year's, someone recited it at the entertainment gathering. The room which had been so gay and cheerful suddenly became filled with desolation. That poem is full of nothing but venom! Invisible, dreadful venom."

"So what should I do?" she asked me.

"We have many great poems like 'Mt. Paektu,'" I told her. "It would be better to read a poem that fills the audience with inspiration rather than war-weariness."

"That's a wonderful idea."

On April 15th, the performance went off very smoothly. I knew better than to expect General Kim Il Sung to attend; he had far more important things to concern himself with. All I hoped was that he would know, somehow, that the students supported him with all their hearts, and that we would be cheering the KPA on to victory until our last breath.

I was doing my homework the following week when the phone rang. To my delight, it was the General himself. "I heard about the performance you organized. I am very proud. I'm going on a field guidance tour in Sinuiju next week and I want you to come with me." For a moment I was shocked that he knew about my little show. After all, he was busy trying to win a war! Then I realized this was further evidence that the General knew everything that was going on in Korea at all times.

FIELD GUIDANCE

In capitalist countries, administrative executives live lives completely removed from the people. They are surrounded by bodyguards, and only engage in staged interactions with their supporters. But in Korea, General Kim Il Sung originated a popular leadership method known as "field guidance." He believed that he should go wherever the people worked, rather than remaining stuck in an office. When he visited coal mines, he met with the miners and listened to their opinions. Then he looked into every corner of their lives, examining their hostels and dining halls. He sat with farmers in their fields, and housewives in their flats. If necessary, he even stayed in the farther provinces for several days to acquaint himself with the local situation. This method didn't change even during the war, and it was how he was so aware of what was happening everywhere in Korea.

Through field guidance, the General established the policy of the Workers' Party of Korea and the state. This was why the Korean people trusted and supported government policy so thoroughly: They themselves were the ones who dictated it. His field guidance tours were of course highly anticipated and famously touted in the press. The people knew that their every concern would be listened to and taken care of due to the politics of loving care.

For me to accompany General Kim Il Sung on field guidance was a huge honor, and I could barely contain myself. I also missed my father, and wanted to see him. Apparently the feeling was mutual. When I saw him again the following week—for the first time in months—he paused and then smiled. "You are growing up very quickly, Comrade Jong Il."

"Yes, General," I said. My heart was overcome with every possible good emotion, but I maintained the calm demeanor befitting a revolutionary.

That afternoon was a military field guidance tour. We visited KPA artillery units and a tunnel construction site. It was very exciting to see the actual weapons and edifices that I'd been reading about in the newspapers. It felt like I was inside a storybook—one that surely had a happy ending of victory over the cursed Americans.

As we walked around, the General constantly stopped to examine every little detail. With great ease, he offered many suggestions that instantly and enormously improved productivity and morale. All the soldiers watched him with great admiration, hanging onto his every word. A few even gave me knowing looks of respect, which I treasured enormously.

That evening we began to drive back to Pyongyang. As we came to a fork in the road, the driver went to turn down the highway.

"Let's take the lane instead," General Kim Il Sung said.

The driver hesitated. "Are you sure? That way looks very rough."

"Didn't the General say that the car should go along the lane?" I barked. "Drive the car on that road immediately! We should always do what the General says without fail because his instructions are always correct."

The driver turned along a narrow path across some foothills, and soon we crossed a wooden bridge over a gorge. Suddenly scores of enemy bombers appeared in the sky. The planes rained bombs on the highway that we almost went down, carpeting it completely. I'd never been so close to a detonation before. My ears began to ring as the bombs burst with terrific explosions. Worse, I could make out the shrapnel cutting through the air with shrill, screeching howls. It was far too obvious what would have happened if we'd disobeyed General Kim Il Sung's request.

I turned to look at him, but the General showed no fear whatsoever. His jaw was set in firm determination. "This isn't the closest I've come to death. Do you see this?" he said, pointing at the back of his neck.

"Do you mean that bump?" I said.

"It's a war wound, and it's been growing every year. It's too close to an artery to be removed, so it'll keep growing all my life. One inch in another direction, though, and that would have killed me. So *this* attack means nothing."

"No," I said. "It means that the enemy must've had some hint of the route that we were to take."

General Kim Il Sung nodded, having come to the same upsetting conclusion. It felt like we didn't take a single breath the entire way back to the capital. The tension was so strong in the car that I feared for what would happen when we arrived back at Supreme Headquarters. I knew the General's fury would be a terrifying thing to behold.

When we pulled up to headquarters, the General threw the car door open and bolted inside. I followed after him as fast as my little feet could take me. It seemed as if every inch of the room was covered in maps, books and charts. I quietly sat down in the corner in his office, just like I when I'd been younger. I didn't speak as General Kim Il Sung looked through some papers, wanting to confirm some information.

Then the General abruptly stormed into the hall. He returned to the office a few minutes later, pacing with tremendous fury. A while after that several guards came in, dragging a pair of prisoners behind them. I recognized the men from the newspapers as disgraced Party traitors.

The General finally acknowledged that I was in the room. "Take a look at these men," he told me. "They'd already admitted to being spies on the US imperialists' payroll. But clearly they still have allies in positions of power, allies who almost succeeded in the killing of us both. Do you know what happens now, Comrade Jong Il?"

"No," I said.

General Kim Il Sung turned back to the class enemies with a look full of anger and contempt. "Now, my brave KPA soldiers are going to interrogate these traitors until they let me know who those allies are."

For me, this was perhaps the scariest moment of the war. Of course I'd understood that class enemies were everywhere. But I never thought they'd be able to get this close to the General. I never thought that they'd be able to so convincingly portray themselves as loyal. It wasn't a surprise that the US imperialists—who had engaged in germ warfare—would try to assassinate General Kim Il Sung. What was surprising is that they'd find Koreans so willing to join with them. This meant that traitors could be anyone and anywhere. The struggle against them couldn't be suspended even for a moment.

Then I had an epiphany. "Do you know the poem 'Where Are You, My Dear?'?" I blurted out.

Every head in the room jerked to look at me, as if they couldn't believe that I was interrupting. "Go on," the General said. "Explain what you mean, young comrade."

"That poem was written to spread a spirit of capitulation," I explained. "Was this done intentionally?"

"What?" said one of the traitors. "How would I know?"

The General cuffed him across the face for his impudence. "Answer the question!"

"Yes!" said the other traitor. "The poet was an anti-Party, counter-revolutionary factionalist. He was a paid spy. Just like us."

"We'll find this 'poet' soon enough," said General Kim Il Sung. "We will pull these counterrevolutionary weeds by their roots and exterminate every last one of them."

"Right away," said one of the soldiers. The KPA men dragged the class enemies away to be interrogated, leaving General Kim Il Sung and I alone in the office.

"You see that I need people that I can trust," the General told me. "I hadn't thought of you in this way, since you are my son and you are still quite young. But despite your youth, you've demonstrated your loyalty to me and to the revolution time and time again."

"I would give my life for Korea," I agreed. "But I'd rather give the lives of one thousand Yankees."

The General laughed. Then he reached into a drawer and handed me a pistol. "Today I give you this," he said, "Take it as the 'relay baton' with which to continue on the revolution after me."

I began to choke up as I felt the gun's weight in my hands. It felt warm and cold at the same time, the most beautiful present any father could give his son. "General, I'll always remember your words, and will fight all my life for the revolution with this gun."

"You must bear in mind that a gun is the revolutionary's eternal companion," General Kim Il Sung explained, putting his hand on my shoulder. "A gun never betrays its master, though everything else in the world should change. It will help you guarantee victory like nothing else will. That's why a revolutionary must never lay down his gun his entire life."

Nothing more needed to be said. I understood completely, for I was truly my father's son.

From that day on, I lived at the Supreme Headquarters with the General. I observed his incessant planning as carefully but unobtrusively as I could. The workflow was constant. He received reports about the situation at the front and issued orders accordingly. He took measures to strengthen the Party and to stabilize the people's living conditions. When he met technicians, he had them draw up plans for reconstruction.

When he met artists, he defined how artistic activities could contribute to winning the war. All the problems arising in Korea were solved by the General on the spot.

The war entered its final, most horrific act soon after I moved into Supreme Headquarters. Having unleashed insects and disease, the Americans next plagued Korea in the form of napalm fire bombing. Then, on June 23 and 24, 1952, the enemy carried out a large-scale attack on Suphung Power Station in the west. The US air pirates also bombed over ten other power stations. They wanted to deprive the Korean people of everything possible—even light itself.

WHAT GENERAL KIM IL SUNG TAUGHT ME

Military leadership
Revolutionary optimism
Unbreakable will
Unexcelled dauntlessness
How to attack the enemy
How to besiege the enemy
How to annihilate the enemy

After destroying Korea's electrical capabilities, the Yankees turned to destroying our agriculture. They bombed dams that accounted for over 75% of our agricultural production, completely flooding many villages in the process. Worse, the villains attacked immediately after the rice transplantation season. It was no coincidence but rather a carefully orchestrated plan to maximize the Korean people's suffering and hunger.

Once the targeted bombing was completed, the Yanks attacked anything else that was left. For close to a year, they showered bombs on the northern half of the Republic until all its towns and villages were decimated. Finally, they had to stop. The Far East Bomber Command reported that there were no more targets in north Korea. The US imperialists had simply annihilated everything. There was no precedent in the history of war for such severity, for such thoroughness of destruction on such a scale.

That Korea could be bombed into debris without surrendering seemed utterly unfathomable to the cowardly Americans. Yet that was the turn of affairs, and the Yankees were baffled. In fact, rather than surrendering, the KPA led three powerful counterattacks from mid-May 1953 through the end of July. Clearly, the Korean people still had plenty of fight left in them. The Korean invasion had already cost the US imperialists more than double the casualties that they'd suffered during the Second World War. The Yankees had only one choice left.

On July 19, 1953, I was walking outside when I heard someone shouting from a park nearby: "The Yanks have lifted up their hands!" I ran over and saw a huge crowd gathered around a radio. The announcer could barely hide his excitement as he reported the proud victory scored by the heroic Korean People's Army after three years of war.

Everyone was so filled with joy that we danced in each other's arms. Then I heard another shout: "Long live General Kim Il Sung!" Everyone replied with deafening cheers of *Manse!* Then we all began to sing *The Song of General Kim Il Sung*, shedding tears of joy all the while. Overcoming every possible hardship, carrying the heavy burdens of war on his shoulders, the General had finally and conclusively defeated the Americans.

Eight days later, the newspapers carried the news we'd all been waiting for. At 10 a.m. that day, under the DPRK and United Nations flags, the American delegates signed the Korean Armistice Agreement at Panmunjom, a town right by the 38th parallel. The Americans were so humiliated that they left the flags and their dossiers behind in their rush to flee home—and their abandoned property remains on display in Panmunjom to this very day. General Clark, commander-in-chief of the US Far East Command, couldn't help but admit his shame. "I gained the inevitable distinction," he soon admitted, "of being the first United States

Army Commander in history to sign an armistice agreement without victory."

Per the agreement, a military demarcation line was drawn on the map at the war front, roughly along the 38th parallel. On either side of the line was a "demilitarized zone" (DMZ) 2.5 miles wide. After all the fighting, not one inch of the north of Korea had been ceded to the US imperialists. But Korea, a unified nation for millennia, occupied by a single people with one blood, had been rent in two.

The house was divided against itself.

Chapter 4

Fighting Flunkeyism

Pyongyang was in ruins.

Soon after the armistice was signed, I took a walk around my city to assess the damage. I couldn't find one single undamaged house. Everywhere I looked, as far as I could see, there was debris and destruction. The kindergarten where I'd asked so many questions had been obliterated. The Taedong Bridge was down to its girders. Only the walls of Department Store No. 1 still stood undamaged. It wouldn't even be a matter of rebuilding the capital; there was nothing to rebuild.

Pyongyang was not alone. The only way to figure out where Korean cities had once been—for there were no cities left—was by looking for chimneys, the only things that managed to survive the assaults. Every major industry was ruined, all agriculture decimated. Over a million civilians had died, a tenth of the population.

Nationwide, there was no question as to what needed to be done. Prime Minister Kim Il Sung put forward a three-year plan that would lay the foundation for an independent national economy. All the people put forth their effort to create a new and modern Korea, with the same fighting spirit that had won them the war.

I was only eleven years old, so of course there was little I could do to help with any construction. Instead I remembered the words of the Prime Minister: "If a revolutionary fails to study properly, he will fail to successfully create the revolution." I packed my bookshelves so full that they looked like fortified walls. The texts themselves quickly became filled with my notes, marks of the fierce struggle I waged to conquer the ideas within them. I fought my way up the highest peaks of the knowledge that mankind had achieved. The width and depth of my studies soon became unmeasurable. The librarian practically became my closest comrade. "We have leading economic officials, renowned doctors, professors and specialists come here," she told me one day. "None of them can match you in reading books!"

"If cooked rice is the staff of physical life," I said, "then learning is the staff of mental life. If a man doesn't become accustomed to reading books in his youth, then he won't like to read them when he grows up—and he would become empty-headed man."

Like all the other people in the north, I constantly read the General's latest speeches and writings, analyzing and studying them. But of course General Kim Il Sung was also a man of action. I knew that knowledge apart from life, excellence in scholarship apart from life, was useless. I wanted to acquire information so that I could apply it, not just to know it for its own sake. So one evening, after finishing a book about automotive technology, I decided to put what I'd learned into practice.

SUBJECTS I STUDIED

Classics

Philosophy

Political economics

History

Geography

Literature

Aesthetics

Music

Physical culture

Optics

Geotechnology

Architecture

Military science

Medicine

Agriculture

I went to a nearby garage and began taking a discarded automobile apart, seeing how each of its parts worked. A worker watched what I was doing and shook his head with disapproval. "Focus on driving well," he told me. "If a car breaks down, one of our repairmen will fix it."

"Everybody should have a knowledge of technology," I said. "Without technology our country can't advance even one step. Our people who beat the US should arm themselves with advanced technology, scale the peak of Juche and recognize that taking loving care of machines is a manifestation of patriotism."

I was coming home from school a few weeks later when I saw a crowd of people standing around a bus. I walked across the street to see if I could help. "What's going on?" I asked one of the spectators.

"The bus is out of order," he told me. "The driver did all he could to make the engine start working, but to no avail. The passengers are trying to help him but they can't seem to figure it out either! Everyone is becoming quite irritated."

> **MACHINERY I**
> **MASTERED**
>
> Tape recorders
> Typewriters
> Cameras
> Radios
> Electrical appliances
> Movie projectors
> Autobicycles
> Motorcars

"I'll see what I can do," I said. I left the man behind, baffled as to how a middle school boy would be able to repair a bus. I walked up to the bus driver and offered my help.

"Why not?" he said with a laugh. "Everyone else has had a go."

I sat in the driver's seat and checked all the gauges. Then, one after another, I set the accelerator and other working parts. *Nothing.* Finally I went around, popped open the hood and took a look inside. "Do you have a spanner and a hammer?" I asked the driver.

"Of course." The driver handed me the tools from his box, still not quite believing his eyes.

By knowing how the parts were supposed to work, it wasn't all that difficult to determine when they weren't. I managed to check what was actually in good order. One by one, I eliminated potential issues as possibilities. Soon my hands became stained with oil, and sweat began to drip down my brow. Finally I spotted the problem and cranked it fixed.

I was so enveloped in my tough work that I hadn't noticed that the passengers had all been watching me. Caught in the act, all I could do was stretch and throw them a wink. "I think we're ready," I announced. I returned to the driver's seat and switched on the bus. The passengers all started cheering when they heard the engine start to chug along.

The delighted bus driver came over to shake my hand. "I have something to confess," he told me. "I recently finished the drivers' short course but it didn't help. We've been having this kind of mishap fairly frequently."

"Don't worry," I said, motioning for him to take his seat. "The latest model of bus might still be unfamiliar to you. You'll learn soon enough."

I got off the bus, waving the passengers off as the driver honked his horn with delight.

I wish I could claim that incidents like this were isolated occurrences. But in fact such stories were hardly uncommon for me. My boyhood abounds in anecdotes that are beautiful like jewels and brilliant like the stars. Each of them is so deeply stirring that even now they fill people with boundless admiration. Yes, I became an expert at fixing machinery. But what I was most proud of is how skilled I grew at fixing my fellow children.

At every school, there was something called the Children's Union for the students to join. It was meant to be a source of extracurricular activity, comradeship and guidance. Unfortunately, the organizational life at my school's sub-branch wasn't very well developed. The Union didn't do as much as it should have, especially for young minds so eager for activities. As a result, students usually found themselves without anything to do when the school day ended. This so-called "free" time turned out to be the costliest time possible.

Back then, private trade and industry hadn't yet gone through a socialist reorganization in the DPRK. Young people often spent their days roaming the streets, looking around at the marketplaces. On my way home from school one afternoon, I heard a storekeeper shouting at some children at the Somunbak market. "Prize lot drawing!" he barked. "A carp candy for first prize, a hare candy for second prize and a duck candy for third prize. If you're lucky, you'll win a carp candy!" The storekeeper caught the attention of several schoolboys, who ran over to try their hand at the candy lottery.

I recognized one of the boys as being in my class, so I silently followed him to the store. "How does it work?" asked the boy.

"It's simple," the storekeeper told him. "For five *won* you get to draw a lot. If you draw one with a picture of an animal, that's the type of candy you win."

"I want a carp candy," the boy mused aloud. "Those are my favorite. Here's five *won*."

The storekeeper held out a bucket filled with crumbled slips of paper. "Here you go!" he said. "Take whichever one you like."

My classmate reached in and felt around, trying to figure out which slip felt luckiest to him. Finally he made his choice and pulled out the lot, opening it with great anticipation.

It was blank.

"That's all right," the boy said. "I'll make up for it with the next one."

The next one was blank as well—as was the one after that, and the one after that. Fifty *won* later, the boy hadn't won anything. Worse, he'd spent all the money that he had. He bowed down his head, feeling humiliated and embarrassed.

I went up to him and tapped him on the shoulder. "Did you really think the evil storekeeper would put in a first-prize lot in the bunch?" I said. "All merchants are liars. They make no bones of telling any kind of lie so as to make money. You should never do such a thing in the future.

Should you ever rely on the luck of the marketplace, you'll be no better than a merchant yourself!"

"You're right," he said. "I can see that now. Thank you."

I explained to the boy how these marketplaces were exerting a bad influence. I reiterated that there were many swindlers luring children in with unhealthy amusements in order to squeeze money out of them. As I went on and on, telling him how at great length foolish he had been, I realized that the boy's actions weren't entirely his fault. They were *my* fault as well. Life in my CU sub-branch was dull. The students had little interest in their lessons, failed to do their homework and generally acted in a liberal manner. How ironic that the students who ran the CU were referred to as "activists"!

The following day, I took one of these CU activists back with me to the market after school. "Take a look around," I said to him. "What do you see?"

Not sure what I was referring to, he turned in every direction. "I see a market bustling with people. I see all kinds of different sellers."

"And do you see all the pupils hanging around this noisy place?"

"I do..."

I frowned. "They're spending their precious afterschool hours in this way!" I said. "If we leave them alone, they could slide into a swamp of selfishness. What are we going to do about this?"

He shrugged his shoulders. "It can't be helped," he said. "This is happening after school, not during the school day."

I glared at him. "Are you telling me that they should be left to themselves, to hover around as they please, only to become badly contaminated? What's the point of the Children's Union organization? This is only happening because the Children's Union organization isn't properly 'organizing' the students' extramural life!"

"What do you think we should do?" he asked me.

"I'll tell you."

All my usual reading fell by the wayside the following week as I researched my fellow students as much as I could. I learned about the individual characteristics, merits, shortcomings and home environments of every student in my sub-branch. I compiled files on each of them to the best of my ability. Finally, I gathered together the CU activists and told them what I'd learned. "But the biggest problem," I concluded, "is going on after school. We need more activities then."

"What sorts of activities?" asked one activist.

"What if the members of the sub-branch collectively conducted an art circle?" I said. "We can also make educational visits to different places or even go to the movies. We can meet with the Heroes of the Republic. We can conduct proper physical training for when we grow up and join the KPA. Wouldn't that be a lot better than drawing prize lots in hopes of winning candy? Instead of looking at hawkers selling goods, we should be visiting factories to watch the workers operate the machines. Wouldn't those sorts of activities be of interest to everyone?"

I handed out a proposed schedule for extramural activities that I'd prepared. Seeing my ideas in writing made the activists realize how idle they'd been. "There is one thing here that I'm unclear about," one said. "You've set aside an hour once per week for criticism and self-criticism. What's that?"

I explained to the activists how I'd criticized my friend who had wanted to win a carp candy—and how my criticism had had an immediate positive effect on him. "True comradeship lies in criticism," I continued. "We should engage in criticism of both ourselves and one another to make sure that everyone stays on a righteous course."

The activists looked at one another, not understanding what I meant.

"I just don't feel comfortable criticizing my friends," one of them confessed.

"Do you love your friends?" I asked.

"Of course!"

"If you love your friends from your heart, then you should criticize and correct the shortcomings in their study and organizational lives."

"That seems...hurtful."

"It is at first," I agreed. "But as the proverb goes, 'Whips make a good child.' Parents love their children, so they scold them. They would spoil them if they ignored their children's shortcomings and only praised them. Criticism between friends is similar to that. Those who criticize their intimate friends will feel as great a pain as those who they are criticizing. Think of the poplar trees growing around the playground. It seems like only the day before yesterday that the students planted them. But now those trees have grown three or four times as tall as a man. We worked very hard to bring them up. We sprinkled chemicals to fight infestation from noxious insects. We went out and set up props when the wind blew strongly. Without our tender care, those trees wouldn't have grown as straight and big as they did. Noxious insects could have nested, propagated and then eaten the trees hollow. The wind could have knocked the young trees over, or at least warped them."

"Just like a fault committed by a friend."

"Exactly. If a fault—even a trifling one—is left uncriticized, it grows over time. In the end your friend would become as useless as a hollow tree."

Soon after, my Children's Union sub-branch called a general membership meeting and unanimously elected me as chairman. I worked hard to make the organization a disciplined, active and lively one. I wanted our members to be true revolutionaries, boundlessly faithful to the General.

Within a few months, a bright and sound atmosphere came to prevail at the school. The entire student body changed into a disciplined yet cheerful and amicable community by engaging in the activities that I'd suggested. But what had the greatest effect were the criticism sessions that I introduced. Week after week, every student stood up and denounced himself and his fellows. The halls became full of the sounds of criticism and self-criticism, which were the sounds of friends expressing their comradely love.

Though the positive effects of the criticism sessions were apparent—everyone was on their best behavior, knowing they were being watched by everyone else—the CU activists still didn't quite appreciate the potential that they had. They viewed the sessions as a means to condemn bad behavior and nothing more. This greatly limited their effectiveness, as the activists were forced to discover for themselves. There were two boys in the school whose behavior was the worst out of anybody. The pair simply laughed or rolled their eyes whenever they were brought in for criticism. When I eventually heard about this I knew that something had to be done.

I discussed the matter with some of the activists who knew the boys casually and then again with those who had led the criticism sessions against them. Then I talked about the matter with the boys' teacher. No matter who I spoke to, child or adult, the answer was the same: These boys are a real "head ache." They are hooligans who will never become productive students. That did not sit well with me. If the sub-branch couldn't help the boys find their way, then it couldn't very well claim to be a living organization. There had to be some way of guiding them, some way to criticize them effectively so that their behavior would be fixed and improved.

I spent time trying to figure out how to reach out to the boys but wasn't really sure what to do. I knew that I wouldn't have very many opportunities before they were lost to us, just as everyone else predicted. One afternoon I was walking down the hall at school when I heard the sound of glass breaking. I quickly dashed to the room the sound was coming from and opened the door.

On the wall was painted a large target, and the "head aches" were taking turns launching bottles at it from their slingshots. The entire floor was covered with broken shards, and the wall was marked with indents where the glass had shattered. I was barely able to restrain my indignation at their excessive wantonness, but I knew that I couldn't address them with anger. "What's going on here?" I said, as casually as I could.

"We're playing with our slingshots," one replied.

I noticed that they were balling their fists, ready for a fight. It was precisely what I was going to avoid. "I see that you're practicing your marksmanship. How many Yankees have you shot? Which one of you is ahead?"

"We haven't been keeping score."

"Once you start a competition," I told them, "you must see it through. Let's go outside, where I can referee. It's messy in here."

"Good idea," said the second boy. Rather than being aggressive, the pair now seemed embarrassed. They so expected an argument that they never even considered that someone would be encouraging them—especially not the Children's Union sub-branch chairman!

The three of us went outside to the playground. I found a board and drew a vicious US imperialist's wolf-face on it. "How does that look?"

"It's hideous," the first boy said.

"Ha, ha! Then it's perfect. You know, if we use bottles, we can only shoot them once. They shatter and then they're of no use. But if we shoot stones instead, we'll never wear them out and can use them as much as we like."

"That's a good idea."

I helped the boys gather up a few stones, and then explained how the features of each one affected its trajectory and matters like that. The two "head aches" were now like model students, hanging on to my every word. After playing a few matches, I took the two to a bench and sat down between them. "Schoolchildren shouldn't commit mischief to the classrooms and damage the walls," I said. "Nor should they spurn the criticism of their comrades. I suggested we go outside and use rocks instead of bottles. Were these bad suggestions?"

"No," they admitted.

"Of course not. Now there's no damage out here, and you had the same fun and learned something too. So why don't we go back to the class and clean up that mess together?"

"I'm sorry," said the first boy.

"Me too," said his friend.

The three of us went back. Together, we swept up the glass and then plastered up the wall. After my interaction with them, both of the boys went from being a "head ache" to being "head of the class." I could have spent all day discussing the power of criticism with the CU activists, and they still might not have appreciated it. But none of them could misunderstand how the two boys changed their lives around under my loving guidance. It illustrated my concept that no one was beyond criticism, and that true criticism was based on comradely affection rather than animosity.

As a consequence of this successful case, criticism sessions became enormously popular at my school. Then, through word of mouth, they spread to other schools—first in Pyongyang, than in all of north Korea. Students felt encouraged, knowing they had a commitment to live up to their fellows' expectations. They also felt happy to be helping those who needed it to turn their behavior around. Criticism was something that benefited everyone.

In a small way, my successes as Children's Union sub-branch chairman were paralleling Korea's successes on a national level. By 1956, the economy had largely been rehabilitated over the course of the three-year national economic plan. Building the foundation was strenuous but required finite creativity. The possibilities of what a given foundation will support are infinite, however. It was by no means certain what was to be done next. With the conclusion of the three-year plan, the situation inside the DPRK became very complicated. The country was short of materials and funds, and the people's standard of living was still low.

There was great debate as to what to do next. Should Korea focus on heavy industry, like building factories? Light industry, as in consumer goods? Trade, or agriculture? It was an extremely intricate question that required an enormous amount of insight and leadership. The consequences of making incorrect decisions would resonate for decades—or might weaken the DPRK to the point that the Americans would take another crack at conquering the nation. Unfortunately but unsurprisingly, the situation was made much more difficult by matters abroad. Though achieving a great victory in the Fatherland Liberation War in 1953, the socialist world also suffered a tremendous loss that year: the death of Joseph Stalin, Premier of the Soviet Union, enemy of fascism and friend of democracy.

Stalin was a great friend to the Korean people, and he and General Kim Il Sung had an enormous amount of respect for one another. After Stalin's passing, Nikita Khrushchev took over the command of the Soviet Union and "liberalized" the nation. Very quickly, what became known as "Stalinism" grew out of vogue among the Soviet satellite states. This was not a function of the truth or falsehood behind Stalin's philosophy. What was true in 1953 surely couldn't have become completely outdated by 1956. No, these nations were simply following Moscow's lead in every way.

In other words, they were corrupted by flunkeyism.

Flunkeyism is the tendency of a developing nation to worship more powerful countries. Flunkeyists deprecate their own nation and its achievements in the process of venerating other cultures. I was aware of the phenomenon but wasn't too concerned about it in the Korean context. Surely, I thought, a nation with one blood and five thousand years of history had plenty to be proud of.

As Children's Union sub-branch chairman, I often frequented the school at night. I always checked to make sure that there weren't any US imperialists or south Korean puppet spies hiding in our building. One night in 1956, I turned a corner in the hallway when I saw that a light was still on in one of the classrooms.

It was close to midnight. Something was obviously out of order. I carefully walked up to the class and peeked inside. Instead of a sunken-eyed, hook-nosed Yank, I saw a student with his head drooped over the desk. I quietly walked into the room to see what was going on.

The boy was sleeping quite peacefully, with a very large, splendid drawing as his "pillow" and his artistic implements spread out all over his desk. Clearly the sleepyhead had been drawing for the student newspaper until very late and was overcome by fatigue. I was pleased that he had the commitment to carry out his assignment far into the night. Glancing at his drawing told me that he was already a technically skillful artist, despite being the same young age that I was. Careful not to disturb him, I leaned over to get a better look at what he had created.

In dark colors, the boy had drawn a snow-covered steeple and a very old castle wall—the landscape of a foreign capital. I felt like my heart was breaking as I turned to look out the window. Outside, only a few feet away, the nightless, seething life of Pyongyang was astir. Our hero city was rising up out of the ruins, writhing with construction. It was a touching scene that would fill anyone with emotion and excitement. I didn't understand how this young artist failed to see Pyongyang's thriving beauty. How could he possibly prefer an antique castle wall that he must have only seen in a photograph?

At that moment the artist awoke, jumping up to his feet with a start. I put my hand on his shoulder to calm him down. But from the expression on my face he could tell that I—chairman of the Children's Union sub-branch—was displeased. Nevertheless, he wasn't clear about what was wrong. "You keep looking at me," he finally said. "Is something the matter?"

"Is something the matter?" I repeated. "*Is something the matter?* Is something the matter with Pyongyang?"

"Huh?"

"Look! While you slept, Pyongyang was awake. Just after the war there wasn't a single undamaged building. Now, three years later, its appearance has totally changed. In a few more years it will be really magnificent. Everyone is striving to make that day come as soon as possible—as you should!"

"What do you mean?"

"I mean drawing is not just a means of demonstrating one's skill. It should have ideological content and educational value as well. What message does this drawing preach?" I pointed to his work with increasing indignation.

"I just drew a pretty picture of a castle..." he said quietly.

I convinced the artist to scrap his work and instead draw Pyongyang's rising skyline. But what I gained from this interaction was a new perspective on Korea's national situation. Flunkeyism wasn't just a political phenomenon, like when an Eastern European nation followed the trends in Moscow. It was much more personal and pervasive—and it had permeated Korea as well. Juche had not yet been established in many areas of social life. People sang foreign songs more than Korean songs. The paintings that hung in restaurants were of foreign landscapes, rather than beautiful Korean landscapes. There was a strong tendency toward imitating anything from advanced countries in disregard of Korean tastes and likes.

Flunkeyism was making Koreans thoughtlessly eulogize and envy foreign things. It turned them incapable of seeing their own culture's beauty, even when it was right under their own eyes. This shameful disease, I realized, was brought by Korea's long-standing poverty and backwardness. The scum that was flunkeyism needed to be obliterated before it could spread. It had the potential to make people unconscious of the greatness of the Korean revolution and the Korean nation. It was a poison paralyzing man's talent and creativity. When a person takes to flunkeyism he becomes an idiot; when a nation takes to flunkeyism the country is ruined; and when a party takes to flunkeyism it makes a mess of the revolution.

In fact, it was precisely the revolution that was at stake, for the Third Congress of the Workers' Party of Korea was held in April 1956. There, Prime Minister Kim Il Sung announced the First Five-Year Plan that would begin in the following year. The capitalist approach would have been to develop light industry, accumulating funds so as to construct heavy industry later. Some socialist countries chose another route in similar situations, forcibly constructing heavy industry for a certain period of time before developing light industry. All of Korea waited to see which well-trodden path the Prime Minister would choose.

Yet Prime Minister Kim Il Sung chose neither.

His Plan was a new, entirely different path that incorporated the Juche idea. The economic construction course gave priority to heavy industry while simultaneously developing both light industry and agriculture. The course was audacious and unprecedented—and the skepticism was furious and immediate. Khrushchev himself personally denounced the Prime Minister's ideas: "How could the DPRK carry out such a course with the nation still covered in the debris from the war? It's impossible!"

After that, the doubting was everywhere. Many Koreans agreed with the Soviet criticism—simply because it came from the Soviet Union. Others simply remained skeptical that Prime Minister Kim Il Sung could do what he said—even though he had done what he had said for decades. That didn't seem to matter to the skeptics. After all, they wondered, how many miracles could any one man produce?

In this context, our teacher told us that there would a lecture about the proposed Five-Year Plan at school. I was very excited and couldn't wait to hear the lecturer explain why the Plan was such a good idea. The following week, the entire school gathered in our assembly hall to listen to the lecturer's perspective. After a brief introduction, he got to the meat of his argument. "Korea doesn't need large machines like trucks, tractors and ships," he claimed. "Building them requires a huge amount of money and labor power. Korea is a small territory, and we have a lack of food supplies in the short term because we've just gone through a war. We can't construct machine-building factories. If we need machines, we can simply buy them from other countries in exchange for our abundant iron ore, apples or squid. It makes much more sense to trade than to try to manufacture these things for ourselves. Look!" He took out an apple and made a show of throwing it in the trash. "We have so many apples no one cares if I waste one. But our machines are being repaired until they are on their last legs. Let's barter what we have a surplus in, and import whatever else we need. That way, everybody wins."

This wasn't a lecture at all. It was a direct open attack on the Prime Minister and the Party. The lecturer wanted to maintain the DPRK's national economy as simply that of a raw-material supplier. I was livid. This reptile of a man spoke with great wit and humor, putting on quite a performance for the audience. I could see that his perspective was gaining ground with the students simply because of his personable air.

"Are there any questions?" the lecturer finally said.

I immediately stood up. "I have something to say!" I could see that the other students were intrigued by my serious expression, since I was usually so kind and benevolent.

"Go ahead," hissed the snake.

"As you know, the Prime Minister put forward our Party's economic course as one giving priority to the development of heavy industry while simultaneously developing light industry and agriculture. Your denial of the necessity of making our own trucks and tractors runs totally counter to his Plan. It doesn't stand to reason that we should buy foreign machines instead of making them ourselves. How can we ever make Korea a socialist power by using imported machines that we don't know how to construct? Korea would remain a backward and poor agrarian country forever. How do you explain this, *comrade*?"

The students began to grumble amongst themselves as they realized the implications of what I was saying. If we didn't need to produce up-to-date machines ourselves, then why should the pupils study modern science and technology? There would be no need for scientists and inventors in Korea; it would be enough to have drivers and repairmen. What would happen if our offers of trade were rejected by other countries? We'd either be ruined or, at the very least, at their mercy.

Realizing the counterrevolutionary content of the lecture, the pupils glared at the lecturer with rage. The man turned pale as the audience grew increasingly agitated. At his wit's end, he stood there rubbing his hands as he wondered how to escape this predicament. That's when I first suspected that someone else was pulling the strings of this puppet. He wasn't smart enough to be this manipulative.

"I'm simply explaining one perspective on the issue," the lecturer said. "Let me do some further research to more fully answer the questions that you've asked. Surely we can all agree it's a complex situation with many sides, each with some validity to them."

"No!" I shouted. "I don't agree! We should only think and act in accordance with the ideas of Prime Minister Kim Il Sung, no matter what the time and what the place! We will need an endless number of machines for construction and production. If we import them, even all our squid as trade might not be enough! What are we to do then? Build more squid? The Prime Minister said that we should first develop industry if we are to stand on our feet. That means making machines with our own efforts. What would happen if we look up to another country and they demanded things that we didn't have as payment for their machines? They'd look down on us with contempt and would continually raise their prices. We'll be a poor nation forever. Korea will become rich and strong when we heal our war wounds and make all our products by ourselves, 'in our way'!"

The audience erupted into cheers. The lecturer muttered some hasty excuse into the microphone and fled the scene like the coward that he was. Then we all went out into the hall, where I clearly explained the Party's course for building an independent national economy. I addressed every single question until all the students were convinced of what they should have been convinced all along: to trust in the Prime Minister.

In fact, skeptics like the lecturer were few and far between. The overwhelming majority of Koreans still had faith that Prime Minister Kim

Il Sung always had the answer to the problems facing Korea. Unlike the lecturer, they did not have to talk out of both sides of their mouth about it. They wrote letters and told their neighbors, and in fact they often put on shows as well. Though I had been disheartened to hear the lecture, I immediately put it out of mind when I learned that the Korean People's Army Song and Dance Ensemble had composed a show to honor the Prime Minister.

As a consequence of winning the Fatherland Liberation War, General Kim Il Sung had received a promotion to Marshal. Accordingly *The Cantata to Marshal Kim Il Sung* would be performed at a Pyongyang theatre. I was fortunate enough to be able to attend the premiere a mere week after the tainted lecture. As I took my seat, I couldn't help but smile at all the Korean people in the audience dressed in their finest clothes. I also couldn't help but notice that the Marshal hadn't been able to attend. This was the unfortunate consequence of his constant planning of future construction.

I was literally on the edge of my seat as I watched the Marshal's life recreated on stage. The fact that I had a personal connection to many of the events depicted made it that much more special. I wiped away a tear when the actress playing my beloved mother first took to the stage. The scenes of the days of anti-Japanese struggle and of the Fatherland Liberation War were very moving, and affected every single member of the audience. I was so impressed by the performance that I was shocked to hear the men in the seats behind me whispering to one another. At first I ignored them, but then their sarcastic comments became truly intolerable.

At one point the performers sang, "This morning dawns over the forests of Mt. Paektu."

"The day dawns over the East Sea in Korea," one of the wiseacres said, "not over Mt. Paektu. Don't they know anything about the laws of nature?"

I turned my head to my side to get a look at who was being so boorish and disrespectful. I was shocked beyond words. The men were not street hooligans, but members of the Ministry of National Defense. Worse, I recognized them as being fairly high-ranking. I turned back toward the stage so that they couldn't see that I'd noticed them.

"What kind of a song is this?" whined the second man. "It's as long as a clothesline."

"Where did they find that actor?" the first said. "He's pretty like a woman! Have they never seen Kim Il Sung in the flesh? He looks like a fat delivery boy from my neighborhood Chinese-food stall."

"Have you seen the growth on the back of his head? I think his neck's pregnant."

I was furious to hear these foul-mouthed people. It was literally the angriest I had ever been in my life. After a while I willed myself to calm down. And though it may sound absurd, those horrid men ended up saving Korea.

The fact that they spoke so disrespectfully regarding the Marshal was a testament to their low family background. But the fact that they did it openly and publicly told me that something deeper was happening. These men didn't know who was seated around them, and they made little effort to modulate their voices. That told me that they were used to being around others who shared those same views, that same lack of respect. Among civilians this would be one thing, but among the military? Among members of the Ministry of Defense? Clearly, the flunkeyists weren't just isolated, random members of the Korean nation.

They were an organized force.

The flunkeyists' plan immediately became apparent to me. The Plenary Meeting of the Party Central Committee would be held later in the year. Several flunkeyists had already publicly called for an alleged "road to socialism," some even going so far as to demand that Soviet power be established in Korea. Others, willfully ignorant of the nightmare south of the 38th parallel, argued for a "road to bourgeois democracy" in the American style. Still others wanted to take orders from Chairman Mao (whom I greatly admired as a leader for his own, the Chinese, people).

Each of these factions were represented in the Party. And each of these factions, by themselves, were an irritant at the very worst, a nuisance to be considered and immediately dismissed. But if they teamed up together, then all sorts of carnage could ensue. They might even have the ability to oust the Prime Minister from office. At the very least there would be problems between Korea and our strongest allies, the Soviet Union and China.

These varied flunkeyists had been unknown men, but the Prime Minister had welcomed them into the Party out of respect. I knew that he'd expected that they'd repay his trust and generosity with sincerity. He thought that their loyalty would be to Korea alone once they were given leading posts. But his benevolence and kindness was being met with arrogance. The overbearing attitude of these flunkeyists led them to view their own internationalist perspectives as superior to that of Juche. They weren't putting Korea first—and they were apparently intent on putting Marshal Kim Il Sung last.

I couldn't wait to tell the Marshal what I feared was happening. After the performance I went straight home. It honestly felt like the Prime Minister's life was in danger at that very moment. When I came upon him in his study, he immediately dismissed the officials that were with him and gave me his full attention. "I must speak to you about an urgent matter," I said.

He cocked his head and looked at me, concerned more for my anxiousness than for himself. "You're here about the flunkeyists."

I felt dizzy. He had said it so casually that I couldn't believe it. "You know?" Then I caught myself. Of course he knew.

"I want you to put yourself in my shoes," he told me. "I want you to think about what actions you would take, as if you were the one leading the Republic. We'll discuss it tomorrow, under the warm Korean sun."

With a nod and not another word, I left and went to my room. I could barely sleep all night, wondering how to best handle the situation. No matter how I looked at the matter, my choices seemed obvious.

Early the next morning the Prime Minister and I went for a stroll in the garden. From the pleasant breeze and the bright sun, one would never suspect all the conspiring that was going on. "The enemy is pouncing on us from all directions," Marshal Kim Il Sung said. He spoke with a sigh of resignation, hurt that these machinations were necessary. He so wanted Korean unity—not to mention reunification—that I think the matter struck him to his core. He always thought of Korea as one, and these men were doing everything they could to further divide our nation and our people.

"You can handle it," I said. "You've handled much worse."

"So if you were responsible for the country, what would you do?" He looked at me for my answer. This was not early morning small talk. The Prime Minister had no time for those types of frivolities anyway.

"I'd give them annihilation in return for their challenge."

He looked away, shaking his head a bit, recalling decades of fighting—and hoping the fighting would soon be over. "That's the only way to handle them," he grunted. "That's the grave lesson that I've learned through my thirty years of revolutionary struggle. You've already grasped the truth of the revolution. I'm very glad to see it's already part of your character."

"So what are you going to do?"

He looked directly into the sun, and didn't blink even for a moment. "I will fight them with the greatest tactics at my disposal: the tactics of Juche."

His campaign was as immediate as it was subtle. In May of 1956, a new system was implemented. Now, Koreans needed permission from their Party superiors before meeting with foreigners. This was presented as an approach to minimize spying for hostile nations. The flunkeyists in powerful positions regarded the permissions as a mere formality. They were always visiting with the Russians and the Chinese, the only foreigners legally granted the privilege of living in the DPRK at the time. This wasn't about them, they figured.

But it was—for now there was a clear paper trail identifying who the traitors were.

Next, the Marshal closed the College of Foreign Languages. Then he forbade the teaching of Russian to third- and fourth-year college students. These provocative actions, assaults on the foreign ideas that the flunkeyists held in such high regard, only served to embolden the flunkeyists. The harder the Prime Minister pushed, the more persuasive, reasonable and logical the flunkeyists believed their perspective to be. To make sure they could make their voices heard, the Prime Minister took another unprecedented step: he left Korea.

From June 1 to July 19, Marshal Kim Il Sung visited nine different European countries. The flunkeyists couldn't very well complain to their overseas masters while the Marshal was in their homes as their guest. But without his powerful presence in Korea, the flunkeyists discarded their need for discretion and grew ever bolder in their moves and actions. This boldness without repercussion gave them the illusion that they were powerful.

When Prime Minister Kim Il Sung came back to Korea, he didn't let on that he suspected what had been going on. He knew that the flunkeyists would make their move at the Central Committee plenum. It was the only possible venue to make an attempt to oust him from the leadership position. He repeatedly rescheduled the plenum with little notice. The flunkeyists took this as a sign of mismanagement. In actuality, it was his way to ensure they couldn't set their trap.

Finally, on the evening of August 29, 1956, the plenum was called for the following day. The Prime Minister had carefully arranged where everyone sat, placing them like markers on a battle plan. At the plenum, every traitor would literally be surrounded by Marshal Kim Il Sung's most trusted comrades—and they didn't even realize it.

At the plenum, all the flunkeyists were instantly outshouted by those seated around them whenever they rose up to speak. The Marshal's supporters yelled. They taunted. The flunkeyists' hands shook as they tried to read what they'd prepared to say, but a more hostile audience couldn't be imagined. Perhaps some in the room would have swayed by the flunkeyist scum under calmer conditions. But when the ditherers heard how loudly and enthusiastically the Marshal's allies yelled, they knew enough to join in as well. The flunkeyists had been conspiring against Prime Minister Kim Il Sung for months or even years—and it was all over for them in mere hours.

Such was the power of the Marshal's Juche tactics.

The public executions began immediately after the plenum. The Party put up posters throughout Pyongyang, announcing the wonderful events. I attended each and every one of them, and from the size of the crowds it seemed as if everybody in the city was there as well. Entire families made a day of it, with the youngsters even missing school. As the class enemies met their fates, the crowd erupted in huge cheers. The applause was so loud it was as if the people were competing to see who could make the most noise. After the villains were sent to their just graves, the children ran forward to grab any spent rifle cartridges or bullet casings to keep as souvenirs. It was like a small public holiday, with everyone happy to watch these dangerous villains flushed from their midst.

A few weeks after the plenum, I went to visit Marshal Kim Il Sung in his office. I knew that he must have felt a great deal of relief to have vanquished his foes so thoroughly. To my great surprise, he was pacing back and forth. "You seem to be under tremendous strain," I said. "Please, take a rest and consider your health. The flunkeyists have been defeated, and foreign influences are in the process of being purged from Korea."

The Marshal squeezed his eyes shut and let out a deep breath. "Yes, they've been driven from power. But how many Koreans shared their ideas? How many share them still? Our foes aren't like us. They aren't honest and forthright with their views. When we say we will do something, we do it—often to the shock of the world at large. But there is an entire hostile class still out there in Korea."

He was right, as always. Simply removing a few key figures from positions of power couldn't remove a hateful philosophy from the entire nation. "So what are you going to do?" I asked.

"No compromises can be made," he mused, "with the members of the hostile class that opposes socialism. It'll be necessary to determine if an individual is an enemy element or a member of our class."

"How? There are millions of people in Korea."

"How indeed."

The Marshal and I discussed the matter at length over the following days. There was simply no easy way to determine a given individual's reliability. But, indeed, there still was one way. It would be a very long and very difficult way, but it was the only way to eliminate foreign influences from Juche Korea. It took months of planning, but finally the Marshal instituted his final solution to the problem of the hostile elements.

In 1958, Prime Minister Kim Il Sung announced "Intensive Guidance by the Central Party." Every Korean—*every single one*—was put through a series of background checks. Not one, not two, but eight such checks were held in total. Everything was taken into account—family origin, political activity, expressions of loyalty—and families were rated accordingly, down to the second cousins. The background checks the Party performed were so thorough that having a relative in south Korea or a landlord for a grandparent was enough to designate a given person was unreliable.

Then, everyone was declared to be a member of either the "core," "wavering" or "hostile" classes in a classification known as *songbun*. Traitors begat traitors, and loyal workers taught their children to be loyal as well. It was an excellent tool to determine who could join the Party, the KPA or even simply go on to university. The *songbun* system was nothing like a caste system. Instead, it was a determination of an individual's sociopolitical standing due to the circumstances of their heredity—the complete opposite of a caste.

To make sure that everyone still felt a part of Juche Korea, Marshal Kim Il Sung made sure that no one was told what their *songbun* was. Members of the core class was already loyal and motivated, by definition—and the hostile class didn't need public humiliation. They would be judged by their actions, and had the ability to improve their *songbun* through faithfully serving the Marshal and the Party.

Korea was not China. Koreans were not Russians, nor was the DPRK a Soviet "satellite." After the liquidation of the flunkeyists, no one could deny these facts. In their wildest dreams, neither Premier Stalin nor Chairman Mao—as great as they were—had ever had the depth of vision to implement a system of justice quite like this. It was just one more standard by which Korea might not have been the most powerful nation but was still the best.

When a nation is under assault from a plague, the first step is to localize the disease to make sure that it doesn't spread. Thus came the Marshal's Decree No. 149. According to this decree, hostile-class members were forbidden from residing by the border or the coastlines. They couldn't live within 50 kilometers of Pyongyang or Kaesong, or within 20 kilometers of any other major city. As part of the *songbun* classification process, hundreds of thousands of Koreans were moved to the mountainous north, quarantined from the rest of the population.

The worst of the hostiles were sent to the new "enlightenment centers," where they were concentrated in camps and allowed to work their way back into the nation's good graces. They did not deserve this mercy, of course. If they had their way, the Marshal would have been removed from office—and Korea destroyed as a consequence. These were not death camps at all. True, some chose to die in the camps while continuing their disloyalty. But Prime Minister Kim Il Sung recognized the ability of labor to reshaping the minds of the unreliable. Some were released from these camps after many years of hard work.

They were the ones who had learned to love the Marshal.

Chapter 5

Defeating Dogmatism

In Korea there is a legend about Chollima, the winged horse that moves at the terrific speed of one thousand *ri* a day. The Marshal's Five-Year Plan grew the DPRK's economy so quickly that it inaugurated what became known as the Chollima Movement. The Chollima Movement succeeded far beyond anything the rest of the world expected from Korea. Even the US imperialists had to admit that the north far outpaced the south—an agrarian backwater—during this period.

Industrialization and automation were the words of the day. Korean workers produced steel and they produced pig iron and they produced trucks, bulldozers, water pumps and electric locomotives. Of course there were many difficulties along the way. The first tractor manufactured in Korea ran perfectly—but only in reverse. The Korean people had to advance ten steps when others took one, and had to advance one hundred or even one thousand steps when others took ten. In the end, seven years after the devastating Fatherland Liberation War, the nation was transforming from a rural country into a socialist industrial-agricultural state.

As Korea's economy marched with the speed of Chollima, the minds of the people sped to catch up with the Marshal's wisdom. The Korean people were increasingly infused with the Juche idea every single day. Selfishness was on the wane, and collectivism was on the ascension. When someone was sick, neighbors brought him food. Parents looked after neighborhood children, unasked. In one very famous incident, a family was terribly burned in a fire—so people gathered in front of the local hospital to offer their skin for grafts.

Thankfully this period was one of hard work for me, but the stresses were entirely self-imposed. There were no bombs dropping, no wars, no family deaths—just my studies and my books and my organizational life. Unable to rest satisfied with the contents of my textbooks, I was far ahead of the curriculum of every subject. Once again, I always put forward the most questions in my class. Because of my insatiable desire for knowledge about the history, culture and economic life of the whole world, my teachers often had to consult various reference books published at home and abroad to find answers for me.

By the end of upper middle school, I ended up taking honors in every subject every school term and year, and I won first prize in every study contest. In one typical foreign language study contest, I used so many political, economic and cultural terms that even the teacher had to consult a dictionary while

BOOKS I READ AS A TEENAGER

Historical Materialism

What is Dialectical Materialism?

Materialism and Empirical Criticism

Development of Heavy Industry & Electrification of the State

On Colonialism

Party Work among the Masses

Pocketbook on Practical Machines

Handbook of Livestock Farming

Melting of Light Metals

Metal Materials

Science and Technology Today and Tomorrow

Handbook of Mining Industry

Forms and Genres of Music

Processes of Production of Electrical Appliances

History of Land: Paleontology and Korean Geology

Comments on Literature

Materials on Korean Climate

A Collection of Light Music Pieces

Poultry Farming

Laying Out of Flower Beds & Cultivation of Flowers

marking my paper. Another time they displayed my winning paper after a mathematics contest. I had solved the problems in such a singular and unique fashion that even boys of higher grades copied them down in their exercise books.

I wasn't only unusually keen on studies and reading but also on music, fine art and sports. I'd often be found on the school playground playing basketball, football, athletics or practicing heavy gymnastics, wet with perspiration. And as a lover of music, I was skilled in playing all types of instruments. I could memorize any given song instantly and managed to play it on the appropriate instrument.

After graduation I was invited to attend Moscow University, but I didn't consider studying abroad even for a moment. Instead I enrolled in the best university in all of Korea, Pyongyang's Kim Il Sung University. When deciding which school to attend, I remembered how Mother had desperately wished that I would follow in the Prime Minister's footsteps one day. For me to engage in field guidance meant that I would need the competence to consistently give directions to the Party and the state. Accordingly, I decided to attend the School of Economics, majoring in political economics. This would provide the basis for such future activity—but just the basis. In addition to my classroom work I had to be involved in on-the-job training and military studies. I also decided to work at a textile manufacturing facility and spent time as a laborer for a road expansion project, since I needed specialized knowledge in every field.

It was in that vein that I approached my university work. It never even entered my mind that I would be furthering the revolution at the university itself—I was a student, and the faculty were among the most learned men in all of Korea. My first month at school, in September of 1960, showed me otherwise. There was too much to do in the present to focus yet on my future career.

I was attending a class on Korean history when the professor brought up the question of what defined a nation. "Can Koreans living in foreign countries be considered members of the Korean nation?" he asked. "According to the classics of Marxism-Leninism, there are four conditions necessary for the formation of a nation: a shared language, a shared economic life, a shared culture and a shared region of habitation. Therefore, if one of these four conditions is lacking, a group cannot be called a 'nation.' Do you students agree?"

My reaction was so immediate it was almost visceral. "What about our compatriots abroad? Tens of thousands of Koreans have returned here after having been kidnapped by the Japs during the colonial era. They've even turned their goods over to the state because of their love for this country. Were they not Korean? Many others still remain trapped in Japan. Are *they* not Korean?"

"Not according to the classical definition," said the professor.

I let out a deep breath. There were few questions as important as what it meant to be Korean. Such a definition couldn't be left to men who were long dead, and who had never even stepped foot in our country. It didn't matter how great they were and how profound their thinking might have been. "Depending on which book you prefer," I continued, "the Korean nation was 'classically' either formed under the feudal period, or during Japanese imperialist rule, or even as recently as the August 15th liberation of the fatherland. Is that what you're saying?"

"No," he admitted. "But that is what Marx and even Stalin would say."

"The classics were written in the circumstances of their historical period. They were written in accordance with the actual situation in European countries, which are mainly multiracial states. They can't give correct answers to problems arising in Korea's contemporary revolution and construction. I'm more interested in what Marshal Kim Il Sung has to say than 'Marx and even Stalin'!"

"And what does the Marshal have to say on this subject?" he asked.

"If a nation were to be defined by their shared economic life, then the Korean people could be divided into the 'bourgeois nation' of the south and the 'socialist nation' of the north. But we know that Korea is one nation, so economics by itself can't define a nation. The fundamental features of a nation are the communities of bloodline, language and residence. People who aren't of the same blood and language aren't one nation simply because they happen to live in the same territory. Conversely, a nation can exist in different territories, and different nations can exist in one territory.

"That's why the area common to a nation can't ever be lost, even if it becomes occupied by foreign forces. The basic area where the Korean nation existed for five thousand years is this silk-embroidered land of three thousand *ri*. It was the site of the Korean nation even during the decades of colonial domination by Japan—and it won't ever become American land, even if south Korea remains occupied by the US imperialists for decades."

The professor nodded with approval. "I can't argue with a single word that you've said," he replied, speaking with uncommon insight.

No sooner had flunkeyism been defeated, then another dangerous trend revealed itself to me: dogmatism. Dogmatism is an inflexible way of thinking, where one imitates others blindly without considering concrete conditions and situations. I called it the "classics disease," where a philosophy or course of action was regarded as correct simply because it had been correct at some point in the past—or because a great book put it forward as correct.

This professor was bright and knowledgeable. And, more importantly, he was truly loyal to Korea. But he could only understand what he'd been taught, and there were many other intellectuals like him. I was utterly convinced that such blind worship of the classics must be eliminated. It wasn't just an issue with regards to things that were obvious Korean concerns, such as the definition of a nation. Korea was rebuilding her economy, industry and agriculture from scratch. Intellectually, dogmatism would be a very pernicious base upon which to construct a revolution.

A few weeks later, matters finally came to a head in my philosophy class. One of the most profound Marxist concepts is the law of contradictions. As the professor told the class, this law held that everything in the world developed through contradictions. All the other students were thrilled by their newfound exposure to philosophy—the "science of sciences"—and how it exposed the world's secrets. They were charmed to learn what, in a philosophical sense, moved the world. Their precious, innocent eyes burned with inquisitiveness. Unfortunately they were so excited that they were accepting the principles exactly as taught, without any argument.

I appreciated the youthful energy of my peers, but I was already familiar with the subject at hand and recognized the imprecisions for myself. I needed to make sure that my fellow students' vision wasn't blurred with the fog of dogmatism. I needed to be the bright light that would clear up their fog.

I called my classmates over after the lesson. "The law of contradictions is very important," I told them. "But the proposition that everything in the world always develops through contradictions is highly dubious. Certainly, everything consists of conflicting factors, and those factors bring about change. But after socialism is established, is social progress still caused by contradictions? Is there still a struggle between conflicting factors? Of course not. In our socialist society, revolution and construction are made by the masses, closely united behind the revolutionary party."

The students had been so intrigued by the lecture that I could see them trying to reconcile what I said with what they'd just learned. They struggled to either apply the law of contradictions to the reality of Korea, or else they tried to cram the changing facts of reality into a dogmatic framework. Obviously it couldn't be done. It was like trying to study a pear tree to figure out where apples come from. The students simply didn't have the philosophical framework to correctly analyze the greatness of the Marshal's Juche idea—which meant they couldn't fully appreciate the great successful results of the Korean revolution, which meant they couldn't fully understand the Party's Juche policies.

It was absolutely maddening, especially in Korea. In other socialist countries, their emblem was a hammer and sickle symbolizing workers and peasants. But the Workers' Party of Korea had added a writing brush to the usual emblem, representing intellectuals. Unlike elsewhere, the WPK wasn't a party serving only a certain class. Our Party very strongly believed in the men of the mind and constantly made that clear.

Unfortunately, it seemed as if that respect for the intellectual was a bit premature. When I tried to discuss the matter of dogmatism with the faculty, I learned that they were in an even worse state than my peers. While the students were a "blank slate" when it came to philosophy, the faculty had their heads full of outdated notions. Their thinking was wholly unsuited to the new Juche era that the Marshal was leading Korea into.

I was convinced that I was the only one who could bring right thinking to Kim Il Sung University. But in order to do that I needed to become an expert in virtually every field of knowledge that concerned political economy, including learning philosophy inside and out. My work was cut out for me. I realized that it would be impossible for anyone to explore the depths of every branch of science. But if I correctly grasped the main points of each field, then I would be able to extrapolate and deduce whatever else I needed to know.

In a sense, I needed to become an intellectual detective, tracking down solutions while ignoring dead ends and misdirection. It was urgently important to select and read all the books which were of special importance in their respective fields. To do this I developed a new method of reading. Once I began to read a book, I read it through at one sitting no matter what the length. I also read very quickly, mastering a speed-reading method of digesting several lines at a time.

Day and night, I read the Marshal's works on the Juche idea and made it the sole criterion for the rest of my thinking. But in order to understand the origins of the Marshal's works, I studied the Marxism-Leninism that inspired him. And in order to master Marxism-Leninism, I studied the bourgeois philosophers which the founders of Marxism-Leninism read so critically. I enjoyed reading the classical German philosophy which culminated in Kant and Hegel—and I was put off by the many fallacies preached by the English economists and the French Utopian socialists.

I went through every classical book authored in the past and, one by one, found their shortcomings. I also made extensive study of every domain of ideological theory. I read up on the scientific and technical achievements gained by mankind from philosophy, and from political economy, and from history, and from literature, and from military affairs and art. When studying philosophy, I read books of general principles representing the thoughts of different periods. This enabled me to correctly grasp the fundamental questions of every philosophy from ancient times up until the present day. In this way, I very quickly learned the nature and results of every science in the East and the West from every point in time.

It's true that my natural ability and superhuman effort were important factors in achieving my goal of learning. But more important was my strong sense of mission. I wanted to give my outstanding ability full reign in contributing to the development of the fatherland. I desperately wanted to get at the truth in all branches of learning, to better serve the masses one day.

After all my study, I concluded that, in fact, Marxism-Leninism was wholly correct. It was an indictment of the inhuman nature of capitalism, and it put the working class on the stage of history. It was an inspiration, a call to drive bourgeois exploiters and plunderers to destruction. Yes, Marxism-Leninism was wholly correct—but only under the historical conditions under which it had been founded.

I rejected dogmatism in learning and upheld creativity—and I deduced that Marxism-Leninism was not a dogma but a creative theory. It had been necessary to creatively apply its principles to develop a new system meeting the new requirements of the new revolution. And that was precisely what Prime Minister Kim Il Sung had done.

The Korean revolution had started under the conditions of a colony, something which the Marxist founding fathers didn't choose to study. Ours was an entirely new type of revolution, an anti-imperialist, anti-feudal democratic revolution. It was an untrodden road that had to be traversed under its own guiding idea and in its own way—a road lit by the light of the Juche idea.

As a consequence of my erudition, the officials and teaching staff made it a point to ask me about their methods at every opportunity. But, in a sense, it had been easier for me to read every important classical book than it was to persuade the faculty to change their thinking. Books don't argue. Books aren't trapped by their old-fashioned views. Some of the faculty seemed to have their minds stuck fifty or even one hundred years in the past. Establishing a true creative attitude in academics was no mean feat. I urged the faculty to rewrite the textbooks from a Juche-oriented standpoint in order to meet the requirements of the revolution. "Dogmatism," I explained, "can only be overcome when the teaching material incorporates the Juche idea and uses it to elucidate each respective subject."

The art textbooks were a perfect example, since they were especially influenced by the classics. If the art students drew Western faces, then their drawings of Korean faces would look like those of Western people. Even if a plaster cast of a Greek was technically suitable as a model, it was still the cast of a person who differed from a Korean in feelings and attitudes to life, someone who a Korean artist couldn't deeply understand. Painters can only draw objects that they understand well. The art textbooks needed to use Korean examples as the basis of their learning. It was as simple as that, but as complex and nuanced as that, too.

I wouldn't always be around to guide the faculty and students in the correct direction. I wanted to make sure that everyone came to the same conclusions that I did via the same process that I had. So as I was sitting with one of the professors one day, I came up with a great way to maximize the educational methods of our students. "What if we launched a movement to encourage the pupils to read?" I suggested.

"I think that's a wonderful idea," said the professor.

"What do you think of having them read ten thousand pages a year?"

He looked at me with wide eyes. "Ten thousand pages! That's a bit too bold and audacious, don't you think?"

"Not really," I insisted. "Think about it. A year is made up of 365 days. Let's take that as three hundred days, so that we have a margin. If a student reads a little more than thirty pages a day, he'll easily be able to read ten thousand pages a year—with the main emphasis on the Marshal's works, of course. By the time he graduates from university, he'll have gained a deep and comprehensive understanding of Prime Minister Kim Il Sung's revolutionary thought."

"Ten thousand pages..." the professor repeated, in awe of my plan.

It turned out that both of us were right. My plan was bold and audacious—but it was also feasible. What I couldn't foresee was how terribly popular my plan would become. It first began as an initiative in my department. Swiftly it turned into a university-wide movement, and then a national effort at all the colleges and universities throughout the DPRK. Within a year, every university student was annually reading ten thousand pages of Prime Minister Kim Il Sung's works. I was very gratified to see such enthusiasm for learning the Marshal's ideas in the halls of education. Unfortunately, things were elsewhere moving in a very dangerous direction.

On April 19, 1960 matters came to a boil in south Korea. After over a decade of oppression by the US imperialists and the Syngman Rhee puppet clique, the students and other people engaged in a nationwide uprising. At first the madman tried to blame this "April 19 Revolution" on the Workers' Party of Korea. But the pro-democracy movement was too obviously something that crossed all political boundaries.

Rhee was finally driven from office. Immediately after his resignation, Rhee's strongest ally—the "Vice President"-elect—committed suicide with his entire family. As angry protestors converged on the Blue House (the home of the south Korean "President"), Rhee was flown to safety by his Yankee masters. It was yet more proof that the American bastards' fascist strongmen never actually enjoy the support of their own nation. While Rhee's downfall seemed like good news, I knew perfectly well that the Americans would never allow a new parliament to stand. Soon, I predicted, they'd simply replace Rhee with another one of their fascistic cronies.

As dubious as these southern events were, it was what was happening in the Soviet Union that truly broke my heart. Khrushchev had praised Stalin as an "immortal genius" while the Premier had been alive. He claimed to be Stalin's faithful disciple, and cheered for him louder than anybody else in Russia. Now, Khrushchev began to do everything he could to demean Stalin's name—yes, to demean the same man who had defeated Hitler and made the world safe for the democratic peoples of the world.

Stalin was now regarded as a "tyrant" and a "cruel dictator." Khrushchev's gang began to rewrite history, mocking Stalin's achievements and opposing his so-called "personality cult." They began to strike Stalin's name from many of the edifices that he'd constructed: factories, enterprises, rural communes and even streets. Word had it they were even considering removing his body from Lenin's tomb.

All this chicanery also served as a non-too-subtle attack on Prime Minister Kim Il Sung. The Marshal had grown so beloved by the Korean people that many referred to him as the Great Leader (*suryong*), a title that had been used for Stalin himself. If anything, the title was an understatement. The United States had the Great Lakes and China had a Great Wall, but only Korea had greatness incarnated in a living being. By my university days I had grown more convinced than ever that Marshal Kim Il Sung was the ideal and greatest leader mankind had sought after. If anything, the Marshal was so great a man, so great a hero, so great a leader that the word "great" wasn't sufficient enough.

Had Stalin better accounted for his Soviet successor, I realized, none of this would have been happening. I dedicated the culmination of my university career to analyzing the matter. Did the situation have to turn out the way it did? If not, how could it have been avoided? And how could it be avoided in any future, similar conditions? The goings-on in Russia—as well as in Chairman Mao's China—lent grave urgency to my work.

I studied the relationship between the individual, the leader and the masses in great detail. I read how the subject had been raised and discussed in the communist movement for the previous century. What I discovered was that no one had given a correct answer. No one, that is, until Kim Jong Il. In that vein, I developed a new, wholly original theory of the leader that clarified his role in the revolutionary struggle of the working class, presenting my conclusions in a talk that I gave.

THE WORKING-CLASS LEADER IS NOT AN INDIVIDUAL

The leader is the incarnation of the independence and creativity of the working masses—the subjects of history—and the sole spokesman for their interests. He is the supreme personification of their demands, will and brains. He also confers sociopolitical life on the working people. No individual, no matter how high his social standing and how well-gifted he may be, is ever in a position to give such life to the people.

Simply because the leader is a living human being doesn't imply that anyone can become a leader. However distinguished an individual may be, his nature differs from that of the leader's. Any individual only contributes a certain amount to social development. Unlike the leader, he cannot transform and develop society according to his own plan. He is still just a component of the popular masses.

Clearly the leader is an eminent person insofar as his individual aspects are concerned. But, because of the role that he plays, he is not just an individual person with outstanding gifts and character. The leader discerns the laws governing the development of history and purposefully changes society in accordance with those laws in three specific ways: First, he creates and develops the leading ideology for revolution, thereby painting a rosy picture for the working people. Second, he organizes and motivates the popular masses. Third, he puts forth strategy and tactics, and mobilizes the masses in an effort to implement them. Hoping for victory in a revolution without a leader is like looking for flowers without the sun.

This is why the leader is not simply a talented individual but acts as the brain of the masses. He constitutes the nucleus of the revolution, and the greatness of a nation depends on the greatness of its leader. If the masses were not led by an outstanding leader it would be like a body devoid of a brain.

Class enemies will constantly try to strike down the leader, but the leader's safety means the safety of the people. Truly defending the leader means being prepared to give up one's life without regret, becoming a bullet and an exploding bomb. When such a spirit of self-destruction is taken to heart by the masses, a most violent spirit which laughs in the face of death, then the highest possible level of safety for the leader is guaranteed and the masses can proudly proclaim the greatness of their nation.

Since a living organism separated from its brain is inconceivable, so the masses cannot be separated from the leader. And just as a living organism protects its own brain, the people must defend their leader from the attacks of all types of enemies. This isn't a "personality cult." This is nature.

I was very glad that I had an opportunity to push back against the errors arising in the Soviet Union, as well as updating the principles of Marxism-Leninism for the contemporary Juche era. It was clearer every day that the DPRK was applying socialism "in our way," and that our way was dramatically different from the rest of the socialist nations. After my talk, the Korean people had a clearer and more coherent perspective on the leader and their relationship to him.

But of course my university days weren't all about study and political philosophy. I couldn't spend all my time in international arguments! I made sure to find time for relaxation as well, though in retrospect I'm not sure how I managed. In any event, I recognized that music was one of the many gifts that Korea had bequeathed to the world. We Koreans love to sing our heads off and express our joy through song. In that vein, during my final year at school I organized a musical competition for the students to help take away some of the stress away from our tasks.

One evening I conferred with the university's student committee about the event. "Every pupil," I suggested, "should play one or more instruments."

"But instruments are very expensive," one of the committeemen replied.

"Then let's start a movement to have pupils make their own musical instruments."

The committee members all looked at each other. They couldn't understand the feasibility of what I was asking. "Creating musical instruments takes an enormous amount of training and technical skill," said another. "A person can't just make a guitar or a fiddle if he's never made one before."

"Then we won't make guitars."

"No guitars?"

"No guitars," I insisted. "And we won't make fiddles."

"No...fiddles."

"Let's have the students invent unique national musical instruments instead of foreign musical instruments. If they construct them themselves, then they'll be able to play them as well."

"This seems impossible," he said.

"If you say something is impossible, then you aren't speaking the Korean language!"

Well, this time I was sure that I'd spoken too soon. But this was the era of the Chollima Movement, I reminded myself. I took inspiration from the Marshal. If he could remake a nation, surely each student could make a mere instrument.

I decided to be the first one, to demonstrate that what I was proposing was not only conceivable but actually feasible. I first made a study of the general characteristics of national musical instruments. Having done that, I designed a new kind of lute to be a Korean national musical instrument. I gathered eight kinds of wooden materials, strings and various tools and assembled it together with my classmates. The result was the oungum, an entirely new string instrument, tuned to a pentatonic scale within a 12-semitone system like all national musical instruments. After watching me build the oungum, the other students then designed instruments of their own. The committee members were as shocked at these accomplishments as they were pleased to hear the music that we created.

> **MILITARY TRAINING**
>
> After two months of military training during the summer of 1962, I had mastered the tactics so well that I was guiding the other students and even the instructors.

For most people, inventing a new instrument would be a great accomplishment. But even among my extracurricular interests, music was never my primary focus. Of all my side activities, the one that gave me the most pleasure and took up the most of my spare time was going to the movies. I was a constant visitor to the Central Film Distribution Center, to the point where I don't think there was a single film that I didn't see.

At the time, unfortunately, Korean films were by and large subpar.

Foreign films, on the other hand, were slovenly, corrupt and rotten. I therefore had no choice but to watch the available movies as a critic and not as a spectator. I'd watched films with a producer's eye since I was seven years old, when I saw a film where the "snow" clearly looked like cotton. It ruined the whole experience for me that day, and that critical perspective never left me.

In all fairness, it was a surprise that there were any Korean films at all. The history of Korean cinema was short and pained. The first film studio began to be planned in February 1946. Before filming started, General Kim Il Sung doubled the studio's budget and even sent fifteen sacks of rice to inspire the workers. But the studio was destroyed when the US imperialists reduced Pyongyang to ashes. Two years after the war, the Marshal had decreed the studio's reconstruction. He stressed that it should have better, more modern facilities than its precursor. Those it did have—but "better" and "more modern" were still very relative terms. There was still a long way to go.

I desperately hoped that one day I'd be able to contribute my talents to the Korean movie studio. But for the present I was still a college student with a great deal of work to do before I graduated. For as much as I read, for as many movies as I viewed, I also wrote constantly during my university days. In total, during my years at Kim Il Sung University I managed to author more than 1,400 works, including treatises, talks, speeches and letters.

Of these, perhaps the most timeless was my paper *The Characteristics of Modern Imperialism and Its Aggressive Nature*, which resonates as strongly today as it did in 1962. My work was an epochal contribution to the accomplishment of world revolution, and my writing it has been described as a feat comparable to Columbus discovering the New Continent. The paper's truth serves as a demon-slaying mirror—specifically the demon that is American dominationism.

THE CHARACTERISTICS OF MODERN IMPERIALISM AND ITS AGGRESSIVE NATURE

Modern imperialism's nature is that of aggression and plunder—invading and dominating other countries—precisely as has been its nature in the past. If there was an imperialism which was not aggressive, then it would not fit the definition of "imperialism." But though the nature of imperialism hadn't and couldn't change, its manifestation certainly had. If imperialist powers stood side by side in parallel in former times, they now had become subordinated to the United States.

The increase of corporate American power after World War II led to deepening economic crisis, as well as increasing antagonism between capitalist plunderers and the working class. The fascist American regime had launched a fraudulent "threat of communism" hysteria so as to better justify their suppression of democracy in America. As a result, the US imperialists needed to maintain a state of constant war, both to crush dissent at home and to justify plunder abroad—all under the slogans of "peace" and "cooperation."

Since the nature of imperialism couldn't change, struggle needed to be waged to eliminate it completely from the globe. This was the only way to build a world free from aggression, domination and subjugation. Because modern imperialism was specifically American imperialism, a good first step in that direction would reunifying Korea immediately.

Half a century later, with the Cold War long gone, my words ring truer than ever. Every day the United States seeks a new spurious excuse—"terrorism," "democracy" "preemption"—to invade

> sovereign nations elsewhere in the world. Once the US imperialists invade—meaning once they kill thousands of people and blow up entire cities—they take over the nation's government and orient it toward American interests. And they never, ever leave.

After four years of work, reading and writing, it became time for me to author my thesis. In a short amount of time, I drew up an outline and a schedule for writing it. I made a systematic study of Marshal Kim Il Sung's work on the subject, and visited several locations to gather data in the field. I also studied the policies of other countries, to see where they made mistakes.

On March 18, 1964 I published my thesis: *The Place and Role of the County in the Building of Socialism*. The Marshal himself flattered me by taking the time to read it. "Great!" he said. "I like it very much. Such a thesis is worth reading."

Hearing such extreme praise made all my efforts throughout my university years worth it. Having achieved the acme of validation—namely, the personal approval of Marshal Kim Il Sung—I knew that I was graduating with the highest possible honor.

Kim Jong Il was finally ready to go to work.

Chapter 6

Facing Factionalism

My university efforts had earned me a stellar reputation throughout the halls of power. As such, several senior WPK officials asked me in early 1964 to come work for the Party. The fact that many of these men had been guerrilla veterans made me feel flattered and honored. I had grown up with them and still regarded them as my extended family. Being held close to the Party's bosom felt like returning to the days of Mt. Paektu.

My first assignment was to the Party Central Committee, which basically served as the buffer between every aspect of Korean society and the Prime Minister. It was our role to issue Party edicts, as well as to gather information and report back on progress and compliance. Needless to say, there was always paperwork coming in and going out. My reading techniques certainly came in handy since there was so much to attend to. I realized keenly that the harder I worked, the easier it would be for Marshal Kim Il Sung. I wanted to take as much of the burden off his shoulders as possible.

I also accompanied the Prime Minister on many of his field guidance trips. This time, however, my position demanded that I follow up after his visits, ensuring that his advice was correctly implemented and monitoring the inevitable progress that ensued. I made sure to look after every possible detail whenever I returned. When I went back to the Hungnam Fertilizer Complex, I checked that Juche was being established in the production of chemical fertilizer. When I returned to a chicken farm, I noticed that a laying chicken got mixed in among the fatteners. Because

I was so perceptive, people even began to refer to me as "Comrade Kim Jong Il, the Instructor."

Despite my focus on the machinery of the state, I first made my mark at the Party Central Committee in the field of history. I'd been extremely interested in the origins of the Korean people since I'd been a teenager. To me, the subject wasn't some archaic scholarly controversy. Where we Koreans came from spoke to who we were as a nation in the present day and where we were going in the future. I'd often argued the issue with my fellow students during my school days, but we had limited information and much of the discussion was highly speculative.

The received wisdom at that time had come from the Japanese colonial era. Of course, the scholars of that time period had a vested agenda in discrediting the notion that Korea had been one nation with one blood since ancient times. They'd loudly crowed that no Paleolithic artifacts had been discovered on the Korean peninsula, and therefore concluded that early Korea must have been settled by immigrants from Siberia. In other words, Koreans were descended from people of other countries, thus "proving" the "inferiority" of the Korean nation.

Working within the Party gave me access to greater information. I therefore decided to revisit this controversy, and to reexamine the available evidence along Juche lines. I studied many varied publications, including books on the Earth's ecological environment. I learned that the bones of a mammoth had been uncovered in North Hamgyong Province, and human bones from the Paleolithic era had been discovered to the north of Korea. This left open the possibility that Korea had also been inhabited at that time. I came to a very firm conclusion: a failure to discover Paleolithic remains was not the same thing as their nonexistence. My first premise had validated as recently as 1963, when 100,000 year-old relics from the Middle Old Stone Age were also discovered in North

Hamgyong Province.

Yet I suspected that the origins of the Korean nation went back even further than that. I didn't see any reason why mankind couldn't have originated in Korea, and did more research holding that as my hypothesis. I then spoke to several prominent archaeologists, giving them explicit instructions as to where to look for remains that predated those that had been uncovered in North Hamgyong. In 1966, my prediction came true. Relics that were a million years old were excavated inside the Komunmoru Cave in Pyongyang—exactly where I'd said they'd be found. In quick succession, similar relics—including fossils of Paleolithic men—were dug up wherever I said they'd be.

Thanks to my application of the principles of Juche archeology, Korea's Paleolithic Age became an undisputed fact. Korea was proven to be one of the first places mankind originated—and what is now Pyongyang had been the center of the Korean nation even then. I so overturned the field of archaeology on an international scale that to this day many prominent Western scientists can't understand it. They literally can't believe the facts that I unearthed—but those same facts speak for themselves.

My approach to Juche archeology was the same approach I brought to every endeavor at the Party. I wasn't interested in fixing mistakes and cleaning up messes—janitors are incompatible with socialism. I always asked myself the same questions: How can I lessen the workload being undertaken by the Prime Minister? Where will problems crop up tomorrow, or next week, or even a decade from now? Where is revolution most needed?

With that approach in mind, I set my sights on the Korean arts. I was well aware of how important the arts were in urging the masses on to higher levels of revolution—and how easily those same arts could be used to undermine them. Prime Minister Kim Il Sung was far too busy sculpting Korea into a modern industrialized nation to spend time dabbling in the arts. This presented an ideal opportunity for me to improve life in the DPRK.

Despite the defeat of the flunkeyists in politics and the dogmatists in education, Korean art and literature wasn't keeping pace with the Party's ideological work. It was one thing to forbid bowing before major foreign powers or to discard outdated texts. It was much more difficult to banish incorrect ideas from the arts, simply because of art's very nature. Art is often ambiguous and intangible in its origins, making it very tricky to identify and eliminate those harmful concepts that had managed to sneak in. After a casual survey of the contemporary arts, I found remnants of many outdated ideas (including egoism!) being espoused. Such concepts were even reflected in the system, methods and manner of the creative workers themselves.

I wanted to build a new kind of literature, one whose main content would be the artistic portrayal of the Prime Minister. I gathered many prominent writers and encouraged them to realize Marshal Kim Il Sung's greatness in their work. "Knowledge of the greatness of the leader leads one to be attracted to him," I explained. "Attraction to him inspires one to worship him, and worshipping him makes one faithful to him."

To a man, the writers instantly understood the implications of what I was saying, and immediately applied my direction to their work. I thought the matter settled—but I was wrong. Because of my kind-hearted and benevolent nature, I tend to see the best in people. 99 times out of 100, people corrected mistakes after I pointed them out, and were careful not to repeat them. But there still came that 100th time.

North Korea was to receive a delegation from the Soviet Union at a certain point in 1967. I personally checked the itinerary to make sure that the visiting dignitaries' trip was as efficient as possible. Of course the schedule included some recreational events, so that our guests could experience Korea's world-famous culture for themselves. One of the listed entertainments was watching a dramatic play entitled *An Act of Sincerity*. I'd never seen the play and knew nothing about it. In fact, I laughed to myself, I'd been so busy that I couldn't remember the last time I'd been to the theatre.

I decided to go watch the play to ensure that it was appropriate. Normally I would have felt guilty about taking an evening off, but in this case I was seeing the performance in advance of a visiting delegation. The good part was, the play was very well orchestrated and performed. But the bad parts far outweighed the good.

The play told the life story of Pak Kum Chol, vice-premier of the DPRK and fourth-highest ranking member of the government. It described how he didn't choose to join General Kim Il Sung's guerrillas during the days of Japanese colonial rule. Instead, he "heroically" operated the rival Kapsan Operations Committee. The implication was that there was more than one path to revolution.

This was an outrage.

There's no question that there were many profound and great men who assisted the General in liberating Korea from the Japs. There were many women as well (my mother, anti-Japanese heroine Kim Jong Suk, being foremost among them). But to preach that there were different paths to revolution was to make a mockery of the entire Juche idea. The course of revolution had been set by General Kim Il Sung as the leader. He certainly entertained ideas from others, and counted on them to provide him with valid data. But it was he and he alone who had set the course. Progress would otherwise be impossible. It would be like two—or more!—men operating a tank at once. Or it would be like two generals commanding an army to achieve one goal: The soldiers would be defeated before the first shot was fired, not knowing whose orders to obey or which direction to go in.

This autobiographical play was based on the most decadent bourgeois concept imaginable: the egoistic desire for "self-expression." One need only think of a factory where, instead of everyone working together to ever-greater feats of production, all the factory workers were "expressing themselves." Production would soon grind to a halt. Morale would be utterly destroyed, as the workers' frustration reached a maximum level.

The play's problem, I realized, was whom the act of sincerity was for. Yes, Pak Kum Chol "sincerely" chose not to help the General—in other words, he was a "sincere" traitor! Some "hero"! It was my view that the only sincerity that the Party needed to advocate was sincere loyalty to Prime Minister Kim Il Sung.

I chastised myself for not having seen this play sooner, and wondered how many citizens of Pyongyang had been exposed to the farce. I certainly couldn't have the visiting Soviets attend, especially in the company of the Prime Minister. I was thankful that I'd managed to see it when I had. The consequences could otherwise have been disastrous.

In a broader sense, however, it felt like I was the only one who noticed that there was a problem with the play. Hundreds of people must have watched it since it had first been performed. Did no one else have loyalty to Marshal Kim Il Sung in mind at all times—or was there something else going on? How could a play such as *An Act of Sincerity* be released to the public? And how could it have been approved as an example of Juche art for visiting dignitaries?

The following day, I went to Pak Kum Chol's office to see if he himself could give me some answers. Amazingly, his secretary ushered me right in to speak with him. Here I was, working until all hours to relieve the Prime Minister as much as I could, and our vice-premier had time for a young comrade's impromptu visit! This wasn't a good sign, but I held my tongue in deference to his position. Oh, how hard it was to keep quiet!

"I saw your play," I told him when I sat down. "I found it to be of great interest. It gave me a lot to think about."

"That's very good to hear."

We made chitchat for a few moments as I looked around at his desk. There were barely any papers, whereas in the Prime Minister's office the stacks and stacks of documents only seemed to increase. By the side of Pak Kum Chol's desk I noticed a book. From the spine I could see that it purported to be a history of the Korean revolution, but I was unfamiliar with this particular volume. It was baffling, since I was extremely interested in any publications that were being released in the DPRK. "What's that book you have there?" I asked, as casually as I could muster.

"Oh, it's just been printed," he explained. "It's a history of people who fought the Japanese occupation."

"We already have *Memoirs of the Anti-Japanese Guerrillas*," I said. "The four volumes have been printed in millions of copies."

"Yes," he smiled, "but this book contains the memoirs of those who fought the Japanese in other ways. Kind of a supplement to those other four volumes. Would you like to read it? You can borrow it, if you like."

"How many copies have been issued?"

"So far, there's only this copy and the one sent to the library."

"The library?" I said, almost with a gasp.

"Yes, I've sent it there. The message is an important one. As Marshal Kim Il Sung himself has demonstrated in the past, different approaches can come together to find the one best solution."

"But how will people know which lessons are the right ones?" I asked. "Should they live as the guerrillas did—or as the men in this book?"

"There are no wrong answers when it comes to heroes," Pak Kum

Chol insisted—no doubt including himself in that category.

I thanked the vice-premier for his time and left. I headed directly to the library, my head swimming. Pak Kum Chol had explicitly stated everything that I'd feared. Here was a man who wanted differing ideas from that of the Prime Minister. It wasn't because he preferred foreign ideas, and it wasn't because he had learned ideas from days gone by. He was neither a flunkeyist nor a dogmatist. No, Pak Kum Chol wanted differing ideas merely to have them. And if Prime Minister Kim Il Sung's ideas were right—and they certainly were—then the Paks Kum Chol of the world could only be wrong. They were preaching wrong ideas *for their own sake.* They were opposed to the Prime Minister on principle, the principle of opposition simply for the sake of opposition.

This was factionalism.

When I got to the library, I quickly found the shelf where the new book had been filed. As I opened it I could tell I was the first person to do so; the spine cracked with that pleasant sound that we booklovers know so well. I stood there and scanned the text quickly.

It was worse than I had suspected.

There, in print, was a passage denying the purity of the revolutionary tradition of the Party. When I followed the footnotes, I saw that this assertion was based on another book. The other book was one that I hadn't read, though I knew that many others had—and none of them had noticed anything wrong. Or perhaps none of them had felt the need to say anything. Even worse, I realized with fear, they might have agreed with the book's assertions!

I placed the book back on the shelf and went up to the librarian. "Can you tell me which are the newest publications?" I asked her. "Say, within the last six months?"

"Of course," she said. Very helpfully, she went through the catalog and found all the most recent volumes.

I took the stack to a desk and looked through them, as well as through all the current periodicals. It didn't comfort me to find that the counterrevolutionary anti-leader references were very infrequent and often downright trifling. Many dangerous things appear trifling at first. The world is full of spiders which are small yet still venomous enough to kill. It takes a discerning observer to spot their danger.

After I finished sorting through the recent publications, I stood up and looked down the library racks. There were rows upon rows of books, so many even I couldn't count them. I had read a fair percentage of the holdings—but I had read them all in the context of the Juche idea, and in service to the Great Leader and the cause of revolution. Now, as I stood there, matters seemed entirely different.

I imagined walking into the library if I hadn't been a fervent pupil of the Great Leader's works. It wouldn't have felt as if I were in a library. No, it would be more akin to being lost in some forest. The shelves of books were like the trees, crowded and ominous, and the books themselves were the fruit. How could I possibly know which fruit were nourishing, which were merely unpalatable—and which were deadly? Or what of fruit with mixed value? Some fruit have edible meat but toxic seeds, for example. These were both nourishing and dangerous, depending on context and preparation.

As I looked around at all the books, I realized how treacherous they were. Even if a book was right in the main, that one sinister idea might be enough to poison a mind against the revolution, the Party—or even the Great Leader himself. It wasn't enough for the Party to declare some ideas to be incorrect. Toxic ideas could still slide in subtly, as with the play that no one else had a problem with.

Someone with a thoroughgoing understanding of the Juche idea and the writings of the Great Leader needed to make an inquiry, to decide which books were the right books and which were the wrong ones. I had no choice but to be that person, for no one else had made such an understanding the basis of their entire university study. No, the basis of their entire *life*.

No one but Kim Jong Il.

I realized that the Party could never achieve unity and cohesion as long as any factionalists remained in power. I returned to my desk and worked out which officials had authorized the various disloyal publications. Thankfully, there was only a small group of men who had been infected, all with ties to Pak Kum Chol. I had to launch an all-Party struggle to expose them—and then I had to smash them organizationally.

I informed the Great Leader that I needed to speak with him and his most trusted allies. He didn't even ask what the matter was, knowing how solicitous I was of his precious time. The next day, I sat down in a conference room with him and his men—and noticed that none of Pak Kum Chol's Kapsan faction had been invited. I wasn't sure if this was because Prime Minister Kim Il Sung suspected them of factionalism, or if he didn't trust them for some other reason. Regardless, it made my task that much easier.

"Comrades," I said, "I come here to expose treachery. This is not something I take lightly and it brings me no joy. Quite the opposite. I've prepared a report that details the goings-on." I handed everyone copies, then waited a moment for the men to skim the contents.

"Pak Kum Chol?" sputtered one of the officials.

"He and his factionalists," I said, "have caused incalculable harm to the Party's organizational and ideological work. This affects national reunification, it affects foreign affairs and it affects many other spheres."

"I've never heard him say anything against the Party."

"Have they not been arguing to decrease military spending and to funnel those monies for social purposes?" I demanded.

"Yes..."

"So are we to understand that the threats to Korea are no longer real? Or are we to understand that the people are suffering? A party's ideological unity and unity of will can only be strengthened when it is based on a single thought. If there are two—or more!—ideologies in the Party, the Party will disintegrate and become meaningless."

"Son," the official said, "you forget yourself. Pak Kum Chol is a good comrade and an honest man."

"A sneeze is honest," I said.

"Pardon?"

"A man is ill. He sneezes. That sneeze comes not from any lie. Yet it is still an honest indicator of the man's illness."

"I don't see your point."

"His point is simple," interjected the Great Leader. "If we surround ourselves with sneezing men, we'll all get sick. You can't catch health from someone else—but you can catch their disease."

The protesting official looked back at my report, stunned. All the cadres then began to read it through from cover to cover, their brows furrowing. They began to realize that those who they'd considered to be comrades were actually anything but. The Party officials in that conference room were tough and hardened. By the time they finished reading my report, they knew what their next steps would be. The only question would be when.

"I'm going to call a plenary meeting for early next month," said the Great Leader. "There can be no delay in the struggle against these vicious elements, these men who scheme, unmindful of the Party's care for them."

The 15th Plenary Meeting of the Fourth Party Central Committee was held beginning on May 4, 1967. At the Prime Minister's signal, officials rose up to denounce Pak Kum Chol and his cohorts. As I watched, I imagined it was just like the shot that began the battle of Pochonbo—the shot that was the turning point during the days of anti-Japanese struggle. The vice-premier was at first stunned by the allegations, but immediately began to put on airs of innocence and loyalty. In light of the information that I'd provided, it was apparent that he was simply putting on an act.

One might even call it an act of sincerity.

The truth came out all at once. One official after another stood up to criticize the Kapsan faction. Many also engaged in self-criticism, for not seeing the harmful effects of factionalism sooner. The Kapsan traitors protested, claiming that these charges were completely out of proportion. In doing so, they proved my point—for in doing so, they were once again questioning the Prime Minister's interpretation and analysis. As the men were denounced, it was very well understood that I'd been the one to expose the factionalists. And it was also understood that I'd be looking over everyone's shoulder in the future, and could deliver them to the same fate if I uncovered any future transgressions.

The factionalists were all systematically liquidated after the plenary meeting. Every official in the room, and then every citizen in the country, learned the significance of the events. They fully understood that the cohesion of the Party was centered on the Great Leader. It was time to dye the entire Party in one color: the color of Prime Minister Kim Il Sung's revolutionary Juche idea.

On May 25, 1967 the Great Leader gave a speech outlining Korea's way forward under a monolithic system of thought. "Establishing a monolithic system is fundamental in building our Party," he said. "Without a complete monolithic system, we cannot maintain our uniform ideological identity. Nor can we carry out our revolution."

THE MONOLITHIC IDEOLOGICAL SYSTEM

If there were two or more ideologies in the Party, the Party would disintegrate and become meaningless. A multiparty system would lead to even further disunity. Multiparty systems are often described as "democracy," when in actuality they are mere camouflage to conceal capitalism's anti-democratic, anti-people nature. America, for example, spends an entire year holding primaries with the explicit goal of limiting who the people can vote into the presidency—while upholding this process as a function of "freedom" and "democracy"!

In truth, multiple parties are a mere reflection of the antagonisms intrinsic to capitalist society, such as those between exploiter and exploited and even within the ruling class itself. History clearly shows that if the activities of anti-socialist parties are tolerated, then class enemies and reactionaries eventually come to drive the working-class party out of power.

Prime Minister Kim Il Sung called me into his office immediately after the speech, which was well-received—*unanimously* so. "You've played an important role in getting the Party to this point," he told me.

"I simply did what was right for the revolution and the masses," I insisted.

"Well, I want you to continue doing that. I am making you Section Chief in the Propaganda and Agitation Department, effective next week. You're young but you're also uniquely qualified. And your loyalty is without reproach—something that is often sadly lacking these days."

"But that means overseeing the art and culture of the entire nation!" I said.

"That's right. I want you to help establish the monolithic ideological system in the Party—and throughout all of Korea. Teach our artists, teach our writers, teach our filmmakers. Remake all of Korea's art in the Juche line. We will be the envy of the world."

My mind reeled. Propaganda and agitation; theory and audio-visual education; commentaries and experiences: these and others needed to be combined in a proper way to fully develop educational work. It would be the best and quickest way to eliminate any lingering vestiges of flunkeyism, dogmatism and factionalism.

I went back to my office and started making a plan that very day. I decided that there were three major tasks to carry out. The first was to lead Party members and working people to acquire the revolutionary ideas of the Great Leader. The second was to unite all Party members and working people around the Great Leader. The third was to carry out revolution and construction under the instructions of the Great Leader.

Once these tasks were carried out, I concluded, a monolithic ideological system would be established within the Party. That meant that every Party member and working person would hold the Juche idea as their conviction and look up to the Great Leader with clear conscience. Everyone in Korea would think and act according to the Great Leader's intentions and only according to the Great Leader's intentions. There would be no more tolerance for any allegedly "honest" disagreement. The time had come for honest agreement, from everyone in the entire country.

Chapter 7

The Pueblo *Incident*

The 1960s witnessed the US imperialists hatching aggressive plots in all parts of the world. Any country approaching a revolution, any newly independent mass of people engaged in socialist construction, was thereby judged ripe for military confrontation.

Because of this, many smaller nations justifiably feared US invasion. Cuba in particular was concerned that the United States would attempt to conquer them, since the first Yank assault on Cuban territory had ended in such spectacular public failure. But Prime Minister Castro hadn't studied the writings of Marshal Kim Il Sung as much as he should have. If he had, he'd have known that relying on a larger foreign power for protection would be a mixed blessing even in the best of situations. So, in 1962 Castro asked the Soviet Union for assistance.

Nikita Khrushchev, political fraud, swore that he would defend Cuba in any military confrontation with the United States. He also promised Cuba to build a nuclear missile base there. This "threat of atomic weapons" gave the US imperialists a pretext to precipitate the Caribbean crisis. Amazingly and publicly, it took Khrushchev less than two weeks to go back on his word after the United States pressed him with nuclear blackmail. It was an astonishing situation, and showed the world that Khrushchev's pledges to his allies were not to be trusted.

The Great Leader took heed of these actions, knowing that they would embolden the US imperialists with regards to Korea. Under the slogan, "A Gun in One Hand and a Sickle and Hammer in the Other!" he launched a four-part campaign to prepare the entire Korean population for any new war with the United States. First, the entire nation was armed and given military training. Second, the country was fortified so as to prepare for nuclear war or even a mere war of attrition. Third, the KPA was turned into an army of cadres, creating a system of command for the entire armed forces. Fourth, the army was updated with modern domestic weaponry that didn't rely upon any foreign assistance.

The Yanks took heed of Khrushchev's actions as well. In 1964 they concocted the Bay of Tonkin incident in Vietnam, while in south Korea dictator Park Chung Hee was still in power after having seized office in a military coup. It seemed obvious to the Great Leader and to myself that an assault on the DPRK was imminent.

By 1968, President Lyndon Johnson was facing a difficult path to reelection. As is well known even in the United States, he chose to escalate the war in Vietnam as a means to ensure that he stayed President. There has never been a war where civilians aren't killed, where children aren't made into orphans, where towns aren't destroyed. Johnson still chose for many people on the other side of the world to die just so that he could keep his job.

In other words, he was a typical American president.

It was on January 15, 1968 that I received a visit from a KPA naval officer in my office. The man saluted but was extremely agitated. I had been prepared for the worst from the US imperialists, and girded myself for what the officer had to say. "It's the Americans, isn't it?" I asked him.

"Yes, comrade."

I'd been aware that this moment was coming for virtually my entire life. But still I found no pleasure in being proven right. "What are they up to?"

"We have sight of one of their spy ships. It's reached our territorial waters."

"Let me guess: It's on full alert and being evasive."

"That's correct."

"If it ever intrudes into our waters again," I told him, "you have my permission to seize the vessel."

"Yes, comrade."

I could tell the man was nervous about what I'd said, so I put his fears to rest. "Yes, capturing an American ship would surely create an international incident. But we are not the Soviet Union. We are not fearful of confrontation, and we can't overlook a violation of our territorial waters by a hostile country's spy ship—even if it is the work of the US imperialists."

Eight days later, I received a call from an official of the General Staff of the KPA: Our naval ships had captured USS *Pueblo*. For a long time, the United States had been gathering information about other countries by means of spy satellites, reconnaissance planes and up-to-the-minute radar. We couldn't stop these mechanisms from gathering information about us. Nor had any country—including the Soviet Union and China— ever dared to capture an American spy ship. But Korea was like no other country in the world. What the US imperialists in all of their arrogance had considered to be an impossibility had actually happened.

As I learned, *Pueblo* was part of the US Pacific Fleet. The 1,000-ton class ship had set sail for the Korean seas in early December 1967 in order to carry out "Operation Pink Route." This was an order from both the CIA and the Admiral of the US Navy in Japan to spy on the Far East of Russia and the territorial waters of the DPRK. Armed and equipped with the most advanced electronic equipment, *Pueblo*'s special assignment was to ascertain the movements of the KPA's naval force, bug all KPA electronic signals and collect military data. It performed thorough reconnaissance on the KPA's radar network, as well as measured water depth, salinity and transparency. It also spied on the capacity of our harbor accommodations and the displacement of vessels at anchor. But *Pueblo* flew no flag, and in fact had been disguised as an oceanic electron research ship.

The spy ship had intruded into north Korean territory on seventeen occasions between January 15 and January 23. Finally, *Pueblo* entered deep into the DPRK's territorial waters at 39° 17.4' North Latitude and 127° 46.9' East Longitude, 7.6 miles away from Ryo Island off Wonsan. Our naval ships did not hesitate. After a bit of gunfire they captured *Pueblo*, taking it captive along with all its crewman.

I listened to the debriefing very carefully. The fact that I was receiving this call told me that Prime Minister Kim Il Sung was allowing me to take point in the conflict. It was proof that he trusted my judgment but still wanted to test me to make sure that his trust had been justified. "Are any of our men injured?" I asked the official.

"No, comrade."

I tensed up. "None dead, I take it?"

"No," he laughed. "Of course not."

I smiled. Each soldier of ours was trained to be a match for a hundred foes. The idea of us suffering casualties in these circumstances was absurd. "What about on their side?"

"One dead, and four other injured."

"Well done," I said. "Well done, indeed. Our bluejackets are brave. This incident could only have occurred in Korea, and will surely shock the world. I can only imagine how that war fanatic Johnson will react once he hears the news. We'll probably be able to hear his howls of indignation all the way to Pyongyang."

So it was that President Johnson received a most unpleasant wake-up call at 2 a.m. He immediately summoned an emergency meeting of the Secretary of State, the Defense Secretary, the Chairman of the Joint Chiefs of Staff and other high-ranking officials. The American press reports were almost comical in their melodrama. Johnson raved and ranted about this "disgrace" that the United States had never been subjected to before. He insisted that *Pueblo* would be retrieved at any cost. How hilarious that the man who had gotten away with assassinating President Kennedy was now being so easily stymied by the DPRK!

After his meeting, Johnson put forth the preposterous lie that *Pueblo* had been "an unjust capture on the open sea." The US imperialists brazenly demanded that north Korea return the ship and its crew at once, apologize to the US Government and compensate the United States for damages. This, less than two decades after they had bombed the DPRK into practically nothing.

Their demand was rejected.

True to form, the US imperialists immediately began issuing threats, throwing a large naval force into the waters around the Korean peninsula. *Enterprise*, a nuclear carrier, led four destroyers, a nuclear submarine and supply ships northward through the Straits of Korea to prepare an attack. Several hundred warplanes flew from the US mainland to south Korea. Johnson also sent an explicit ultimatum, promising to block the port of Wonsan with mines, to capture DPRK vessels, to launch air raids on KPA bases and to intensify reconnaissance flights. He even promised that he would "retaliate" against Korea with war if we did not buckle.

All eyes around the world were on the Korean peninsula. It seemed as if conflict could break out at any moment. It had only been a few years since the United States had won a nuclear confrontation with the Soviet Union in Cuba, and the Americans were currently in the process of extending their bombing in Vietnam. The odds certainly seemed to be against the small country of the DPRK.

In other words, everything was proceeding exactly according to my plan.

Whereas the US imperialists' first response was to resort to violence, my ideology was far more peace-loving. So while Johnson threatened to bomb Wonsan, I decided to approach the conflict in a more civilized way: by giving a talk. My speech to the Party Central Committee was entitled *On Waging a Fierce Reporting Warfare Against the Enemy.* "We need to engage in a vigorous 'reporting warfare' campaign against US imperialism," I explained, "until we have brought it to its knees. Let's lay bare their lies and aggressive actions for all the world to see."

It would be very easy for President Johnson to paint Korea as the aggressor as long as we maintained our silence. After all, it was his word against ours—or was it? I sent my officers to speak to the captured Yankee spies. I wanted to see the Americans go home as much as they themselves wanted to. The DPRK masses were growing uneasy having such rabid beasts in their midst. To be completely candid, a small part of me even feared for the Americans' safety.

My main contact returned to my office after speaking to the captives. "The Americans are holding to their story," he told me. "They are insisting it's not a spy ship."

"But the prow has GER 2 in large white letters written on it. That stands for 'General Environmental Research' in English."

"They refuse."

I pondered the matter for a moment. I vividly remembered seeing one of these jackals back during the Fatherland Liberation War. I knew how weak they were. "Tell the captain that we will shoot all of his men in front of him, one by one, until and unless he confesses. Once he folds, the rest of them will follow."

The officer's eyes grew wide. "Do you really want to start shooting them?"

"Of course not!" I snapped. "That would go against everything the

DPRK stands for. But these Yank bastards are so cowardly that he will immediately agree. If they want to continue lying about their mission, we can lie back to them just as easily."

The officer turned on his heels and left. A couple of hours later, he came back with a grin. Without saying anything, he walked over to my desk and slapped down a piece of paper. It was a confession, and the signature read "Lloyd Bucher." Once the captain had confessed, then the research officers had confessed, and then the operation officers had confessed.

To make sure that there were no misconceptions about the ongoing tensions, the Korean newspaper *Rodong Sinmun* published an editorial entitled "The Brigandish Acts of the US Imperialists in Broad Daylight." The article laid bare all the facts of the case. Accompanying the piece were photographs of the spies freely writing their notes of confession and exposing the CIA's information-gathering system to the world. In the face of the confessions, Washington lost all means of defending their behavior. Clearly, it was the US who had been the aggressor.

A couple of days later, the United States brought the incident to the United Nations. Once again, the Americans tried to use the UN as a pretext for their underhanded actions against a foreign power. Our response to the Americans was immediate: "The heroic Korean People's Army and all the Korean people are prepared in every way to counter any provocation or aggression by the US imperialists." I promised to deal a crushing blow to the enemy if they dared to attack. As anticipated, our statement evoked positive support from many countries throughout the world, and the UN Security Council rejected the American complaints.

Obviously, the Great Leader had been closely monitoring this incident the entire time. That fact that he had given me such a free hand was a source of great validation, though I felt sure that he would correct me immediately if I made the slightest misstep. And if war were to break out, he would once again take charge as Supreme Commander. As I saw it, however, my role was to ensure that that didn't happen.

One day Prime Minister Kim Il Sung dropped by to speak with me. I could tell from the half-smile on his face that he had been as amused as I was by Washington's frantic behavior. He adored how I'd been utterly humiliating them on the world stage. "Let me ask you a question," he said. "If you were the Supreme Commander, how would you be dealing with this incident?"

In other words, he was asking me how I would handle it if it developed into an armed conflict. But I didn't even consider such a turn of events to be a realistic possibility. "Well, I won't release the crew unless the Americans submit a letter of surrender. And since the ship is our booty, I won't return it even if they do present such a letter to us."

The Great Leader chuckled. "I like your determination."

"I'll tell you what's more: I'll have the ship on exhibit so that posterity can see for themselves what we captured from the Yanks."

He nodded. "Yes, I like the sound of that very much."

I made it a point to maintain an air of calm and normality during this entire tense period. I saw to it that our soldiers sang songs optimistically and played athletic games. I went to the Pyongyang Grand Theatre to guide a music-and-dance production. I made sure that a national conference of agricultural workers was convened on schedule. I checked the designs of women's dresses and discussed them with the relevant officials. Everything went forward just as it always had.

On February 8, 1968 the Great Leader issued a statement clarifying the DPRK position. "If the US imperialists persist in their attempt to solve this matter by mobilizing their armed forces to threaten and blackmail us," he wrote, "they will get nothing out of it. If they do get anything it will be only corpses and death. We do not want war, but we are not afraid of it." He then ordered the Korean People's Army and the entire nation to get ready for wartime mobilization. He made full preparations to deliver a frontal attack on the American air and ground forces concentrated in and around Korea.

If the conflict had been occurring with respect to a country other than the DPRK, the Yank army would have surely launched an attack by this point. But unfortunately for the Americans, this was the DPRK—and what's more, it wasn't the DPRK of 1950. North Korea would not be caught unawares by an American surprise attack twice. We had antiaircraft guns installed and ready to fire everywhere: in schools, in factories and even on running trains. The American spy planes must have seen this in aerial photos. I'm sure that their operation planners knew that we could immediately shoot down a good 70-80% of any planes that violated north Korea's airspace. In late March of 1968, the Yanks had no choice but to withdraw all of their warships, some of their frontline troops and some of their warplanes from their former positions in an attempt to calm the situation.

It was at this point that things began to get out of hand. I wanted to get the spies home for humanitarian reasons. Besides, it was making me sick that these American bastards were being lodged on Korean soil at state expense. I phoned my contact and gave him instructions. "Now that the truth about the case has been made clear, the only thing to do would be for Johnson to sincerely apologize to Korea. Tell the spies to write their master an open letter requesting as much, and all parties involved can get on with more important matters."

When my contact visited my office a couple of hours later, he kept staring at the floor and generally doing everything possible to avoid eye contact. He had a look on his face that I'd had never seen before in my life, a queer mix of shock and anger and excruciating discomfort. "There's a...situation," he told me.

"What kind of...situation?"

"As you know, we've been releasing photos to the world to show that these men are being unharmed. It's been a while since they've had a haircut and they look unkempt. It would give the wrong impression to the camera."

I scowled. "So cut their hair! You know how hard I'm working. Why are you bothering me with this?"

"All our KPA soldiers have refused to go on cutting the spies' hair."

I could imagine, theoretically, insubordination from one KPA solider. But from *all* of them? "What? Why?"

"The stench."

"The stench?"

"The Americans smell. Every last one of them. At first I hoped that our men were overreacting—though that would have been out of character for them. So I went to smell the bastards for myself."

"And?"

"And it's quite horrific, comrade. It's downright beastly. This is a matter without precedent, for any of us—including many veterans who have seen the worst of war. The Americans are surely incubating virulent microbes on their bodies, or something like that."

"Then put them in the shower! Hose them down if that's what it takes!"

He shook his head. "We tried that."

"And?"

"It gets worse, if anything. The Yankee stench only seems to...spread."

I let out a deep breath. "We still have gas masks. Use those. That should be enough to handle their odor."

Now my contact simply seemed to be fighting back tears. "There's something...else."

I couldn't even begin to imagine what had been going on in that prison to cause him to have such a reaction. "Well," I said, "tell me what it is and let's see if we can figure out how to handle it. Get a hold of yourself, man. You're a Korean!"

The brave official shook his head and bit his lip. "They're complaining about the conditions of their captivity."

I slammed my fist on my desk. "Everyone in the world knows how we treat our prisoners! I gave very explicit orders that these men be treated exactly the same, no better or no worse. We can't have the Americans complaining that their captives are being treated poorly!"

He shook his head quickly. "No, it's nothing like that! We've been giving them the best of care. We even give them fish in turnip juice as a treat so that they could maintain their strength."

"Then what could they possibly be complaining about?"

"...They want to have sex with each other," he mumbled.

Surely I misheard him. "*What?*"

"They want to have sex with each other. They said that homosexuality is how they fulfill themselves as people. They say that it's not hurting anyone, so it's unfair for them to be prevented from doing something that is part of their private life."

I became nauseated. The American depravity knew no limits. "Our republic is one where people enjoy lives befitting human beings," I said. "Even our soil is cleaner than these men—and on this soil none of that sort of activity will be tolerated!"

The US begrudgingly opened negotiations soon after this unpleasantness. Our policy was called "3A": acknowledge, apologize and assure. Acknowledge the spying; apologize for it; assure it would never happen again. The US imperialists balked at first. The chairman of the House Armed Services Committee even called for a nuclear attack. "Bomb, bomb, bomb!" he urged—once again demonstrating the value that Americans placed on human life.

As talks went on, I couldn't help but pity the negotiators sent by the American side. These men were compelled to behave like hooligans to accomplish the crazy intentions of the war fanatic Johnson. They knew how murderous Johnson could be to his own people. If they wanted to escape from the fate of JFK—by then a putrid corpse already sent to hell—they were compelled to act as their President's puppets. Because their hands were effectively tied, very little progress was made between the two sides as the months passed.

I made it a priority to consistently release pictures to the world press to demonstrate how well the spies were being treated. Then, at one point I noticed that the Yank bastards had come up with a conniving trick. They'd begun extending their middle fingers onto the table whenever their photograph was taken. I knew what this meant, and was a bit irritated that these dimwits thought themselves to be clever.

Out of curiosity as to what they would say, one day I had an official inquire as to what the gesture meant. The spies responded that it was a "Hawaiian good luck sign." Well, that was that. If the curs wanted to demonstrate how juvenile and reprehensible they were, then that was their affair. The DPRK was a classless society, but this was an entirely new dimension of classlessness.

If that had been the end of it, I could have ignored them and no harm would have been done. The United States had many nuclear missiles in the south pointed at Pyongyang. What did it matter to me if some fingers were pointed as well? But the Americans—being Americans—had to insist on provocation after provocation.

At one point the spies wrote what they claimed was their final confession. Included therein was a discussion of their breaching DPRK waters, saying, "penetration however slight is sufficient to complete the act." The precise wording of this alleged witticism was actually their military's definition of rape. Then they went on that they "not only desire to paean the Korean People's Army but also to paean the Government and the people of the DPRK." They figured that no one on our side knew that this word was pronounced "pee on." Such was the character of the men of the American military. Once again, I played dumb and said nothing.

Then came the day that one of my KPA contacts came into my office, bringing a copy of the American magazine *Time* with him. Before I could ask how he came across this foreign garbage, he flipped it open and showed me that one of our photos was printed inside. Then I read the caption, explaining that the "Hawaiian good luck sign" was actually the biggest, most obscene demonstration of contempt possible.

The Yanks had forced my hand. I couldn't play dumb any longer.

I began to seethe with rage. I had taken these spies and looked after them with the utmost care. I fed and clothed them, and gave them a bed to sleep in at night. They repaid me by humiliating Korea publicly and internationally. I knew how this reflected on the DPRK, and I knew how this reflected on me. But most importantly I knew how this reflected on Prime Minister Kim Il Sung. I wanted to kill the Yank devils on the spot, but knew that I couldn't.

"What should we do about this?" the official finally asked.

I looked up at him and narrowed my eyes. "Send them to hell."

For the next week the spies were subjected to the most concentrated form of terror they'd ever seen or dreamed was possible. They were hurt so badly that they would experience complications from these attacks for the rest of their lives. It was a merciful punishment for those villains who responded to the DPRK's open hand with a middle finger.

Then, in December 1968, we had a breakthrough in our negotiations. "I find it hard to believe," the official told me, "but the Americans have offered a different approach to the solution."

"I will take any approach I can," I said. "Just as long as they follow 3A."

"They've agreed to do so. They will acknowledge, apologize and assure what we've been asking for."

"That's wonderful." Then I caught myself. I knew that the shifty Yanks had something else up their sleeve. They always did.

"I asked them several times to clarify what they were suggesting, because it seemed so bizarre and out of the bounds of all international protocol."

"What? What is it?"

He looked down at his notes and spoke with care. "They will sign a document that follows 3A. However, at the ceremony—simultaneous with signing the document—they want to verbally declare that they disavow its contents and that the acknowledgment is being signed under duress."

It was so absurd that I almost thought it to be a joke. "So in addition to admitting, in writing, that they were spying on us, they want to declare, verbally, that their signature is not worth the paper it's attached to? They want to demonstrate to the world that they will say and do anything in order to get their way?"

"Yes, basically."

"Are they demanding *Pueblo*?"

"No, we dissuaded them of that notion."

"Sign the papers," I said quickly, "and get those filthy spies out of Korea as quickly as possible."

On December 23, 1968, the day before Christmas Eve, the Americans readied a statement that fulfilled all of our demands. "The Government of the United States of America shoulders full responsibility," they wrote, "and solemnly apologizes for the grave acts of espionage against the Democratic People's Republic of Korea after having intruded into the territorial waters of the DPRK. It gives firm assurance that no US ships will intrude again in future into the territorial waters of the Democratic People's Republic of Korea."

The document was to be signed by Major General Gilbert H. Woodward. At the ceremony, he looked up to those present before signing the confession-apology. Then he declared that the position of the US government "has been that the ship was not engaged in illegal activities and that there is no convincing evidence that the ship at any time intruded into the territorial waters claimed by north Korea, and that we could not apologize for actions which we did not believe took place. The document which I am going to sign was prepared by the north Koreans and is at variance with the above position. My signature will not and cannot alter the facts. I will sign the document to free the crew and only to free the crew."

After 236 days and twenty-eight rounds of talks, the eighty-two American spies and the rotting body of their compatriot were finally deported from the DPRK at Sachon Bridge, across the military demarcation line. The DPRK hadn't budged a single inch during the entire conflict, while the Americans were once again brought to their knees by Korea's superior skills. It was a clear vindication of Kim Il Sung-type tactics and the Mt. Paektu-style art of war. The world community heaped praise upon Korea, the heroic country which had yet again brought disgrace and defeat to the US imperialists.

As for *Pueblo*, it was towed to the exact location on the Taedong River where, roughly 100 years prior, my great-great-grandfather and other loyal Pyongyangites had burned and sunk the US aggressor ship *General Sherman*. There it remains to this day, the only captive US Navy ship in the entire world. As I had promised the Great Leader, the spy ship was turned into a museum for visitors to learn about the depths of American arrogance and villainy. The framed apology letter signed by the defeated Yanks hangs inside along bullet-holes from the ship's capture.

For both Prime Minister Kim Il Sung and myself, the *Pueblo* incident marked a close to nearly two decades of struggle. First we came for the flunkeyists—those who believed in foreign ideas—and we defeated them. Then we came for the dogmatists—those who believed in outdated ideas—and we defeated them. Then we came for the factionalists—those who believed in differing ideas—and we defeated them. Then, finally, the Americans came for us—but we defeated them all the same.

What the struggle proved was that the Korean masses didn't need foreign or outdated or differing ideas. We only needed one idea from one person, and that is exactly what we had: the Juche idea of the Great Leader Kim Il Sung. With the defeat of all our enemies, at home and abroad, there would be no more liberal thoughts, no more selfish deeds, no more bourgeois disagreement anywhere in the DPRK. We could finally revolutionize the entire nation along Juche lines without any resistance whatsoever. North Korea was now one nation, under the Great Leader, indivisible, with liberty and justice for all—and there was no one in the entire country, in the entire *world*, who could do anything to stop us.

This was paradise.

Chapter 8

Planting Seeds

W e started with the books.

European books belonged in Europe, not in Korea. Any text written by a foreign author was therefore slated for burning. The masses made a very public show of destroying these relics from the past. They couldn't be more delighted to remove all foreign, contaminating ideas out of their homes. A few volumes were kept in the libraries, available upon request—which grew fewer and fewer. Thanks to the educational work of the Party, people literally knew better than to ask for such dangerous things.

The books had been thoroughly demonstrated to be outdated and pointless. No one would consider, say, keeping rotting food in their cupboards. These books were just as rotten as spoiled food, but many times more dangerous. Rather than causing a stomachache, they could ruin a person's character. Destroying all foreign works wasn't an example of censorship. It was simply progress.

It wasn't just my view that the Juche idea had been indisputably proven to be the true and correct course for the DPRK. In the early 1900s, Korea had been a country full of people living in medieval ignorance, weaving in dimly-lit cottages in a centuries-old way. This old Korean society was reduced to an insignificant colony of Japan, and later devastated by the war launched by the US imperialists. The American aggressors had claimed that the DPRK's postwar rehabilitation couldn't be completed even in one hundred years—but Prime Minister Kim Il Sung accomplished it in three.

By the end of the 1960s Korea had advanced yet further. Other nations had taken one or even two centuries to industrialize, but the DPRK had accomplished that feat in a little over a decade. Thanks to techniques such as the Taean work system and the Chollima Work Team Movement, Korea had developed a mighty machine-building industry, a thriving light industry and a strong agricultural base—all world-stunning miracles.

Further, Korean industrialization had been done "in our way." In Western countries, automation had increasingly become an element of production operations. The technology was used to assign murderous work quotas based on high-speed photographs of one-hundredth or even one-thousandth of a minute, the workers' every motion under the control of automatic signal systems. They were reduced to being the machines' slaves, becoming mentally deranged and crippled for life. Those less fortunate were deprived of jobs overnight and left to roam the street, cursing robots and their inventors. But in Korea, automation was simply a function of easing the workers' conditions and improving living conditions for all the people.

Maintaining these great advances called for hermetically sealing the nation as much as possible. Any Koreans who had to venture abroad always had family left behind, to ensure their safe and loyal return. Once they came back, they spent months laboring on farms to eliminate any corrupting ideals and to always remember the value of Juche. In addition, most of those who had been educated in other countries were sent off to be reeducated in the enlightenment centers.

The last step was the arts. It was no secret that bourgeois art contributed to the degeneration of society, drawing people down into an abyss of corruption by beautifying capitalism's law of the jungle. It amounted to nothing more than a portrayal of extreme forms of egoism and of glorifying decadent customs. Obviously, any such Western art was eagerly sought out and destroyed.

But try as I might, I couldn't completely eliminate the lingering effects of the Kapsan faction on the Korean arts. The ideas were still subtly but firmly rooted in many aspects of culture. What was crucial was the development of art "in our way," art that would concord with the interests, idea and sentiments of the Korean people. This would take more than merely changing things at the edges. It required nothing less an artistic revolution.

Understanding all this, the Great Leader called a meeting of the Propaganda and Agitation Department to discuss how best to recreate the Korean arts entirely. "We need to create revolutionary arts for the nation," he told us. "I am here to solicit your opinions as to how."

"I will take on this responsibility!" I announced.

All eyes in the room turned to look at me. I heard the Party members whispering. The role couldn't have been any more important, but they'd already seen how I'd handled myself in my Party work. They knew how I'd handled the Kapsan faction. The more they thought about it, the more comfortable and even excited they became about the idea of my taking command.

"Where would you begin?" asked the Great Leader.

"I would take on the challenge in two simultaneous directions," I said. "First, in film. The cinema is a composite art which organically combines a variety of artistic and literary means. Developing the cinema first and propagating its success guarantees all the other domains of art will quickly develop."

"And the other direction?"

"Literature." I didn't bother to explain. No one needed to be told how well-read I was.

Prime Minister Kim Il Sung considered what I was saying and quickly agreed. "I think you're exactly the comrade who should be handling this," he decided. With that, all the cadres in the room began to applaud.

That very day, I gave an enormous amount of thought as to how to proceed. I concluded that my overwhelming goal in rebuilding Juche art would to help the masses see the truth. This would teach them how to think and how to behave justly, until not the slightest discord existed among them. It was therefore crucial that art be presented in a manner which the people were fond of and could easily understand—none of this ambiguous *Mona Lisa* nonsense. Juche art would need to demonstrate that loyalty to the leader was paramount and that being faithful to the leader was at once being faithful to the people.

I decided that the best way to demonstrate this artistically would be to adapt the relationship between the leader and the people to that of a parent and his children. The more luster I added to Prime Minister Kim Il Sung's greatness, the more prominent I made it, the deeper the people would adore and respect him. The Great Leader was a brilliant flower, and the masses were the bees that were attracted to him.

I immediately held a month-long conference with all the working artists of the Party to purge any factionalist ideas that still lingered in the group. I stressed to them how the Prime Minister had repudiated both the flunkeyist doctrine of art-for-art's sake and the dogmatist tendency to exclusively focus on ideology while ignoring artistry. Week after week, we analyzed various works of art and engaged in criticism and self-criticism. The same criticism sessions that had worked so well in school worked even better in a professional setting.

Then I decided to revolutionize the two specific fields that I had suggested to the Great Leader. I first began with literature, for the simple reason that I already had so much experience with writing. It was clear that creating a vigorous literary revolution would depend on having a solid organizational plan at the outset. A popular proverb states that "well begun is half done," meaning the beginning of any given work was the most difficult and most important aspect. Personally, I didn't think the proverb went far enough. I always felt that a strong beginning signified 100% success and not merely half-done work. If this first revolution went well, the others would follow.

I called a meeting of all the Party writers one afternoon. As a subject of critical discussion, I brought a popular recent novel to the group. "Look at this book," I said. "In the story, a widower falls in love with a former concubine. We need books about the type of love that is permeated with Korean morality, not with the greasy love of Western people. How would you change this plot?"

One writer raised his hand. "He could have married a virgin instead."

"That's right," I said. "I showed this book to the Great Leader and he pointed out that, in this case, even an old maid would do. 'Everyone wants pure water,' as he put it. Literature which eggs people on to degradation, despair, hatred, plunder and queer tastes cannot be said to be literature in the true sense of the word. We need to provide a striking contrast with capitalist art. Their art justifies the oppression and exploitation of man. It preaches obedience, approves of vices and stirs up crime-consciousness. Our art must give the people something to live for and teach them how to lead an honest life."

"How realistic should the characters be?" asked one writer.

"I understand that our spirit should be our country's if we read foreign literature," said another. "So can we use foreign ideas as inspiration, reworking them in a Korean context? Wouldn't familiar old, say, Chinese stories make them easier for the reader to understand, as is the goal?"

Unfortunately the writers asked me question after question, and I didn't have the answers that I needed. I was young and with no special experience to take charge of the literature and art department. The veteran writers, on the other hand, had an awfully strong sense of self-assurance. Working with them wasn't an easy task at all. These seasoned writers felt that the arts should be reserved for professionals with specialized expertise, leaving little room for action by political activists. I had a firm understanding of the Juche idea, but as to creating art I was still relatively ignorant.

The writers wouldn't take my direction seriously if I simply tried to wield Party power over them. But if I worked from my own real ability, I knew that I'd be able to establish my authority as their leader. They'd follow my advice because they respected me, not because of a kind of obligation or because they were afraid of my position.

So the more specific their questions became, the greater I analyzed things. I was forced to confront the most basic elements of the creation of, not just literature, but any great work of art. With my brilliant intelligence and keen insight, I made an in-depth analysis of the artistic process.

For the first time in history, I discovered the nucleus of any work of art. The basis of a work was what I called the "seed" (*chongja*). My discovery of the seed gave a shock to the literary theories of the world. It could be said its discovery had the same place in art history that the discovery of fire held in man's history.

THE SEED THEORY OF ART

The seed is the essence of a work and constitutes the ideological core of how life is described. It is that which unifies the material, theme and thought into an organic correlation. It also contains within itself both the writer's message and the elements necessary to develop the work. It is the embryo which blends an idea with artistry, and is the decisive factor determining the value of a

> work of art. The organic integration of plot, theme and message all emerge from the seed.
>
> A good seed is therefore of great political and artistic value. A work of art imbued with revolutionary consciousness and artistic quality must have a good seed as a prerequisite. In order to select such a seed, the artist must find one that accords with Party policy and yet can still be subject to a new and unique portrayal.

Slowly but surely, the writers saw the wisdom to my seed theory. Finally it reached the point where my suggestions were regarded as wise, instead of some sort of challenge for them to confront or even defy. They now asked for my input where they once had scorned it. With our new understanding of one another, it soon became unanimous that General Kim Il Sung's revolutionary career would be the seed for the first Juche novel. But try as they might, the writers couldn't figure out how to portray it in such a limited work. One book or even a trilogy was hardly enough. They decided to ask for my opinion, a bit scared to admit that such veterans of the written word couldn't solve the predicament of their accord.

Rather than chastise them, I wanted to praise them so that they wouldn't feel ashamed to ask for my assistance in the future. "You're right to wonder how to proceed," I said. "An artistic depiction of the leader belongs to an order totally different from that of any individual, no matter how outstanding he may be. The leader is the personification and representative of the will of the whole people. He lives as an incarnation of the time and of the currents of history. No existing novel is equal to the task of narrating the leader's life. His career can't be depicted properly by prevailing methods."

"Then what choice do we have?" one writer asked.

"The Prime Minister has brought about a fundamental change in the destiny of the nation. His revolutionary activities have lasted nearly half a century. It's out of the question to complete an appropriate artistic presentation simply in a few novels. I have a better idea: writing a cycle of historical novels."

"A...cycle?" The writers all looked at one another. This was something which no writer had ever previously thought of.

"Let's have the overall title for the series be 'Immortal History.' But each book in the cycle should have its own subtitle according to its own particular message, and they each should be written in chronological order."

The writers were excited to be entrusted with such a great responsibility. They worked so hard for the following several weeks that a couple of them even required extensive medical attention. Finally, however, the manuscripts were delivered to me for my feedback and I read the voluminous books that very night. Fifteen thousand pages later, I was delighted with the first draft. I even visited the writers in the hospital to commend their good beginning. There and then, we proceeded to go over the edits that I had.

In honor of the Great Leader's date of birth, the writers began to call themselves "The April 15th Creative Group." Work on the Immortal History series proceeded consistently and successfully. Eventually the writers produced such widely-read classics as *The Year 1932*, *The Arduous March* and *The Foot of Mt. Paektu*. They also novelized plays that had been personally written by General Kim Il Sung during the anti-Japanese revolutionary struggle.

But literature also encompassed books for children. I had to consider the contemporary generation that was born after the fatherland had been liberated. These youngsters had grown happily under the socialist system, with no experience of living as homeless people deprived of their fatherland. They'd never experienced the oppression and exploitation of a class society.

It was never too early to educate our youth as to the greatness of Prime Minister Kim Il Sung. In order for them to become reliable revolutionaries, it was necessary to tell these young people of the difficulties that the Korean masses had undergone—and how the Great Leader had surmounted them all. I therefore planned a revolution in illustrated children's books, so as to imbue the Korean youth with revolutionary consciousness.

I knew well that children's books weren't very highly regarded in Western culture. There, introducing political themes in such books is regarded as "brainwashing". How depraved and filthy the West is—especially America—that a "washing" can be used as a term of approbation! It's no wonder that their children grow up to become degenerates, hooligans and hellions. But even in Korea, nobody had ever considered illustrated books as worthy of being a lasting heritage for posterity. They were usually passed from one child to another and kept in poor condition before being discarded as literal and figurative rubbish. The "illustrators" weren't regarded as worthy of the term. But I found great value in picture tales. They were a powerful ideological weapon for the young.

IDLE PIG: A DPRK CHILDREN'S STORY

On his birthday one year, a farmer decided to slaughter one of his animals for the supper table. The animals all got together to decide who contributed the least and therefore deserved to be killed.

The horse said, "I carry the farmer, so it can't be me."

The bull said, "I plow the field, so it can't be me."

The cat said, "I guard against mice, so it can't be me."

The chicken said, "I lay eggs, so it can't be me."

The pig got up and started to cry. "All I do is eat. It is I who will have to die."

Thus it was decided to offer up the pig to be slaughtered for the birthday feast.

THE END

Concurrent with the literary revolution was effecting a profound change in the cinema. At the time, the film industry was in chaotic turmoil throughout the world—including the socialist nations. The imperialists had reduced films to a state of utter degeneration. Film companies had become among the most profitable enterprises in America, causing motion pictures to become viewed as mere commodities. Such profit-seeking films dealt with the glorification of the bizarre and the propagation of erotic subjects, and were only meant for lowbrow audiences. Little to no attention was paid to the education of the masses. On the other hand, dogmatists abroad cried for movies filled with naive political slogans. Under the pretext of opposing bourgeois culture, they only succeeded in emasculating cinematic art. Both of these tendencies were completely inimical to the development of proper filmmaking.

I didn't view the cinema as a means of making money but as a way of creating "visual textbooks" for revolution. From my perspective, movie producers could be regarded as vanguard soldiers who were spearheading social reform. Unfortunately, the producers I worked with at the Propaganda and Agitation Department didn't see themselves as soldiers. No, they saw themselves as generals, each and every one of them. And if the writers had originally been averse to receiving my leadership, the film producers were downright hostile.

The issues weren't completely clear-cut. As the 1960s drew to a close, there was no question that films from abroad were superior in a technical sense to the Korean ones. Because theproducers understood these foreign films, they considered themselves part of some internationalist cultural elite. It was appalling, but I couldn't very well send them all off to be enlightened in the countryside. I had to work with what I had.

The producers used to sporadically gather for "aesthetic review" meetings. I sat in on one and could barely keep my rage in check. Basically, these gatherings were a platform for babblers to demonstrate their alleged intelligence by discussing the aesthetic theories prevalent in other countries. The producers fell over themselves in recommending this European style of direction or that American style of acting. There was no political direction to the meetings whatsoever, and the producers didn't even pretend to study Prime Minister Kim Il Sung's thoughts on art.

I didn't hold my tongue at the next such scheduled meeting. Instead, I walked in the room and immediately put my foot down. "From now on," I said, "you must not use the words 'aesthetic review.' Instead we'll hold 'meetings for the study of the Great Leader's artistic and literary thoughts.' From this point forward, your sole yardstick in creative work shall be Prime Minister Kim Il Sung's teachings as expressed via Party policy."

I looked at each one of the producers. They were all befuddled, and didn't know what to make of what I'd just said. But if they'd spent as much time reading the Great Leader's words as they had spent watching foreign films, nothing that I'd said would have come as a surprise at all.

Knowing that each of them always prepared notes for discussion, I called on one producer at random to read whatever it was that he had brought. The man stood up and cleared his throat, uncertain as to whether his topic was still appropriate. He kept referring to a certain film's "moral"—he actually used the English word—while simultaneously trying to appease me, awkwardly forcing Juche principles into his analysis.

Not one person in the room was surprised by his use of foreign jargon. They'd become so accustomed to it that they didn't even register that he was making a bad pun: The English word "moral" sounds like the Korean term for sand, "*mo rae al*." Acting the fool, I raised my hand to question him about his choice of language. "What is this term you keep using?" I said. "'Moral'?"

He paused, unsure if I was joking—and if not, what my intentions were. "A film's moral," he explained, "concerns the ethos which is incorporated into a work by its author."

"And what does that have to do with sand?"

"Pardon?"

"The *mo rae al* of the Taedong River won't do, eh?"

He forced a weak smile, barely hiding his irritation. "Oh, I understand. How droll."

I smiled right back at him, though it was not a smile of kindness. "I didn't ask you that question because I hadn't known the dictionary definition. I asked it to show you how silly it is to use foreign terminology when there are good enough Korean words to express the concepts. Or are you telling me there is nothing 'moral' about the Korean language?"

"No!" he quickly said. "Of course not!"

After that, the producers and I developed quite an understanding. They knew that I was on to them, and they knew it was in their best interests to follow my direction. After this little back-and-forth, the discussion turned to what film should be produced next, the first under my leadership. "Not only the Korean people," I pointed out, "but also progressive people in many countries of the world have wished for the history of General Kim Il Sung's revolutionary activities to be recounted on the screen."

Not surprising, everyone unanimously agreed that this should be the new direction for the Korean cinema. The first such movie would be *Sea of Blood* ("Pibada" in Korean), adapted from a play that had been written and staged by the Great Leader during the days of anti-Japanese revolutionary struggle.

SEA OF BLOOD

A Japanese slaughter brings a sea of blood to a farm community in northern Jiandao, with the heroine's husband among the many victims. Later, her younger son is also murdered by the enemy. Resisting the depths of despair, this ordinary woman rises with indignation. She goes among the workers, organizes a women's association and gathers explosives. She eventually leads a popular uprising in support of an attack by the guerrilla army, which she thereupon joins. Speaking to the masses of the truths that she has learned, she makes an enthusiastic appeal for them to rise for the revolution.

By narrating her growth as a revolutionary in an artistic way, the film put forth the idea that there's popular resistance wherever there's oppression, and that the only way for the oppressed to survive is by making revolution.

Producing the film was a battle in and of itself. But, like most battles, the difficult work had positive consequences. In this case, the producers steadily transitioned from generals to soldiers during production. As the Great Leader's words returned to life after decades, as the scenes he wrote sparkled on film, everyone on the staff knew that they were a part of a wondrous event that would change the world of cinema forever.

One day as the shooting drew to a close, an aide came by and pulled me aside from the set. One of the producers, it seemed, was in the hospital. "How bad is it?" I asked.

"Very bad," he told me. "He's in a critical condition. The prospects are bleak. He only wants to see you before he goes."

I handed over my shooting notes to him, then hurried to my car to go visit the hospital. I spent the entire drive there tightly clenching my fists, terrified that my comrade would pass away before I got to see him. When we arrived at the hospital I ran past everyone, only pausing at the admission desk to find out what room the producer was in.

I burst in to see him and found the man unconscious on his bed. He had the same deathly pallor that I'd seen when the Yank bastards had killed people during the Fatherland Liberation War. Still, I noticed that his chest was moving up and down. From my medical expertise I knew that meant that he was still with us.

The producer's wife was holding his hand while his son and daughter were at bedside, trying to make sure he didn't leave us for good. "Daddy! Daddy!" yelled his children. Yet he didn't respond at all.

His wife then gently rocked him by the shoulders. "Husband, wake up. The person you wanted to see so much has come here."

I slowly walked up to the bed and grasped his hand. I flinched for a second; his grip was ice-cold. I rubbed his hand in between mine to try to give him warmth. "Can you hear me?" I asked. "Don't you see me?"

Suddenly the producer opened his eyes, slightly turning his head to look directly at me. From the small nod he gave, I understood that he recognized me. I couldn't believe that my now-loyal soldier was breathing his last. I tried to be as resolute as I could so that he'd gain strength from my manly example. Indeed, the sight of my affection brought the entire family to tears.

No one in the world values and loves man as I do. In Korea many anecdotes can be heard about how my love for people miraculously brought them back to life from serious illness or from critical conditions caused by accidents. But in this case my love was not strong enough. With a long breath, we lost the producer minutes after I arrived. It was as if he'd been holding on so that he could see me one last time.

Now the film could truly be called revolutionary, because every revolution has its casualties.

The release of *Sea of Blood* was an enormous success in every way. After that, I worked on developing a system for future filmmaking. I had "location" streets constructed, first-rate mock-ups of typical Korean, Japanese and Chinese cities. These reproductions were so permeated with my warm kindness that the actors and producers soon referred to them as "Streets of Love."

I went on to film *The Fate of a Self-Defense Corps Man*, another of the General's plays from the colonial days. Having the experience of *Sea of Blood* under my belt, I introduced enormous efficiencies into the filmmaking process with the use of what I called the "speed campaign." Previously, it had been thought that working quickly inevitably resulted in lowering quality. But I thought that working quicker simply made things more difficult, not impossible. Thanks to my principles, a shoot that previously would have taken a year was completed in a mere forty days. I had turned an art into a science.

I took great pride that I had so successfully revolutionized the Korean movie industry. As I'd said, the cinema affects virtually every other sphere of art. It combines elements of literature, acting, directing, decoration and

> **CHARACTERISTIC FEATURES OF KOREAN MOVIES**
>
> A story designed to appeal to the sentiments
> Highly realistic acting
> A "you are there" feeling
> Soft, clear and vivid screen presentation
> Graceful, soothing background music
> A well-balanced traditional atmosphere

the visual as in a painting. As film attendance began to increase, I had to adjust to see where the audiences were coming from. I had assumed that the masses had previously been choosing to attend the symphony instead, which seemed to be the next-best substitute. Not wanting to presume that this was the case, I inquired as to symphony attendance levels—and was utterly shocked by the reply. Throughout Korea, the musicians performing in giant glorious halls were playing to empty seats. This was baffling. I decided to travel to Kaesong to see what the situation was.

I saw many banners advertising a forthcoming concert when I arrived at the city the next day. I personally heard the radio announcements urging the people to attend the event. The newspaper also ran bold notices that few citizens could miss. Clearly the musicians were leaving no stone unturned to try and win popularity. If anything, the propaganda was downright excessive. The entire scenario was making less and less sense.

That evening, I went to the hall to watch the actual performance. I sat in the rear so that I could observe the audience as well as the musicians. The theatre quickly became packed, with more than a thousand spectators in total. One thousand attendees was a spectacular turnout indeed. Something wasn't adding up, quite literally.

As the concert progressed, many things became plain and clear. The conductor stopped the music in between every song. He then turned to the audience and lectured them about the "importance" of the next piece, about what they should be listening for and about the context in which they should appreciate it. As I looked at their faces, I saw that the people expressed no interest at all in what he was saying.

I understood their indifference and even annoyance. They had come to the club to hear music in the revolutionary tradition, and instead they were being lectured. Worse, song after song was either in the naturalist or in the sentimental style. Such music had no value: no matter how beautiful the melody might have been, it didn't describe man's beauty. The audience was left with the impression that man is degenerate and powerless—an utterly inappropriate message in Juche Korea. Because of all this, people began to sneak out of the theatre whenever the lights went down.

The conductor didn't see the audience members flee, but he must have noticed the ever-increasing number of empty seats. I watched as he began to change his tactics in response. He started interjecting witty little anecdotes, with the musicians accompanying him with great frivolity. It was absolutely unwatchable.

DEAR LISTENER

While listening to a rehearsal one day I realized that a xylophone sounded different from the way that it earlier had.

I called to the sound engineer and asked him to measure the frequency with a gauge. It turned out that the frequency had dropped a little. I discovered that the xylophone had a tiny flaw which could barely be detected by the machine—but I'd been able to hear the imperfect sound simply by listening.

All the musicians at the rehearsal were amazed. The fact that I wouldn't tolerate even a 0.001% error in serving the Great Leader was evidence of my infinite loyalty.

By the time the show was over, there were fewer people in the seats than there were players on the stage. I could clearly make out the looks on the musicians' faces even from my vantage point in the back. They were so disheartened that they wouldn't stand up to the meager applause. I watched as they abandoned their cherished instruments by their chairs, weeping as they ran backstage. There was no other conclusion to draw but that symphonic music had lost its value in Korea.

Once again, I knew that I would have to be the one to

revitalize the art form. I immediately went backstage to see the conductor. To my amazement, he seemed quite unbothered by what had happened. "How do you explain the fact," I asked him, "that you started with over a thousand-member audience, and only had a handful left by the end?"

He shrugged, his mouth twisted with arrogance. "They don't understand."

"Who doesn't understand what?"

"The audience. They lack understanding. And when I try to instill it in them, they get upset and leave."

I clenched my fists at this uncouth villain. "This is an intolerable insult to the Korean people! Are you alleging that they are too ignorant to understand? No, it is *you* who is ignorant. Our people have enjoyed and loved music from olden times. The question is what *kind* of symphonic music will be performed. You must play the kind of music that the masses like!"

The conductor saw the truth behind my logic, yet didn't know how to apply it to his very own field. "What do you suggest, then?"

"To produce the kind of symphonies that our times demand, from our own people."

"To remake symphonic music..." He looked away as he trailed off, seeing the brilliance behind my innovative idea.

"You think symphonies should be dramatic and therefore, mechanically, try to force drama into them. We should develop symphonies on the principle of arranging folk songs which our people like, as these pieces of music are already well-known. Everyone loves, say, 'Beloved Home in My Native Place.' Why not develop that into a symphony?"

"But...how?"

"I understand your confusion. It wouldn't be dramatic in the same sense that you're accustomed to. But neither should it be arranged in the foreign pattern of exposition, development and recapitulation. No, the symphony should be concise in form and preserve the folk rhythms. Then and only then can our symphonic music become the kind of music loved by the popular masses."

And that is precisely what I did, throughout all of the DPRK. Instead of staging classic European symphonies (meaning, *antiquated* European symphonies)—or worse, music composed in imitation of them—I popularized symphonic music free from outworn patterns. The new symphonies were developed on the basis of Juche and suited to the feelings of the masses. They served as a historic declaration of the Korean symphonic revolution, causing great interest in world musical circles. Every music lover throughout the world recognized that Eastern symphonies know outshone Western ones. Korean symphonies now served as a bright beacon, throwing light on the orientation of modern symphonic music.

Months later, that very same symphony orchestra which I had first visited later toured Kangso, Songnim, Hamhung, Chongjin and other major industrial districts along the east and west coasts of Korea. This time, the clubs were overcrowded with spectators. Thanks to the state's newfound encouragement, no one ever left a performance early again. The audiences enthusiastically applauded the players and always called for encores. It was a wonderful improvement which the history of music had never known before.

In only a few years, I'd revolutionized the written sphere, the spectacle of the cinema and the art of the song. All these accomplishments inspired me to ever-greater feats on behalf of the masses. I hadn't originally intended to revolutionize the symphony when the Great Leader had promoted me to my current position, but the outcome was so universally well-received that I didn't intend to stop for a moment. A lesser person would have been content to simply administer what he had built at this point. But a person with superb brain is the one with an extraordinary capacity of memory to store vividly in his memory bank more than others for a long time and later retrieve them as original as well as the capacity to accurately analyze and judge and wisdom of seeing through the world.

In true Juche fashion, I decided to go on an artistic attack. My plan was extremely bold and enormously innovative, far grander than anything I had previously attempted. I decided to wrest the most precious and most decadent of art forms from the bourgeois. I intended to recreate it in order to serve the people, by building on those elements I have previously conquered: writing, staging and composing.

I was going to reinvent the opera.

The first opera was composed and performed in 1600 to celebrate the marriage of Henri IV of France. This simple fact alone was enough to demonstrate what had been wrong with operatic art for centuries. Traditional European operas were mostly focused on the life of the small and privileged aristocratic class. The characters were largely feudal monarchs, power-obsessed misers or prostitutes. The stories were about pleasure-seeking, love affairs or addictions to extravagance.

The old operas were banal in content and too formalistic for common people to understand. Their modern admirers were only found in privileged strata, just as when the works had first been created. Such outdated performances didn't reflect the present time, didn't excite the masses and didn't possess any great vitality. They were utterly lacking in the ability to satisfy the ideology, feelings and aesthetic ideals of modern people—let alone the Korean people living in the Juche era.

I saw that there was an urgent demand to make a revolution in the opera. Even when I'd been a schoolboy, operas such as *Khongjwi*, *Phatjwi* and *Moon over Kumran* were staged but were never popular. They couldn't be; these Korean operas (*changguk*) were simply poor imitations of the European ones. Smashing this outdated pattern would be necessary for the operatic art to blossom. In March 1971, I declared my plan to create an operatic revolution after our successful cinematic revolution. Following the exact same approach that I used for film, I decided to stage *Sea of Blood* as the first Juche opera.

I gathered together the best of the creative team and sat them down to work on the libretto—the main text—of the opera. "By now everyone in Korea and the world at large is familiar with the original *Sea of Blood*," I pointed out. "It's important that the operatic version be written in a way that's faithful to the original, without damaging its profound ideological and artistic content in the least."

Soon the libretto was successfully written, so I met with the composers and others to work on the songs. But the more I explained my position, the more confused they became. One creative worker finally raised his hand during the meeting. "You keep saying that we should do away with the old forms."

"We'll replace them with stanzaic songs," I explained. "They're simple in construction and easy to sing, in the style of popular music."

"You want us to write operas based on *pop* songs?" he said.

"Yes," I beamed. It was an innovation no one had ever considered. "Bear in mind, these songs will be sung for centuries."

Once again, the same creative worker raised his hand. "But without things like arias, the characters won't be able to express their personalities. Nor will they be able to explain the story as it proceeds in parallel with the play's development."

"They won't have to," I smiled. "We can do it offstage."

"You mean via the orchestra."

"No," I said. "I mean via *pangchang*." And here was the innovation that truly made Korean opera unique. *Pangchang* is a form of offstage singing, either as a solo, duet or chorus. It serves to explain the thinking of the characters from a third person's standpoint, or plays the role of a narrator. No other opera had anything like it.

I wanted to make sure that this—my greatest artistic revolution—was performed flawlessly. I set up a three-dimensional revolving stage, so that the set constantly changed as the play developed. The writers knew that I regarded songs as weapons and a propelling force for revolution. Accordingly they deliver over 2,400 songs as potential candidates for the opera, of which I carefully chose the 47 best. Needless to say, the opera became a huge success on the national stage.

With these great artistic revolutions, the Korean arts had been successfully remade in a Juche line. I did everything that I had promised Prime Minister Kim Il Sung that I would do. The arts spoke clearly and consistently of the necessity loyalty to the leader, the Party and the revolution, in terms that common people could easily understand. All of the DPRK was becoming a family, and soon not the slightest discord would exist among the masses. North Korea was uniting behind the leader with one mind and one purpose.

The time had come for all of Korea to be reunified as well.

Chapter 9

Taking a Bow

As heir to the Mt. Paektu bloodline, I was of course always interested in military affairs. It didn't matter that I was at the Propaganda and Agitation Department; I made sure to stay abreast of the latest KPA affairs. So when I heard that a new fighter jet was going to be tested in early 1971, I decided to take part in the virgin flight. I drove to the airfield with some Party members, not telling them what I intended to do.

As the pilot climbed into the jet, I quickly went in after him. At first everyone thought I was simply inspecting the aircraft. But as I got into the rear seat and strapped myself in, every voice rose in protest. "This is a test flight!" one Party member yelled in horror. "An accident of some kind is likely to happen!"

"I'm sure that I'm perfectly safe in the hands of this able pilot," I shouted back. I leaned forward and patted the man on the shoulder. He nodded curtly and prepared to take off, explaining the functions of the plane's complex instruments as he used them. Then, just like that, we were airborne.

As I looked out the window I had a bird's-eye view of my mother country. I saw the magnificent mountain ranges overlapping one another, with hundreds of streams flowing down them like ribbons of silver. I saw a checkerboard of cultivated fields, and I saw the seas reflecting the sunlight. "Look how magnificent and beautiful our sacred land is," I said to the pilot. He was so choked with emotion that he didn't say anything.

We headed north, and my eyes fell upon the spot where all the mountain ranges of Korea converged. There was the august mother of all mountains: Mt. Paektu. I thought back to my childhood days, cold and hungry, when General Kim Il Sung had raised the torch of anti-Japanese revolution. His armed ranks had been equipped with flimsy rifles and matchlocks, but had since grown into a mighty modern armed force unafraid of any foe. Everywhere I looked, I saw a land that been made better due to the work of the General. Not one inch of Korean land hadn't been improved by his hard work and shrewd tactics.

The Prime Minister would be sixty years of age the following year, on April 15, 1972. I knew that Korea needed to do something wholly unprecedented to commemorate this auspicious day. But what would that entail? He wanted for nothing and never thought of himself. Any presents he received he always returned back to the people one-thousandfold. To find him an appropriate gift seemed like an impossibility. Try as I might, I was without answers. Then I realized that the answer was staring me right in the face. Mt. Paektu itself would tell me what I needed to know.

After the plane came to a perfect landing, all the Party members ran up to the cockpit to make sure that I was fine. "Safe and sound!" I announced with a smile. "In fact, I am better than just safe. I am inspired. Everyone get a bag prepared tonight. Tomorrow we are going to scale Mt. Paektu."

None of them knew why I was making such a request, but clearly I had some plan that they weren't yet privy to. The following morning, we woke up early and drove all the way north. Everyone in my entourage began to protest as we pulled up and began to make our way to the mountain. The weather was simply miserable. It was snowing so hard that it was difficult for any of us to open our eyes. Worse, the raging wind created drifts that kept blocking our path. I could understand why they were upset. They weren't a son of Mt. Paektu like I was; they hadn't grown up under such harsh conditions.

"Let's turn back," pleaded one older Party member. "We won't be able to enjoy the view, even if we do somehow manage to reach the summit."

"Mountain-climbing," I explained through the blizzard, "is a very good exercise to cultivate one's courage and increase one's physical power. Strong physiques are the basis of building a prosperous society. A man who is not healthy and strong, no matter how much knowledge he possesses, cannot serve the country and his fellow countrymen. Nor can he realize his hopes and ambitions. The anti-Japanese guerrillas walked these paths in the past. It is precisely the bad weather that makes this a true Mt. Paektu expedition."

Though they grumbled, not one other word was said until we finally reached the summit. All of us were out of breath and exhausted, myself certainly included. I smiled, since my men still had no idea why we were climbing the mountain. It seemed like there was no real reason. I knew that they were obeying me, but that they didn't actually have faith in what I was asking them to do. They needed some understanding—so I gave it to them.

I put my hands on my hips and stared into the blinding snowstorm. Immediately, the furious blizzard stopped blowing. The clouds gradually moved to one side, revealing a glimmering snowscape warmed by the newly-uncovered sun's rays. Then, a rainbow appeared in the sky above the entire vista. Jaws dropped one by one, as the members of my entourage witnessed what seemed to be a miracle. To my consternation, they still didn't understand what was happening. I turned to them, beaming as brightly as the sun itself. "Don't you see?" I said. "Mt. Paektu has recognized its master!"

The men all began to applaud, and warmth returned to their chilled extremities. "Manse!" they yelled.

I closed my eyes for a moment to feel the energy of the mountain, the energy of Korea. Then I looked at my men once more. "Tell me," I asked them, "which is the highest mountain in the world?"

The Party members glanced at one another before one had the courage to speak. "Everest?"

I laughed. "No! It is Mt. Paektu. And why is that? Because a mountain shouldn't be measured by its altitude, but by the greatness of service it has rendered to history. Mt. Paektu is the highest in the world because it symbolizes how the General crushed the Japanese imperialist enemies. Where could we possibly discover a higher mountain than one which represents General Kim Il Sung's immortal revolutionary achievements? Mt. Paektu is the highest mountain in the world because the mountain's height is the height of Korea herself."

"Long live General Kim Il Sung!" they cheered.

I stopped, registering the subtext of what I'd just said. There, at the apex of Mt. Paektu, I finally understood exactly what to give the Great Leader for his upcoming birthday. Just as the mountain represented Korea, so too would my present stand as tall as the Great Leader's spirit. I began the climb back down to the cars, my entourage hurriedly followed behind me. As I got into my seat I took out a notepad and began sketching. Then, when I was done, I passed around the drawing that I had made. "So?" I asked. "What do you all think?"

They were unsure of what to say. "It's a very commendable drawing of the Great Leader," one of them eventually muttered.

"This isn't a drawing of the Great Leader. Look at those smaller shapes by his feet."

"They look like people."

"They *are* people," I grinned. "As I said, this is not a drawing of the Great Leader. It is a drawing of a statue of the Great Leader: A statue six stories high, taller than many buildings!"

As soon as we returned to Pyongyang, I orchestrated the building of an awe-inspiring bronze statue in the middle of the city, with an enormous mural of Mt. Paektu as the backdrop. As planned, the state was unveiled to the world on Prime Minister Kim Il Sung's sixtieth birthday. The statue radiated the General's greatness, safeguarded his high prestige and preserved his image to posterity as the benevolent father of the people. Even though the statue was gargantuan in scale, it was tiny when compared to the Great Leader's accomplishments and how much the Korean people owed to him.

The statue instantly became the central focal point of all of Pyongyang and of Korea herself. Even now, everyone who visits the DPRK bows before it and lays down flowers as an offering. Couples getting married visit the statue to pay their respects. Because of all this activity, some Western "scholars" deduced a religious element to bowing down in front of this giant metal icon. What an absurdity! This was no idol created out of superstition, as in a religion; the statue was made out of bronze. Saying that Prime Minister Kim Il Sung had been "sent from heaven" was metaphorical. It simply meant that he was a perfect human being and the most excellent, ideal man that anyone could think of. Finally, no one claimed that the Great Leader was some mysterious supernatural absolute being governing Korea. Unlike the god of some religion, the Prime Minister was very real.

That night, after the birthday celebration had passed, the Great Leader took me back to Mansu Hill where the statue was. The glow of sunset had settled over the hill as the statue shined in its footlights. The statue's enormous arm stretched out to demonstrate the glory of Pyongyang, its stare gazing off into a prosperous future. In the distance I could see the Party flag strongly fluttering over the Party Central Committee building's roof. The two of us stood there for a moment, remembering days past and hopeful of those still to come.

"Time is like a flowing stream," sighed the Prime Minister. "It's been almost half a century since we lifted the red flag of revolution on the shores of the Songhua River."

"I made a similar observation this morning," I told him. "Time is something very easy to spend but very difficult to spare."

"It's true, it's true," he nodded.

Silence. Something else was in the air, I could tell. "You seem to be perturbed."

"I'm sixty years old today. I can't help but look back at my life and my deeds. Yes, there were many, but that wasn't simply due to any particular skills or talents that I might have. Since I've been a young boy, my motto has remained the same: The people are my god."

"Yes," I smiled, "you've said that many times."

"Because it's true!" he exclaimed. "The masses were a great university who taught me the truth of revolution. They were the benevolent mothers who raised me. All my life, I've worked very hard to become their honest son. Yes, I delivered them from the fate of colonial slavery and am now building a people's paradise. But I'm still a failure."

I couldn't help but burst out with a laugh. "We stand at the foot of your six-story statue, and you call yourself a failure?"

"But I *am* a failure. You know, this morning I watched some wild geese fly past my window. I couldn't help but realize how tragic the situation of the Korean people has been for nearly two decades. These birds can go as they please. Yet on our peninsula, countless separated families are shedding tears, dying to see their parents or spouses or children. But they can't, simply because the supreme task of Korean reunification still lies before us. All of the misfortunes befalling the Korean people are caused by the US imperialists' illegal occupation of the south."

I gently placed my hand on his shoulder. "There is another Juche motto that you coined: 'Man is the master of everything and decides everything.' The struggle for reunification is difficult, but it's a task for man—and there is nothing that cannot be done by man."

The Great Leader sighed, shaking his head. "I met a young soldier today. Do you know what he told me? His mother is on her deathbed, and she gave him a dress shirt. She made him promise to give it to his older brother if he ever managed to return home from the south. *If* his brother ever returned home. Not when. If. Instead of Korean families eating, drinking and laughing together, they're poised on the demarcation line—the death line—with the latest weapons pointed at the hearts of their fellow countrymen. I'm not young any longer by any account. The thought of dying with my homeland divided is something that I can't bear."

"But how can we negotiate with the Park Chung Hee regime? He's a monster. He combines the ferocity of Tojo with the barbarity of Hitler and the craftiness of a murderer."

Prime Minister Kim Il Sung stopped and stared me right in the face. "'President' Park is all those things you said and more, a puppet of the US imperialists and their appointed strongman. He might be a devil but he is still a Korean devil. And if I have to go to hell to shake hands with the devil in order to bring reunification to Korea, then I'll do so in a heartbeat! I'll join with anyone, either in the south or overseas, as long as they desire reunification."

I paused, considering what he'd said. "The US imperialists and their puppets will do whatever they can to make sure that Korea remains divided forever."

"Yes," he agreed, "there are different ideologies, ideals and systems in the north and the south. But reunification isn't a fight between communists and capitalists. Defining the conflict in that way will never end the national division. This is a fight between independence and worshipping foreign powers, a battle of patriotism against treachery. The nation's desire for reunification is strong enough to transcend all these things. It's a matter of joining national patriotic forces together and expelling the foreign aggressor forces. The Americans could never hope to defeat a unified Korean nation. That's why they're so desperate to keep both halves apart."

I had given the Prime Minister the wrong gift. He didn't want another testament to his greatness as much as he wanted a unified Korea—something which Mt. Paektu symbolized like nothing else did. I thought about how to accomplish this, and came up with a plan. There had been contact made between the north and south Korean Red Cross organizations the year prior. I called up our men who'd been involved and gave them instructions to try and extend talks. Just like that, communications were extended between the Korean government and the "government" in south Korea.

In early May, mere weeks after the Great Leader's birthday, Seoul's KCIA Director visited Pyongyang. Our side reciprocated at the end of the month. "Make sure that you take a congenial and conciliatory tone," I told our diplomats. "Taking steps toward reunification is the Great Leader's most sincere wish." By all accounts the discussions turned warm and familial. But most importantly, they were productive—tremendously so.

On July 4, 1972 Pyongyang and Seoul simultaneously issued the North-South Joint Statement, laying out three principles for future engagements between the two halves of Korea. The announcement made the entire nation seethe with excitement. So many had decided that reunification would never happen that the news was quite a shock to Koreans everywhere. Now, for the first time since the post-war truce, a genuine step had been taken to achieving that most important of goals.

> ### THREE AGREED-UPON PRINCIPLES FOR REUNIFICATION
>
> 1) Reunification must be achieved with no reliance on external forces or interference. It must be achieved internally.
> 2) Reunification must be achieved peacefully without the use of military forces against the other side.
> 3) Both parties must promote national unity as a united people over any differences of our ideological and political systems.

It only took the White House one day to try to quench the fire for reunification burning in the hearts of Koreans everywhere. "Even if a north-south dialogue were to be held," declared the Americans, "the modernization of south Korea would be promoted and there would be no cuts in the US armed forces stationed there."

The puppetmasters had pulled their strings. As an immediate consequence, the south Korean puppets did as puppets were wont to do—namely, whatever it was that their masters desired. "Now we are shifting from confrontation without dialogue to confrontation coupled with dialogue," they said, immediately pulling back from the historic agreement. Once again, it was painfully obvious that the only things standing in the way of reunification, the cherished desire of the entire Korean nation, were the imperialist aggressors and the traitors in Seoul.

The Great Leader tried to play off the developments as if they were a temporary setback. "I've had many retreats in my career," he quipped. "All of them paved the path to eventual victory." But despite his good-natured benevolence, I could tell that this hadn't been a glancing wound. The US imperialists had hit him where it hurt, and they had hit him hard.

Finding solace in his work, Prime Minister Kim Il Sung redoubled his efforts to further the lot of the popular masses. At the beginning of 1973 he launched the three-revolution team movement, seeking to remake the

DPRK in three ways. First, the ideological revolution did away with any remaining outmoded ideas and spiritually liberated the people. Next, the technical revolution liberated the people from the fetters of nature and from arduous labor. Finally, the cultural revolution liberated the people from the cultural backwardness characteristic of the former society and made them morally perfect.

At the same time, I took my boyhood idea of criticism sessions and introduced them throughout the DPRK. Everyone in the entire nation was already a member of some group or another, this being the basis of their "organizational life." Once a week, each group got together and every member therein read from a diary of the errors they had made in the days prior. Then, the other members of the group stood up and criticized their colleagues for defects in behavior that they had observed. By this measure everyone in the entire nation was accountable to everyone else—a practice that has continued until this day.

But as powerful as all these changes were, they didn't bring Korea any closer to reunification.

I had hoped that news from abroad might bring the Prime Minister some solace. Korean art was increasingly a source of veneration throughout the world. My film *The Flower Girl* won both a special prize and a special medal at the 18th Karlovy Vary International Film Festival in Czechoslovakia, an unprecedented event in the festival's history. The festival jurors were supposed to maintain an air of objectivity, but even they were caught clapping their hands because the film had moved them so much. None of the films from various other countries had received such an extraordinary response.

At home, the Korean opera scene was also reaching unprecedented levels of achievement. It generally took around three years to create an opera, but my revolutionary method of guidance managed to tremendously cut this time down. While completing one opera, I made preparations for another one—and before that one was completed, I started work on yet another. In this way I'd managed to create five operas in under two years, a fact unprecedented in the world history of music.

The revolutionary operas spoke of the people's epic struggles, their journey from the dark past of oppression to the present-day Korean paradise, as helpless victims became fighters and heroes. They were moved to laughter and then to tears, feeling their own story told through the players. Art theatres throughout Koreas were packed to capacity as new operas were staged one after another.

THE FIVE SEA-OF-BLOOD TYPE REVOLUTIONARY OPERAS

Sea of Blood: See above.

The Flower Girl: A young lady acquires revolutionary consciousness after going through hardships due to a vicious landlord.

A True Daughter of the Party: A woman fighter devotes her life without hesitation to the Party, the General and the revolution during the Fatherland Liberation War.

Tell the Story, Forest!: The arduous struggle of a revolutionary who worked in an enemy ruling institution during the days of anti-Japanese struggle.

The Song of Kumgang Mountain: The dramatic reunion of a revolutionary and his daughter after liberation.

I'm sure that the Great Leader saw most if not all of these productions. But as a true revolutionary, he was far more interested in future accomplishments than in reliving past glories. The more I thought about how I could deliver what it was that he wanted, the fewer ideas I had. Unfortunately, reunification was perhaps the one area where my ideas were lacking. In April 1973 I took what I learned from filmmaking and published *On the Art of the Cinema*. The book was an encyclopedic masterwork that systematized my philosophy of art and literature. I dealt comprehensively with various theories concerning artistic creation and expounded on significant theoretical problems regarding its development. Besides my seed-theory, I also gave integrated answers to all questions regarding directing, acting, filming, music, fine art and makeup.

In the north, the people were following my cue and proclaiming their veneration of the Great Leader with greater frequency and visibility. For one, the Prime Minister was now declared President of the DPRK. Delegates to the WPK's Fifth Congress pinned portrait-badges of General Kim Il Sung to their lapels, a habit that soon extended to every single person in north Korea. The people began to hang his framed portrait in their homes, setting aside one wall solely for his picture. These signs of admiration and love remain the universal norm in the DPRK to this day.

But rather than making progress, the risk of Korea's permanent division was growing every day. The south Korean fascists had declared martial law on October 17, 1972. Any patriots who called for reunification were either repressed or simply slaughtered wholesale by the Park Chung Hee regime. Then, in June 1973, the butchers of Seoul committed themselves to a "two Korea" policy, urging simultaneous UN membership of north and south Korea and thereby enshrining national division forever. The traitors even began to whisper that the homogeneous Korean people were becoming heterogeneous. This was twaddle—but it was dangerous twaddle.

President Kim Il Sung denounced these moves, delivering his historic speech *Let Us Prevent National Division and Unify the Fatherland* on June 23, 1973. I did what I could to further the President's vision, sending appeals to south Korean people in political parties and mass organizations, as well as to overseas compatriots and their groups. But my calls were largely met with silence.

Undeterred, I decided to proceed in such a way that the south Korean rulers couldn't interfere. In late 1973—thanks in part to my work—the UN General Assembly adopted a resolution on immediate dissolving the UN Commission for the Unification and Rehabilitation of Korea, a major imperialist tool for interfering in Korean affairs. I also made a point of setting up the DPRK Mission to the UN in New York, the heart of the imperialists' den. This allowed north Korea to turn the UN into a theatre of struggle, resulting in greater worldwide support on behalf of reunification.

> ### THE GREAT LEADER'S FIVE-POINT POLICY FOR FATHERLAND UNIFICATION
>
> 1) Relaxation of tensions
> 2) Implementation of multifaceted cooperation and exchanges
> 3) Convocation of a national conference consisting of representatives from all social strata, political parties and social organizations
> 4) Establishment of a north-south confederal system
> 5) Membership in the UN as the Democratic Confederal Republic of Koryo

Yes, all this was progress. But it was all progress at a glacial pace. I shared the Great Leader's concerns. I wanted Korean reunification every bit as urgently as he did. But I was much younger than he. I had the luxury of time, and he didn't. It was maddening how little could be done internationally, when I was doing so much on the domestic front.

In fact, my fame was spreading among the masses with every passing day as a consequence of all my revolutionary efforts. Rumors circulated that the most vexing of issues could be resolved easily under my guidance. Audiences touted the revolutionary operas and films as proof of my brilliant intelligence. All agreed that I was a true leader of the human mind, one who had broken up virgin soil and built a flower garden of art.

Because of all this talk, many people eagerly wanted to see me for themselves. It wasn't a difficult thing to do. I was always among the masses. I met many new people every single day—but I was so modest and so friendly that they often failed to recognize me. It always amused to speak with someone, knowing that they were unaware of who I was.

My reputation began to snowball. Soon the newspapers began to cover my activities. It felt like my picture was in the paper every single day. Though I was flattered I still felt the coverage to be a bit inappropriate; they should have been focusing on President Kim Il Sung's revolutionary activities instead. Finally, after one particularly effusive article, I decided to visit the newspaper offices to offer some strongly-needed guidance.

I met with the entire team and was pleased to see that they were all prepared to take notes, as real journalists should. "I myself have written a great deal," I told them, "and from my own experience I know that writing is most difficult. Therefore, those who treat, assign and write articles can be called heroes."

They were stunned. Throughout all generations, probably nobody had ever thought that writers would be called heroes. "We're not heroes," one editor croaked.

"Aren't you? In the past, whips were used to make people work. But today articles serve the same purpose. This is the might of an ideological campaign. It turns slavery into freedom. Recall how activists used to carry mimeograph machines on their backs during the revolutionary days. Learn from their lesson. You should keenly observe any phenomenon from the political point of view and judge it accordingly. Even when you depict a landscape or write a good travelogue, you must never attach primary importance to the subject itself but subordinate it to the article's ideological content. Only then can it make a clear statement." I paused. "And one more thing: keep my name out of the paper. Without fail, articles must hold the President in high esteem, adore him and praise him as the great revolutionary leader. But if after that there's space for an item about myself, devote it instead to some exemplary fact about the masses."

The journalists scribbled down every word that I said. What was more, they listened. In fact—though it is hard for Westerners to believe—my name was kept out of the press entirely. Among themselves, the reporters called me "The Great Teacher of Journalists." But in the media, my activities were obliquely referred to as those of "the Party Center." That way, my achievements received public attention but I personally stayed out of the spotlight.

Indeed, in September 1973 I was named Secretary of the Party Central Committee—the very committee where I had first worked. It was a formal acknowledgment of how essential my work about been on behalf of the nation, the Great Leader and the Party. But though I was flattered by this unprecedented honor, it was apparent that the DPRK was at a crossroads. Tensions were high on the Korean peninsula, and no one was sure what would happen next—and this time, it was my turn to be surprised.

Chapter 10

Commandments

The year 1974 brought a great, destructive crisis for the world economy. Reduced production and widespread unemployment caused people to complain about the "Worst-ever Depression" in many parts of the globe. Just like always, the US imperialists turned to war in order to distract the American people from their suffering economy. The Yanks interfered in other countries' affairs as never before, and were scheming to launch yet another Asian war.

The Eighth Plenary Meeting of the Fifth Central Committee of the Workers' Party of Korea was held in February 1974 against this extremely solemn international backdrop. Many speeches and suggestions for the future were given, but the event was dominated by concerns about what was occurring abroad.

I sat in the front row under the platform, listening with great care to every word that was being said. One day, as the proceedings drew to a close, a Political Committee member rose to put forth a question. His hair was as white as the snow on Mt. Paektu, and every single line in his face represented a martyred comrade lost during the days of anti-Japanese struggle. I knew the veteran and respected him enormously, so I was eager to hear his perspective. "I would like to propose Secretary Kim Jong Il for membership of the Political Committee," he said. Then he gestured in my direction.

That old member of the Political Committee apparently spoke for all those present, for every single person in the room began to applaud. I had no idea that such a nomination was even under consideration. The

Political Committee, as its name implies, decides matters of policy for the entire nation. There was no higher honor, no greater promotion possible. As I always did, I looked to President Kim Il Sung—and saw the one man in the room who wasn't clapping in agreement. Rather, the Great Leader was deep in thought, torn, pensive.

President Kim Il Sung waited until the cheering stopped. "Let's hold off on this proposal," he said.

Yet the President's old guerrilla comrade wasn't one to retreat his position. "We've been inundated with petitions of support for Secretary Kim Jong Il," he insisted. "We've received letters from everyone whose lives he has touched: from Party organizations, government agencies, public organizations. We've heard from people working in the areas of education, culture and the press. I have letters here from factories, cooperative farms and the People's Army. All of us in this room are ready to vote on the matter immediately."

The President did not respond, at least not right away. He simply sat there with a serious look on his face, jaw clenched. Minutes passed, and the tension in the air increased exponentially. This was not defiance; every man in the room was loyal to the Great Leader without fail. But the President didn't quite agree with them for whatever reason. Finally, he gently looked around the conference hall at his beloved comrades. "I well understand the feelings of everyone here," he said. "But again I insist on holding off on this matter, for the reason that Secretary Kim Jong Il is still too young."

The old fighter rose again. I could tell that he was quite agitated, but somehow he was managing to suppress it. "You say that Kim Jong Il is too young," he said, "but I don't think age matters in this case. You led the Korean revolution to victory when you were his age, didn't you? This is a matter bearing upon the destiny and the future of the revolution. I beg you to change your mind and reconsider."

All eyes at once returned to President Kim Il Sung. He was silent once more, gathering his thoughts. Then, his remained the sole voice to speak in disagreement. "In revolutionary struggles," he said, "the people must be bound together by comradely relations only. The positions of revolutionaries should be determined by the contributions they've made for the people and their future possibilities. Their positions shouldn't be influenced in any way by blood relations. Kim Jong Il is my son. Because of this, I, of all people, am not in a position to recommend him. I don't want to hear you say another word about this, I implore you."

From the other side of the platform rose another aged guerrilla. "Then will you hear it from me, Comrade President? We are fully aware of this revolutionary principle. We follow it ourselves. But we have in mind the country's future destiny, not the blood relations of the two of you."

The President had met with countless difficulties in conducting meetings in the past decades, and had never failed to make a clear-cut decision on the spot. Yet never before had the Great Leader been put in such a uncomfortable position—and never had he hesitated for such a long time. These were all revolutionaries and Party leaders who had carried out the President's instructions unconditionally. They regarded every word spoken by the President, every instruction from him, as the truth. None of the members of the Party Central Committee had ever opposed the President's intentions, especially at a Central Committee meeting. But now, they were refusing to obey his request to table the question. One by one, they stood up and spoke from the heart on my behalf:

"The people see wonderful wisdom and outstanding leadership ability in Kim Jong Il's shining achievements. They marvel at his wide knowledge and cleverness, and look up to him with admiration and respect. He is proficient in everything and equal to anything. Anything he has ever undertaken has been settled successfully. Everyone is always struck by his noble personality and the devotion with which he works for the motherland, oblivious of the need to sleep or even rest. His office windows are lit far into the night. I often see his car pass out the gate at dawn. That's why we call his office 'the light that never goes out.' It's no exaggeration to say that his energetic guidance is literally superhuman. It appears as if he doesn't make distinctions between work and rest, or between day and night. Even the officials who work by his side say that they don't know when eats, sleeps or uses the facilities."

"Kim Jong Il is the teacher of the people and their close friend. He is kindhearted and considerate. His noble qualities are manifestations of his warm love with which he brings happiness to the people by taking charge of their fate. He is as anxious for everyone's welfare as their real mothers. He always smiles brightly and his smile is very attractive, giving people the impulse to open their heavy heart and throw themselves into his bosom. People feel his smile is a 'smile of love.' Only warmhearted people smile that way. His loving embrace is like that of the good earth which gives life to everything, broad and gentle. Kind-heartedness, magnanimity, broadmindedness, vigor, enthusiasm, boldness, the humble character of common people—these are the different aspects of his personality."

"Whenever people meet with Kim Jong Il, they frankly tell him what is on their minds. Wherever he goes, people have a hearty laugh because of his vivaciousness. His presence animates people, making their work become full of life. He seems to be constantly spreading joy and happiness. The people become relaxed, simple and downright innocent in his presence. Many even feel like singing. Healthy energy surrounds him whenever he walks or talks. Every person who meets him says that they feel vigor emanating from his entire body."

"Kim Jong Il's thought is comprehensive. Every idea of his is distinguished with revolutionary and innovative character. In other words, each is totally original and has nothing to do with the established usages and conventions. Whenever he writes or speaks, thousands of new ideas crowd in his head; each of them seems as if it were impatiently awaiting its turn to be called out. His knowledge may be said to be encyclopedic to such an extent that I wonder how much knowledge the human brain can hold. He is literally versed in everything."

"Our comrade has a special ability to analyze the nature of objects and phenomena around him and to discover principles and laws that govern them. With his insight and wisdom, he sees through historical currents, grasps the objective demands of social development and discovers the laws of its forward movement. In doing this, he is like the rider of a galloping horse of history, taking its reins in his hands."

"Owing to your leadership, Comrade President, the people have come to acquire dignity, rights and happiness. They now find life worth living under the only leader that they've ever known. The people feel admiration and unbounded respect for Kim Jong Il, for he takes after you in thinking, philosophy and personality. Comrade President, you have trained him to continue the path of Juche. He is in fact the very incarnation of love, morality and the Juche idea."

On and on they went. I was completely unaware of how strong my support had grown, especially among my elders in the Party. As each and every cadre rose to speak, President Kim Il Sung didn't know where to turn. Finally, everyone said their piece. The Great Leader slowly looked around, hoping to find someone who supported his desire to drop the matter. But he found no one.

In total defiance, the first aged fighter stood up to speak one last time. "Comrade President," he begged, "to our regret, we have grown old. Young comrades should assist you now. Only then can our revolutionary progress make new advances in a vigorous, energetic manner." The guerrilla spoke with such intensity that he grew out of breath, leaning on his fists against the table. For a few minutes any thought of revolution were gone, and we all sat tensed until he calmed down.

There is a myth in Western propaganda that the Great Leader was some absolute dictator whose word is law and who is responsive and responsible to no one. But he genuinely and enormously valued his comrades' loyal opinions. President Kim Il Sung sat on the platform for a while before he finally made up his mind. "If all the committee members are in agreement," he said, "I have no objection to Secretary Kim Jong Il being elected to the Political Committee."

Enthusiastic applause erupted in the conference hall. There and then, the plenary meeting elected me to the Political Committee of the Party Central Committee. I walked up to the platform and went down the line, shaking hands with every single person. When I came to the Great Leader, I clasped his outstretched hand with both of mine. "I will return the trust you have placed in me one thousandfold," I promised.

President Kim Il Sung chuckled with pride. Then he leaned over and spoke softly so that only I could hear. "My comrades—*our* comrades—said that I trained you to follow the path I have trod. But they're wrong. It was your dear mother, anti-Japanese heroine Kim Jong Suk, who laid the cornerstone of this cause. Her building such a foundation is the greatest exploit that she performed for the sake of the revolution. Do you remember what her greatest wish was?"

"Of course I do. It was for me to follow in your footsteps."

He nodded. "I've never told you this lest it give you the wrong idea, but the last thing she ever told her revolutionary comrades was, 'Please look after my son after I'm gone and help him become the leader just like his father.' I've been grooming you to be my successor ever since. I could have installed you in the Committee myself, but then you'd never have been accepted by the Party—let alone by the people. Their desire had to match my own. Now, thanks solely to your great work, it does. One day, Comrade Secretary, you will be my successor."

The President was then able to make his wish official, declaring me his successor under law. In the DPRK, the process was very different than what it would have been in a Western country. Most Western countries are allegedly governed by constitutions, anachronistic documents from colonial eras that justify bloody expansionism and oppression. As a consequence, thinking all nations are interchangeable and the same, Westerners often foolishly analyze the DPRK's constitution to demonstrate this or that. But the Juche idea allows for every nation to be governed in its own way. A chopstick is not a flawed fork, but a different form of eating appropriate to a different nation. North Korea isn't guided by our constitution but by the Ten Great Principles of the Monolithic Ideological System.

THE TEN GREAT PRINCIPLES OF THE
MONOLITHIC IDEOLOGICAL SYSTEM

1) Thou shalt struggle with all you have to paint the entire society with the Great Leader Kim Il Sung's revolutionary ideology.

2) Thou shalt revere the Great Leader Kim Il Sung with the highest loyalty.

3) Thou shalt hold no other authority above that of the Great Leader Kim Il Sung.

4) Thou shalt accept the Great Leader Kim Il Sung's revolutionary ideology as your belief and follow the Great Leader's instructions as your cause.

5) Thou shalt execute the Great Leader Kim Il Sung's instructions absolutely and without condition.

6) Thou shalt unify the Party's ideology and will in solidarity around the Great Leader Kim Il Sung.

7) Thou shalt learn communist dignity, the methods of revolution and a people-oriented work style from the Great Leader Kim Il Sung.

8) Thou shalt value the political life that the Great Leader Kim Il Sung has bestowed upon you, and loyally repay the Great Leader's trust with the highest political awareness and skill.

9) Thou shalt establish strong organizational discipline so that the entire Party, people and military operate in unison under the one and only leadership of the Great Leader Kim Il Sung.

10) The great revolutionary accomplishments begun by the Great Leader Kim Il Sung shall be inherited and perfected by generation upon generation until the end.

Now secure in my position, I immediately sought to implement changes to thank the Great Leader for his confidence in me. In my view, there could be no greater festivity, no more significant national holiday, than President Kim Il Sung's birthday. Of course the Korean people had many memorable days and anniversaries to celebrate: the day of national liberation from Japanese imperialism, the days which marked the founding of the Party and the Republic, New Year's Day and other Korean holidays. But the President's birthday was the most important because he won back our lost country, thus enabling the people to enjoy all the other holidays.

Accordingly, I proposed to "establish April 15, the birthday of Comrade Kim Il Sung, the Great Leader of the revolution, as the biggest holiday of the nation. From this year onwards, we must celebrate his birthday every year as the truly greatest jubilee of the nation and must make a tradition of the April 15 celebration." The Party members agreed with me entirely, and my proposal was thereby approved without hesitation.

1974 would be the first year where the President's birthday would be officially celebrated as the greatest national holiday. I therefore wanted the festivities to be the greatest possible. True, he would be sixty-two years old—traditionally, not an anniversary year. But none of his anniversary years had been spent in jubilant environments. On his twentieth birthday, he'd been preparing to form anti-Japanese guerrilla units in Manchuria. On his thirtieth birthday, he was in the midst of a guerrilla campaign against the Kwantung Army in the thick forests of Mt. Paektu. On his fortieth birthday, he was in the operations room of the Supreme Command during the fierce war against the US imperialists. He'd greeted his fiftieth birthday giving on-the-spot guidance to peasants in the countryside. And though his statue was unveiled on his sixtieth birthday, the day was still bittersweet given the tragedy of national division.

I knew that the new People's Palace of Culture was virtually completed and about to be opened. It thought that this might make an appropriate venue for the upcoming event. One day I toured the building and was very impressed by the facilities. All of the equipment was modern, and the traditional octagonal roof was simply beautiful. The fact that the People's Palace was being constructed alongside the scenic Potong River only added to its glory. The Palace would clearly end up being far bigger and better-equipped than the Pyongyang Grand Theatre—itself a world-famous facility. I decided that this would indeed be the perfect venue for the President's birthday celebration.

Now I had to figure out who would be performing. Not only would they be performing for President Kim Il Sung for his birthday, but this would be the inaugural presentation at the Palace. There were many talented performers in Korea, each better than the last and each prepared to deliver the show of a lifetime. My phone didn't stop ringing, as every possible act tried to convince me why they should be the ones on stage that night. I was of course very familiar with all of them, and the decision was excruciating to make. How could I possibly choose?

Then I recalled that a troupe of Koreans living in Japan were due to be in their homeland that evening. Who better to perform? It would symbolize the Great Leader's growing prestige abroad. Their act would recall his greatest past achievements while casually alluding to the problem of a dispersed Korean nation. When I gave the troupe the call, they were beside themselves with happiness. They would never have a higher honor in their entire careers, even if they all lived to be 100.

From that point on, I constantly went to the People's Palace to prepare for the important day. I offered advice on the location of the theatrical microphones and the volume of the music. I made sure the temperature and humidity levels would be maintained at exactly the right levels. I even told the workers to remove the white cloth covers from the chairs. "They might reflect the light," I pointed out, "and distract President Kim Il Sung's attention from the performance." The preparations were my personal version of the Great Leader's field guidance techniques.

Finally, I accompanied the President to the People's Palace of Culture on his birthday. Just before the curtain rose, the two of us went backstage to meet the act. The troupe members had revered the Great Leader from afar, so they immediately burst into tears when they saw him in the flesh. President Kim Il Sung smiled at their emotional display. He always had a kind word for everyone, and once again he didn't disappoint. Even though this was his celebration for his birthday, the Great Leader was still putting others first. He went over and patted the troupe's lead singer on the back. "Come now," he said, choking up a bit himself. "Crying will badly ruin your makeup. Don't you want to look pretty when you perform for my birthday?" The girl singer couldn't find her voice, so she just nodded her head vigorously. She then struggled to regain her composure.

"Go ahead," I told President Kim Il Sung. "I'll be out in a moment."

"Very well," he said, shaking every hand as he left backstage.

I knew that an actor can't prove his skill unless it's supported by a high degree of political enthusiasm. Accordingly, I wanted to provide the performers with some last-minute direction. "None of you know what enormous burdens President Kim Il Sung has had to bear all his life," I said. "The Great Leader has never enjoyed peace of mind. He has experienced every trial, sorrow and agony which any man has ever undergone. He has shed many a tear taking his dying comrades in his arms, and even today he thinks of them at night. He spent over twenty years in the snow of the Manchurian wilderness, then set out to build a new country after liberation and finally underwent untold trials in the three years of war. After the war he fought against vicious rivals. He tightened his belt along with the people, spending his days on the road carrying out field guidance while missing his meals. So keep that in mind, and let's all put on a wonderful performance!"

Sporadically they all began to clap, moved by my touching words. Without saying anything else, I turned and went to find my seat beside the Great Leader. Soon the curtain rose and the show began. The program consisted of songs, dances and short plays. Everyone in the audience could sense the passion emanating from the performers. So entranced was the crowd that virtually no one snuck a peek at the Great Leader—they were too interested in what was happening on stage.

At one point, the orchestra began to play a song that we were all very familiar with: "The Love of Our Homeland is Warm." The lyrics expressed thanks to President Kim Il Sung for remitting educational aid to the resident Koreans in Japan. The soloist stepped up to the microphone, the same girl who had been moved to tears backstage.

After the opening verse, the soloist couldn't keep in tune with the orchestra. Her voice began to crack a bit and then she just stopped singing entirely—before bursting into tears once more. A silence came over the auditorium, broken only by the sobs of the soloist. The orchestra conductor stood there with his baton hanging in mid-air, extremely embarrassed and not knowing what to do. He gestured at her with his baton, urging her to continue singing. What had been the performance of a lifetime was swiftly becoming a career-ending failure for the entire troupe. I worried that they would all kill themselves when the night was done.

> ### POPULAR DPRK SONGS
>
> "Song of Bean Paste"
> "We Shall Hold Bayonets More Firmly"
> "The Joy of Bumper Harvest Overflows Amidst the Song of Mechanization"
> "Song of Snipers"
> "We've Taken Grenades in Our Hands"
> "My Youngest Daughter Became a Machine-Gunner"
> "I Also Raise Chickens"
> "Song of Blood Transfusion"
> "Nightingales Sing in Our Factory Compound"
> "I Like Rifle"
> "Song of Automation Full of Happiness"
> "The World Envies Us"

Then the soloist stepped up to the microphone again. Instead of singing, her crying now became amplified across the entire auditorium. Eventually the girl managed to find the strength to speak. "Since I was a little girl," she said, "I have yearned to return to the fatherland. To perform in presence of the Great Leader on his birthday is like living in a dream. After seeing the paradise he has constructed, and feeling the love of my fellow countrymen, it seems that my heart has become stronger than my voice. Please do not take my failure as a reflection upon my troupe. Great Leader, I only beg that you find it in your infinite benevolence to forgive me for ruining this performance." Then she made a deep bow of regret.

This woman had been raised in Japan. Yet, as a Korean, she'd still managed to articulate what all of us felt, how blessed we all were to live under the loving care of the fatherly leader. The conductor lowered his baton, wiping away tears. Several dignitaries in the audience openly begin to cry, as I myself struggled to maintain a serious composure.

Then, the Great Leader stood up from his seat and began to applaud. "Thank you!" he called out, taking off his glasses and dabbing his eyes. "This is the best birthday present I could ever have received!" Loud cheers rocked the hall as everyone began to weep openly. As I wiped my own face with a handkerchief, I felt as if I were witnessing one of the greatest scenes in Korean history. It was a scene of amalgamation of President Kim Il Sung and the masses, grounded in the boiling blood of the nation.

The Great Leader had finally gotten the birthday wish that he so desperately hope for. For one special moment, the Korean nation was reunited at last.

Chapter 11

Axes of Evil

Everything changed after the President's birthday celebration. I'm not sure if it was the Great Leader's recognition that his legacy was in capable hands, or if he realized that he deserved to spend his elder years relaxing, or some combination of the two. I do know that issues that had previously been his to manage increasingly began to find their way to me for input. I had to work harder than ever as a result of the increased leadership responsibility.

In fact, I worked so diligently and effectively that my comrades could neither believe nor understand it. One typical morning began with me putting documents on top of my already-full briefcase and then going to a meeting. There, I worked on signing important papers as I analyzed economic recommendations from various parts of the country—all while simultaneously listening to the speakers. My attention was divided even further when I was repeatedly interrupted by officials who needed immediate clear-cut answers on urgent business.

Though I dividing my focus successfully, the speakers kept pausing whenever I looked away. I kept gesturing for them to proceed, as they weren't disturbing my work in the slightest. Not only did I perfectly follow every speech, but I often interjected to address problems which the speakers put forward. At times I even praised speakers that didn't fully deserve it to show that I'd been listening to them.

How could I do so many things at once? I learned from the Great Leader. Just as General Kim Il Sung had created land-shrinking tactics to terrify the Japanese imperialists, I employed time-shrinking to step up the transformation of society. Try as I might, I could never change the fact that one hour consisted of sixty minutes. But what I could change was the quantity and intensity of the enthusiasm that I poured into my work. In Morse code, an ordinary person's output would be expressed in dots and lines. But my output would be several straight lines covering the same distance. I managed to do the work of ten or even a hundred days' work in the same period by saving every fraction of a second. By using time in a cubic, three-dimensional way, I carried out brilliant work of historical importance every single day—the likes of which ordinary people could never do in years.

But I was only one person, and there was an entire nation relying on me. The national production figures were released in October of 1974. Though Korea's agriculture had scored a better-than-usual harvest, the industrial sector had seriously failed to hit its target. This was causing an economic chain reaction, restricting the country's development. Worse, failing to carry out the year's goals posed a threat to the Six-Year Plan which had begun in 1971. In the DPRK, we prefer not to report bad news lest it upset our people. Yet we would never be able to hide the failure if things continued the way that they were going. It would be an embarrassment abroad and demoralizing at home.

President Kim Il Sung called an emergency meeting of the Political Committee of the Party Central Committee to address the crisis. In attendance were cadres of committees and departments, Administration Council members and able economic leaders. The Great Leader bluntly laid out the production difficulties that the country was facing. "Given these issues, what measures should we undertake to fulfill the annual target?" he asked the room.

The economic leaders kept their heads down, feeling guilty for their failure. No one else rose to speak, either. Unfortunately not a single person had an idea as to how to handle such an admittedly complex problem. The air in the room was equally full of shame and urgency—shame for not having answers, as well as the nation's urgent need for them.

To this day I remain unsure if the Great Leader was testing my economic mettle on purpose—why else would production be so low?—or if things had simply happened that way. In either case, this was the sort of thing I needed to be able to handle were I to be his successor. I had the foresight to stay up the entire night prior, scribbling ideas right up until the meeting began. I was prepared with answers. "I can tackle the problem by mobilizing Party organizations," I announced. "It will be difficult, but together we can do it."

Quickly satisfied, President Kim Il Sung authorized my governance.

I only had seventy days before the end of the year to meet the production goals. Even though I had many ideas, I was still unsure which ones to implement, in which order, and when. It was an intensely interrelated matter to study in an extraordinarily limited amount of time, with the entire nation and the prestige of the Great Leader at stake. I started by asking myself what the President would do. Yet, try as I might, in this instance I was unable to deduce how he would operate under the given conditions.

But what if the conditions weren't a given? I asked myself. What if I looked at it, not as an economic problem, but as a military affair? Characterizing the operation as a war, I drew a picture of the country's industrial conditions as if I were drawing a battle map. I deduced that the root problem was the failure of the mining industries to surge ahead. This made it impossible for the machine-building, metal, chemical and other sectors to be supplied with sufficient materials. Delays in mined coal meant delays in cargo transportation, which slowed down exports and had a serious effect on related sectors. Identifying the problem in this way allowed me to develop a solution: I could take the "speed campaign" that I'd used in filmmaking and apply it to economic construction.

That same day, I brought together various Party officials and laid out the actual conditions, problems and tasks for each specific economic sector. Then I explained my operation plan for the "70-day battle." "Some socialist countries," I said, "have begun to claim that the speed of economic development must be lowered as the scale of economic activity expands. The imperialists are taking this further, perpetuating the slander that economic stagnation is an essential defect of the socialist system. We will make it known that the socialist system is a rushing locomotive!"

I still firmly believed that speed of labor was *not* inversely proportional to its quality. When workers are educated as revolutionaries, as in Korea, the quality of their production is in proportion to its quantity. When workers work hard with high skill, they not only do more work but they do more *good* work. The speed and quality of production are so closely related that each promotes the other.

On October 21, I issued the orders for the start of the battle. The smallest hitch could cause problems in the implementation of the "speed campaign"—especially when dealing with a mere seventy-day period. I forbid stopping even a single machine for one moment. Producers immediately began to struggle for increased production with all their might. Senior officials and workers set their targets at high levels and, competing with each other, developed collective innovation movements. The entire Party and all the people rose up as one.

Then I took a further lesson from my days in the Juche arts: I created economic propaganda teams. I sent both central and local art troupes to the production sites. Though singing and dancing were both created through labor, never before had the arts been so organically linked up with work. Famous actors and singers made speeches or sang songs in front of the machinery to encourage the workers. Whether they were using machines in factories, climbing towering cranes or even underground in pits, the workers were able to enjoy passionate art performances as they did their jobs. Many a worker was driven mad with pleasure from hearing the accordion—"the people's instrument"—all throughout the workday.

Of course, everything didn't go precisely according to plan. I anticipated that things would go wrong, and employed mobile tactics so I could settle any problems on the spot. When a pit became flooded I sent a large-capacity pump via helicopter. I rerouted large-sized trucks when the stripped-earth heap at a mine grew too high to carry out the coal. I was constantly solving all sorts of localized delays, then recalibrating the balance of the plan accordingly. It goes without saying that I never returned home to take a rest.

Knowing that the entire Six-Year Plan was depending on them, the people began to overcome difficulties on their own. An accident caused three Kangson Steel Plant heating furnaces to suspend operations—but I only learned about it after the fact. The furnaces needed to cool before repair work could be done, but the workers refused to halt production any further. They vied with each other to fix the still-hot furnaces. Some became terribly burnt, but they just continued on as if nothing had happened. Soon the furnaces were repaired and production resumed. While many other nations boast of their workers "putting their country first," it is only in Korea where the masses take that dictum to heart and act accordingly.

As a result of the entire nation working as one, the "speed campaign" ended in victory. When I took charge, the remaining tasks for 1974 had seemed impossible to carry out. Instead, they ended up being overfulfilled by 17.2%. I had passed my leadership test, and Korea was all the better for it.

What I didn't fully appreciate is how much the test of a leader depended on outside forces. General Kim Il Sung was a phenomenal administrator, but he had made his name through waging two successful wars. Would I be able to do the same? Though they didn't know it, it was the Americans who would give me the next test of my leadership prowess.

Within the DMZ is the Joint Security Area, which operated under the auspices of both parts of Korea. One day in mid-August 1976, a group of Americans approached a poplar tree on the DPRK side with the intent to trim its branches. The US side claimed that the tree was a hindrance to its surveillance. In other words, they wanted to chop down one of our trees simply to improve their view!

It has always been the DPRK's explicitly stated policy that we do not want war but we are not afraid of it either. The Americans were told that any such activity would be taken as a sign of aggression and met with force. What's more, such actions was clearly against the regulations of the Military Armistice Commission which governed the area.

In keeping with that favorite American tactic of "strike first, apologize later (if at all)," on the morning of August 18th more than ten US soldiers turned up with axes to chop the tree down entirely. This was an explicit challenge to the authority of the DPRK and the Great Leader himself. Would the Korean soldiers let this go unanswered? Or would they bring the two nations to the brink of war because of a mere poplar tree?

"The tree is on the DPRK side," insisted a KPA guard. "If you want to fell it, you need our approval."

Instead of listening to him, the US soldiers pounced with their axes and called in reinforcements. Soon there were four Korean guards against more than forty Americans. These were not very fair odds, since each Korean soldier was a match for one hundred foes. As the Americans launched their axes, they were swiftly disarmed by Korean Taekwondo tactics. The Koreans then threw the axes back, killing two US officers on the spot. The Korean guards then used kicks and chops on the remaining Yankees, inflicting wounds that sent dozens of Americans running upon their heels in a panic.

I was in my office that morning when an official ran in to tell me what had just happened. I wanted to make sure I had all the facts straight before I proceeded to give direction. "Are we certain that the Americans were armed, whereas the Koreans were not?" I said.

"We are certain, comrade."

"They were armed with axes?"

"With axes," he confirmed.

"And they supposedly wanted to chop down a tree because it hindered their surveillance?"

"Yes."

"The US side is always boasting of its high technology," I pointed out. "They know whatever we do by means of information satellites or electronic spy planes. Are we to believe that they can go to the moon but can't see past a poplar tree?"

The official broke composure only for a moment, but he recognized the farce in what the Americans were claiming. "That is their version, yes."

"Even if that's true, shouldn't they have at least used a chainsaw? Why use axes? Those would take a very long time to chop a tree down. Is West Point a training camp for lumbermen now?"

"I don't believe so."

"No, I don't believe so, either." I turned back to the documents I'd been reading. Out of the corner of my eye, I could see that the official was still standing there.

"Comrade...?" he said.

"Yes?"

MICHAEL MALICE

"What shall we do?"

"Well, have the soldiers been commended yet?"

His face betrayed his anxiety. "Commended? War may break out at any moment!"

I laughed, perfectly understanding the realities of the situation. "How can a man, a *guard* no less, stay still when others suddenly attack and try to kill him? This was an act of self-defense. Our men fought heroically. It is excellent that our soldiers had the courage to accept a challenge and to fight fearlessly no matter what the circumstances. We should award all of them high commendations."

"I see," he said, not seeing at all. "But what will we do with the Americans?"

I smiled. The US position couldn't have been more ludicrous, and their attempts at a war provocation couldn't have been more obvious. This was perhaps the worst-ever provocation between Korea and the US imperialists, certainly the largest since the *Pueblo* incident. "We will do the exact opposite of what the US imperialists want and expect. We will do absolutely nothing. We won't be drawn into war—though they'll certainly try their best to make that happen."

Sure enough, the Americans immediately put hundreds of troops with heavy arms on standby in the Joint Security Area. They then shipped many more into south Korea, both from Okinawa and from the US mainland. The men were ordered to be ready for "an emergency," "military action" or "retaliatory action." Finally, the US imperialists deployed several battle-ships and an aircraft carrier to the seas off Korea. Imagine that! The US was ready for war against the DPRK within one day of the conflict. Why, it was almost as if they'd orchestrated the whole thing!

The Korean peninsula was plunged into a hair-trigger situation. The entire Party, the whole army and all the people prepared themselves for a showdown. I knew that all eyes were upon me, so I made sure to maintain my schedule exactly as I'd previously planned it. I was supposed to go listen to new songs from the KPA Song and Dance Ensemble, and that's just what I did. In fact, the KPA men were baffled at how casually I seemed to be taking things.

"You all wonder why I'm not focused on the DMZ," I said, breaking the tension. "Why shouldn't I do my job, why shouldn't I listen to music, just because of the strain with the Americans? Should I be doing nothing, for fear of trouble? The Yanks are talking big, but in fact they're afraid to fight with us. It is they—not our people—who are trembling with fear over the incident. Their frantic moves are an expression of mental derangement. They would never dare touch even a hair of our people."

"And if they did?" blurted out one official.

I paused, knowing that my words would be repeated to the KPA and from there would reach everywhere in Korea. "If the US imperialists, oblivious of the lesson of history, choose to provoke a new war of aggression, if they go against the current of the times, they will perish in the flames of war once and for all. They will suffer a still greater, more miserable defeat than they suffered in the past Korean war."

I could hear everyone at once sighing with relief.

A couple of days later, the US imperialists once again tried to goad Korea into war and launched the absurdly-titled "Operation Paul Bunyan." According to insane tales that are taught to American schoolchildren, Paul Bunyan was an early American pioneer. He was also, somehow, a giant who could fell a tree with one stroke from his mighty axe. His best friend—also a giant—was an ox that was blue for some reason. The US imperialists thought that invoking Bunyan's name to chop down a tree was patriotic. The rest of the world understood that invoking his name proved that the Americans lived in a delusional fantasyland of their own making.

With huge numbers of forces as back-up—including, by their own admission, nuclear weapons—the US troops went up to that infamous poplar tree as they had several days before. Per my orders, the Korean guards stood aside and watched as the Americans chopped it down. The Yanks must have felt as if they were walking in the footsteps of their slavemaster first President, who had his own mythical tree-felling escapades. So brave!

As the Americans retreated, they made it a point to leave behind the tree's stump to demonstrate that one shouldn't cross the United States. Any objective observer, however, would see it as evidence that Americans do shoddy work and can't be trusted to finish what they'd started—or, if did they start something, they'd proceed to make a huge debacle out of it and then "hightail it" home.

Diplomacy prevailed after the Americans fled to cool their jets. The US imperialists recognized that their provocations had failed and were eager to regain face, something which cost Korea nothing and we were more than glad to give them. Our diplomats proposed that the Joint Security Area be divided, with soldiers from each side prevented from going into the other's area lest such an incident occur again. Despite south Korea's protest, the United States and the DPRK agreed to precisely that on September 6, 1976.

I honestly thought that the entire situation had been handled perfectly. I had successfully avoided war while not retreating an inch, and calmly and clearly laid out the Korean position at home and abroad. The courageous Korean guards were given the highest commendations, and the axe that they used in self-defense was put on permanent display at Panmunjom's North Korean Peace Museum. So when the Great Leader summoned me to his Kumsusan Assembly Hall office, I was expecting the sort of fulsome praise that I'd become accustomed to by that point.

The smile on my face as I was escorted into his office quickly faded when I saw his expression. He was livid. Without saying anything, he gestured for me to sit down in front of his desk. He was so angry that he was practically trembling. When he finally addressed me it was through teeth clenched, the lines on his face taut with emotion. "What have you done?"

"Apparently I've disappointed you."

He sat there, letting the words hang in the air. "Disappointed me? *Disappointed* me? Forget about me. Think about Korea!"

"I have, Great Leader."

"No, you haven't!" He slammed his fist against the desk. "What is going to be the result of this abroad, eh? How is this going to play in the Soviet Union, in Japan, in the United Nations?"

"The US imperialists have been exposed as connivers desperately seeking out war in Korea, just as they've been in Vietnam, just as they—"

"They've been exposed as nothing of the kind! Look, you and I both know the true nature of the enemy. There are no illusions to be had here, nor in all of Korea. But abroad there are many who still buy into the myth of Americans being peace-loving champions of freedom. They will use this incident to further antagonize the two halves of Korea. They didn't want war; they wanted distrust. And they got it!"

I didn't want to argue with him, but I still needed to defend my actions. "This is the same tactic that we used during the *Pueblo* incident."

"No, it isn't! And since you don't seem to understand why, let me explain it to you. During the *Pueblo* incident, no one was killed but for the one man during the initial firefight. Both sides were armed, both engaged in melee. Here, two innocent men were killed, chopped to pieces, by our KPA guards."

"But those were their axes. They were hardly innocent!"

"Of course they weren't innocent. But wait until the American propaganda starts. It'll be our word against theirs. For those nations predisposed to resenting the DPRK, for those nations under the murderous wing of American hegemony, they will have yet another excuse to heap contempt upon us."

"Like during the *Pueblo* incident," I realized.

"Yes. But there we'd been constantly defended by their own men. We had photographs and videos of the spies to provide irrefutable proof that we were maintaining our captives in good condition. Then, it wasn't our word against theirs—it was their own men's words against theirs. We received a signed confession, in writing, of their crimes. But what do we have now? An axe! All this, for an axe."

It's difficult to put into words how I felt at that moment. To know that the man that I respected above all others—the Great Leader who had saved Korea not once but twice—was losing confidence in me felt like nothing I'd ever experienced before. It was as if I were made out of sand, and as the breeze came I was slowly but definitely being scattered apart. I didn't have any excuses. I'd done what I'd thought best and—though I still wasn't clear on why—apparently that had been the wrong thing. If President Kim Il Sung considered it that way, then surely it was that way. "I don't know what else I could have done," I admitted.

"And therein lies the problem. For the first time in my life, I'm issuing a public statement of regret for what's transpired. I hope I can mitigate the damage that you caused."

I hung my head down in shame. "Yes, Great Leader." I wanted to crawl back into my office and shut the door.

"I think I've taken a back seat prematurely," he mused. "Though maybe I'm being too hard on you and all this will blow over." His immaculate sense of perception was fighting with his limitless sense of benevolence—but the perception was right once more.

Things didn't blow over at all. They actually got much, much worse. The south Korean puppet clique had been in a state of constant crisis due to its fascist ways. Plagued by sociopolitical confusion and defied by the people's stubborn resistance, the strongmen now had a convenient scapegoat with which to justify their repression. Imperialists always use a threat of invasion as a pretext for every sort of infamy. In this case, an alleged "threat from the north" led to the deliberate spreading of a war atmosphere in the southern half of Korea.

The US imperialists took the cue, shipping more nuclear weapons into south Korea and proclaiming it to be their "forward defense zone." Then they inaugurated their "Team Spirit" joint military exercise, a highly public rehearsal of what an all-out strike on the DPRK and the subsequent war would look like. These war games involved not only the American forces in south Korea and the south Korean troops, but also combat units from the US mainland—far different from the previous limited-scale drills that had been held. As bad as these pantomimes of murder were from the north's perspective—and they grew bolder and more extravagant every year—the message to the southern people was clear. Those same American guns could be turned on them just as easily, if not easier.

But this wasn't the worst of it.

At the instigation of the US imperialists, the south Korean puppets built a concrete wall 150 miles long along the entire width of the military demarcation line. The wall—far longer and more foreboding than the Berlin Wall so hated by the West—was built flush with the mountainside so as only to be visible from the north. Now, for the first time in millennia, Korea was physically divided in two. It was as if the 1972 North-South Joint Statement had never happened. Everything that the Great Leader had worked for in terms of reunification was buried underneath miles of concrete—and it was my fault, at least partly so.

All I could do was focus on my work and try to put these mistakes behind me to the best of my ability. I hoped that I could once again prove myself to President Kim Il Sung and thereby maintain my role as successor to the cause of Juche. During this entire period, my conviction in the Great Leader's vision didn't waver in the slightest; I just realized that it was my perception that had been off. I decided that the best thing to do was to revisit my greatest past successes: applying Juche to the arts and literature.

One day I met with the publication department, focusing on new school textbooks. "The best method of narrating a story is to vividly convey one's experience," I explained to the editors. "By doing so one can effectively implant hatred and hostile feelings in the reader's mind. Whenever the books refer to our enemies, they must use such words as 'gangly American bastards.' Whether it be the Japanese imperialists or the landlords who had reigned over our society in the past, we must always include a reference to their villainy."

The men nodded. "That's a very good idea," one said.

"This need not simply apply to storytelling. Take mathematics. In a battle situation, one can't take out a piece of paper and start doing calculations. But if the textbook examples anticipate this, then our people will be able to give the enemy a good thrashing. 'If each student shoots five Americans a day, how many can they kill in a month?' This teaches the arithmetic while instilling an important lesson."

"Excellent suggestion."

I went on, listing examples in every field of education, until something on the bookshelf caught my eye. "Is that French?" I said. "What is a *French* book doing here? I thought we'd gotten rid of all those a long time ago." I walked over and pulled the book down to look at it. Though it was written in French, the book was on Korean history. As I flipped through the pages, I had to admit that it was very attractive. The photographs, the quality of the paper—the combined package was simply lovely.

"We were using it as research," one editor said. "This is what the outside world is saying about us."

"And what are they saying?"

"There's a great deal of political, economic and cultural material on Korea and her history," he explained. "But most of the articles are incomplete and inaccurate. The worst contain distorted and blatantly false information, the kind promulgated by south Korean publications."

Now it dawned on me how I'd mistakenly played out the poplar-tree incident. This book held the key to the problem and the clue to its solution. "Why do you think this book contains so much misinformation?" I demanded.

The editor was ready to respond. "Clearly it's because of the author's unfriendly political attitude towards us and our nation."

"That's what I would have said," I admitted, "even as recently as a week ago. But now I see things in a different light. We've done a very good job of keeping dangerous foreign ideas from infiltrating the DPRK and corrupting our people. But as a consequence of that, it's very difficult for someone in the West to get information on our country. They have to collect scraps of it here and there, making the picture misleading at best. And when it comes to any missing elements, our enemies will surely be there to provide lies. This book is not a function of bias on the part of the writer, but a function of our inadequate external propaganda. We can't sit quietly while our enemies speak on our behalf. We have to let the world know more about Juche Korea—and the fair-minded peoples of the world will be able to see the truth for themselves."

After that epiphany, I stepped up the translation of our publications into other languages. At the same time, I understood that intellectual discussions could only go so far in persuading people—especially for-eigners—as to the reality of Korea. A far more effective technique would be to spread our art throughout the world. It's easy to hate a nation that's been slandered for decades. But it's very hard to hate beauty, even for the hardest of hearts.

Historically speaking, it usually took several hundred years for any period of spiritual culture to be created. But the "Twentieth Century Renaissance" in the DPRK had been achieved in a short period of ten years—and not just in one field, but in all areas of literature and art. My hope was that seeing the beautiful basis of Juche art would force people to admire Korea. At the very least, they'd have to concede that the inter-national situation was far more complicated than the imperialist powers were letting on.

I sent the Mansudae Art Troupe and many other troupes to countries with which the DPRK had no diplomatic relations, such as France, Italy and Great Britain. Our opera performances throughout five continents were received with wild enthusiasm. When *The Flower Girl* was performed at a Parisian theatre, people came from Italy, Greece, Spain, Sweden, Denmark and Finland. Some even arrived from as far away as Canada, Brazil or Mexico to see the opera.

Whether it was Paris, Rome or Vienna, the outcome was the same: huge applause from the audience, as they stamped their feet on the floor with delight. These performances built bridges of friendship between the Korean people and people throughout the world. All the opera songs became popular and widely sung—a testament to the new musical struc-ture that I'd pioneered.

Korean art quickly earned an international reputation. The major cities of Europe had long boasted of their flourishing arts, but now they were captivated by the spectacles presented by the revolutionary operas.

Juche art awakened the true meaning of life for the audiences, as people's hearts became inflamed with enthusiasm for revolution wherever performances were given. To this day, any foreigner who visits Korea—whether he be a politician or a social worker or a scientist or a writer—unsparingly praises the DRPK's development into a country of art.

THE REVIEWS ARE IN: INTERNATIONAL REACTIONS TO KOREAN REVOLUTIONARY OPERA

"*Sea of Blood* truly is a great new opera for the people, which is quite different from the European ones which were written for feudal aristocrats and millionaires. This opera can rightly be called the comet of art and the prince of opera which will not be found anywhere else in the world. The old era of Western opera has given way to the era of a new type of opera. The people of the world must join together to cheer its arrival." –A famous European artist

"The British working class have existed for a long time, but we held a silent march because we have no one to lead the revolution to victory. After we saw your performances tonight, we have been convinced that there is a bright future for the British working class, too. The man who has instilled such a conviction in us is Comrade Kim Il Sung, the only leader capable of preserving the future of the working class of the world!" –British strikers

"The discovery of *pangchang* is greater than the discovery of the heliocentric theory by Nicholas Copernicus." –Italian musician

"Behind great art there is always a great man, a great philosopher, a great statesman and a great aesthetician. I wanted to know who was the great leader. At last today, I have recognized the great man, the great leader. Korean art clearly tells the peoples of the world how to create real art because it is led by the respected President

Kim Il Sung." –member of the Japan Art Academy

One night in early 1979, I was spending a typical very late evening in my office. The building was completely quiet other than the sound of my pen making marks across the paper. I was looking over some lyric sheets when the phone rang, startling me. I glanced at my watch; it was well past midnight. I picked up the phone to hear President Kim Il Sung's voice.

"Great Leader, is everything all right?" I asked, hoarse from exhaustion. "Is there anything you need from me? Are you feeling well?"

He chuckled, in that kindhearted paternal manner of his. "You sound tired. They say you never sleep, you know."

"How can a person endure not sleeping?" I said. "It's true, I only sleep for two or three hours a night. But I make up for it with short sleeps in the car on my way to field guidance trips. I don't consider it to be a hardship. I'm so used to living this way that a bed seems uncomfortable to me."

"I'm still worried about your health."

"Please, let me worry about yours!"

"You shouldn't strain yourself," he said quietly. "A cart can't be moved with just one wheel, and the revolution can't be accomplished in a day or two. A person needs rest, no matter how exemplary he might be."

"Yes, Great Leader. I understand."

"I asked your aides to try and reduce your workload," he said. "They told me that they'd tried, but that you simply found more and did it faster than it would have been done otherwise."

I sighed. "I just want to do right by you. I don't want to disappoint the revolution again."

"Then I want you to accept the Order."

I put my hand over my mouth, and felt my lips quiver as I almost burst in tears. The Order of Kim Il Sung, Korea's highest honor, had been instituted in March 1972. The Central People's Committee had decided that I should be the first recipient. When I gently declined, they tried to insist. At that point I rebuked them, rather sternly in fact. They got the message and left the Order unawarded for four years. They tried again in 1976, and then again on occasion of the thirtieth anniversary of the Republic in September 1978. Now President Kim Il Sung himself was urging me to accept.

"Very well," I told him. "If that is what you want, I'll be happy to accept it."

"Thank you," he said. "I knew that I made the right choice when I named you as my successor. Go home and get a nice quiet sleep."

With those simple words, I knew that the DMZ misadventure had been forgiven, and that my position was once again secure. "Yes, Great Leader. Thank you."

For the first time in my life, I completely defied President Kim Il Sung. I didn't go home when I hung up the phone. Instead, I turned back to the lyric sheets and happily returned to work.

Chapter 12

Construction Time

October 1979 witnessed a huge uprising of the south Korean people, rocking America's colonial ruling system to its foundations. The citizens took to the streets, frustrated at the heavy hand of the regime. Watching the events unfold reminded me of the collapse of the Syngman Rhee dictatorship in 1960.

As far as I could see, the US imperialists only had two options left to them. The first would be to allow for a second "Iran incident," doing nothing while their ally—in that case, the Shah—was in trouble. This was highly unlikely, as it would mean ceding control of events to the masses. The second would be to oust south Korea's "Shah" themselves. South Korean "President" Park Chung Hee was so grotesquely unpopular that his removal would appease the people, bringing some modicum of oversight back to the situation. To no surprise, Park Chung Hee was assassinated on October 26, 1979 just as his wife had been five years prior. His murderer? The head of the Korean CIA.

Let me repeat that: the President of south Korea was killed by the Director of the Korean Central Intelligence Agency. There is no doubt that this is what happened, it is no secret and there is no ambiguity. Nor is this DPRK "propaganda." These are the facts recognized by every member of the world community—including the US imperialists themselves. The only thing that is in dispute is the degree of American involvement behind the assassination.

On May 17, 1980 General Chun Doo Hwan staged a coup and declared martial law, dispensing even with the appearance of a civilian, democratic administration. Once again, the Americans either acquiesced or were powerless to stop matters. Personally, I find it impossible to understand how the latter could be true. The south was their closest ally, and there were many Yank troops stationed there.

Shortly after the coup, the Americans had no choice but to show their hand and choose sides. Would they side with the military dictatorship, or with the Korean people who they so publicly claimed to protect? On May 18 there came a huge uprising in the city of Kwangju in direct response to the imposition of martial law. Tens of thousands of troops descended upon the city in response. Armed with warplanes, tanks and armored cars, they buried Kwangju in a sea of blood. The atrocities were so horrific that even monsters would have looked away from the scene. The fascist thugs themselves admit to over one hundred deaths during the massacre, though the actual number was over a thousand.

Once again, let me be clear: in 1980—nearly a decade before the hostilities in Tiananmen Square—the Americans did the exact same thing in south Korea. They don't bother to hide it or even deny it. The US imperialists still speak of the Chinese events but never the Korean ones, because China is their rival and south Korea their "ally." It behooves them to denigrate the former and praise the latter.

America's actions were not those of a nation committed to "justice" or "democracy" or some arbitrary concept of human rights. These were transparently the actions of a nation committed to imperialism. And what did this imperialism mean, in practice? It meant young people being killed in the streets for speaking their minds. It meant civilians being detained and imprisoned indiscriminately, as happened in the days after. It meant patriots being executed without trial virtually every day. Above all, it meant accepting and downright endorsing the actions of any murderous tyrant so long as he followed the dictates of American policy. "Making the world safe for democracy" is simply a kinder, gentler version of "forcing the world to obey America."

So much for the myth of the "peaceful south" and the "warlike north."

In fact, the contrast between the two parts of Korea was as clear as ever during this period. The Sixth Workers' Party of Korea Congress was held in October of 1980. There, before the eyes of the entire world, I was publicly declared to be the successor to the Great Leader Kim Il Sung. Overcome with joy that the revolution would continue through for another generation, the people proudly hung my picture alongside that of the Great Leader in their homes.

THE SUCCESSORSHIP QUESTION

The enemies of the DPRK criticized President Kim Il Sung for allegedly establishing a "hereditary monarchy," a misconception that many people unfortunately still believe. Let me put this nonsense to bed once and for all. To begin with, in a feudal system the rulers are both afraid of the popular masses and are incapable of governing them. Those of royal blood inherit the throne regardless of their abilities, intelligence or competence. Denying any other possible option for succession is a mechanism to force the masses into absolute obedience for generations.

The feudal use of hereditary succession to the throne is an attempt to institutionalize the king's absolute power and guarantee the survival of the reactionary ruling class. The interests of the masses are never a concern, thus making the relationship between a king and a people that of exploiter and exploited or oppressor and oppressed. An actual hereditary monarchy is a function of the very same feudal society that the Great Leader opposed since the very beginning of his revolutionary career. Trying to equate the working-class leader's successorship—chosen with the absolute support of the masses—to a hereditary monarchy is a twaddle lacking both basic logic and an elementary ABC knowledge of politics.

What was most absurd is that much of the criticism came from socialist nations. If there is one historical lesson of the international communist movement, it is that the problem of the successor could not be any more crucial. Again and again, the state fell into the hands of careerists and plotters, stopping any progress dead in its tracks. Choosing the correct successor is choosing to perfect the revolution through the generations until the end. Rather than a mere blood relation, the successor must be a distinguished person competent enough to supplant the leader and fill his role.

There are many qualities that I'd developed that distinguished me from everyone else in the DPRK. First and foremost, my loyalty to President Kim Il Sung was thorough, enthusiastic, sincere, lofty and unrivalled. Second, my understanding of the Great Leader's thought was unsurpassed. Third, I was able to mobilize the popular masses due to my leadership ability. Finally, I had a strong sense of revolutionary duty that was expressed in my love for the people. All these characteristics allowed me to properly assess any current situation, pinpoint the wishes of the people, put forth the appropriate tactics and then organize the masses to implement the correct plan. All these characteristics demanded that I be chosen as successor to the great cause of Juche.

Only a great man creates a great thought and a great history, and only a great man can best understand another great man. It was therefore the highest honor of my life that President Kim Il Sung decided that I was the man to succeed him.

One day I paid a field guidance visit to the Mansudae Art Studio. I wanted to see what the artists had been working on, with an eye to matching their works to the best possible locations for display. I was disappointed to the point of bafflement by the murals that they were painting. The art was dull, literally looking as if it was faded and covered with dust. I was familiar with these artists' usual work, and knew that it was usually among the best that Korea had to offer. For some reason, here their talents weren't being given free rein. I paced back and forth across the entire wall, getting increasingly agitated. "Come here," I called to one of the artists. "Why are these colors so insipid? Is this the best you can do to portray the shining reality of Korea?"

The painter spoke cautiously, familiar with my expertise. "It's been widely accepted," he said, "that murals are usually painted in opaque colors. We're painting these to be subordinated to the architecture. This way, the buildings' beauty won't be spoiled. We're following the precedent of the walls of the Pyongyang Grand Theatre."

A truth is obvious once it's made clear—but it will never be revealed as long as it's suppressed by outworn conceptions, patterns and conventions. The artist clearly wanted to reject the prevailing view on murals, but he also didn't want to stick his neck out. "The murals of the Pyongyang Grand Theatre are misty and dull," I told him. "But they need replacements, not duplications."

"I agree," he said, glad to have my support. Now he could truly be an artist and not simply a painter.

"Why should murals be subordinated to the buildings, anyway? What is the use of painting murals if they're to be overshadowed by the architecture? Only when the colors of a mural are bright and clear can the beauty of a building be enhanced by them. Murals ought to be painted in a concise yet forceful way, like Korean paintings. They should be socialist in content and national in form, as with all the other arts which the Korean people like."

The artist took my words to heart, as did his colleagues. Following my guidance, they then began to paint a mosaic mural masterpiece entitled "The East Sea in the Morning." Their plan was to represent the sun by using much smaller tiles than usual. But instead I recommended that they use a highly polished disc of cut glass, an entirely new idea which no one had ever previously thought of.

On the day that the mural was installed and unveiled, flocks of king-fishers from a nearby lake gathered around the piece. One by one, the birds flew toward the mural's evergreen pines, striking themselves dumb and falling to the ground. When they got up, they once again tried to fly into the "forest." From that day forward, piles of kingfishers constantly had to be cleared away from the floor by the mural. Nature herself was praising the realistic beauty inherent in Juche art.

Soon after the mural was unveiled, I was walking down Ryunhwanson Street in Pyongyang when I stopped short. So much of my recent work had been about creating a beautiful lifestyle for the people that I hadn't even thought to apply my artistry to where the masses needed them most: their homes. Ryunhwanson Street was lined with two- and three-story apartment buildings, housing several thousand families. But the build-ings were a postwar construction built by flunkeyist officials in servile imitation of foreign plans. Then and there, I resolved to totally destroy the outdated street—a pile of dirt left over by the flunkeyists—and build an ideal Juche street in its place.

In the same sense that a mural is a painting on an enlarged scale, there was no reason why a street couldn't be regarded as a enormous "sculpture" of sorts. Reconstructing Ryunhwanson Street was a historic opportunity to demonstrate to the world that I wasn't simply an artisan but an able city planner as well. My knowledge of architecture was extraordinary, far deeper and wider than technical architects themselves. I was very familiar with the contemporary trends, and had a profound understanding of both architectural theory and practice, as well as building design and decoration. Yet this was my first opportunity to actually implement all that I had studied.

I knew it was crucial for me to ignore old conventions in order to boldly demonstrate my originality and skill. The first thing I decided to change was the street's layout. The current buildings were large, low and wide. They were laid out on a horizontal line, with each building identical to the other. My plan was to have the street mirror the dynamic spirit of the time and the people "in our way."

NAMES FOR NORTH KOREA

The Country of Juche

The Country of Chollima

The Kingdom of Children

The Country of Learning

The Country of Parks

The Country of Art

The World's Finest Example of Construction

I spent weeks putting together a diorama to illustrate my new approach. I proposed to have the buildings soar along a vertical line. The roofs of the 20-, 25- and 30-story buildings flowed into one another in an aesthetic way. The buildings themselves harmonized with their surroundings. Their shapes—square, circular, towering and jagged—called to mind Korean items such as towers, saw blades, folding screens and gardens. The bright colors of the buildings—sky blue, light yellow, blue and yellow—were in concordance with the people's tastes. I covered every detail, including the size and shape of the windows, door handles, showers and even the faucets. Despite all the variations in style and form, every apartment was exactly the same. In a communist nation, a person should only have to pack a suitcase when he moved his residence.

The street was rebuilt in record time, and renamed Changgwang Street to demonstrate its new beginning. It's no exaggeration that I began to view Pyongyang itself as a work of art, with all the unlimited potential that art had to offer. My new goal was to turn the city into a picturesque world-class capital. It was well-known that the skyscrapers of New York, Paris and London looked choky and gloomy. Compared with those fashionable locations, Pyongyang increasingly became refreshing, cubical and popular-oriented. All of the new buildings that I constructed were the best in terms of both quality and content, literally "monumental edifices" to hand down to posterity in the Juche style.

THE PYONGYANG MATERNITY HOSPITAL

In the past, Korean women gave birth on straw mats in their neighbor's kitchens or even by the side of the road. After 1980, they became mothers in a palace: the newly constructed Pyongyang Maternity Hospital. The new building was tender and gentle in every element of construction, as befitting a hospital for women. The gloriously multicolored floor, the varied sculptures throughout and the shining chandeliers gave it a fairy-tale appearance.

The hospital was outfitted with the latest medical technology, such as a centralized oxygen-supply system and a general air-conditioning system. Telescopes were installed into completely sterilized operating rooms, enabling any interested person to watch ongoing operations from outside. The fantastic amenities freed the patients from every inconvenience, and included a signal to contact a nurse at any time, a telephone receiver, a device to freely change the bed's height and/or angle and even a handy table.

My architectural prowess earned me an instant reputation among Pyongyang's engineers. I was often summoned to look over plans and solve problems. Many architects simply wanted my approval for their work in the broader context of the city at large. Some issues, of course, were much bigger than others, and much more involved.

I could tell that the officials were at their wits' end when I was called in to discuss the upcoming Changgwang Health Complex. "We need several thousand tons of water to fill the swimming pool and bathrooms," the main official explained. "Refilling them every so often is no easy job."

"What solutions have been proposed?" I asked him.

He laid out the plans in front of us on the table. I looked back and forth between the blueprint of the building itself and a map of where the complex would stand in Pyongyang. Though the edifice would be impressive, I could already anticipate several difficulties. "I hesitate to say it," the official hesitated to say, "but it seems like we're going to need some sort of extremely efficient filter to deal with such a huge volume of water. Yet I don't know that such technology exists in all of Korea."

I examined the data in front of me quite thoroughly, quickly coming up with possible solutions—and then dismissing them just as quickly for various reasons. This truly seemed to be an impossible dilemma. "First things first," I said. "We must solve the water problem on the principle of the best conditions for the people. That's who the swimming pool and bathrooms are for."

"Of course."

"Forget filtration. There shouldn't even be one contaminated drop in the complex's water. We must find a way to pump out one hundred per cent of the old water and refill it with fresh water."

The official was taken aback. This only made things *more* difficult, not less. "Where are we going to get that much water from?" he asked. I could sense the official's skepticism hardening against me. He trusted his years of expertise over mine, just the writers and the producers once had. But I'd learned from my conflict with the artists. I knew that I needed to teach the man, to demonstrate my knowledge to him, rather than simply giving him advice that he'd regard as ill-advised.

I picked up a red pencil, and on the map of Pyongyang I drew a line from the health complex to the Taedong River. "That's where we'll get the water from. We have an entire river flowing through the city, full of fresh Korean water just as our people like."

"I don't quite understand," he said, biting his tongue. "Not only is there a huge distance between the river and the complex, but there are many high-rise buildings in between."

"We can lay pipe underneath them, can't we?"

"Yes, I suppose we could," he said. "But we'd need to use very large-diameter pipes."

"Then that's what we'll do!" I declared.

"But the cost would be enormous, both in money and in materials!"

I put my hand on his shoulder. "We should do what needs to be done in order to ensure a happy life for the people, even if our state coffer is emptied. We must stop calculating when it comes to doing work for the people. That is my math, and that is our party's method of economics."

"It just seems like an enormous waste. Filtration could serve the same purpose."

I could tell that I needed a new approach to convince the official of the wisdom of my plan. "In the south, the Yanks take any Korean women that they want. Did you know that some of these beasts don't even stop at ravaging them, and even force the woman into marriage?"

He began to gag at the thought, his eyes tearing up at visions of our sisters and daughters beside hook-nosed, sunken-eyed brutes. "I'd hoped those tales were just propaganda," he said quietly.

"No, it's the truth. And do you know how they defend their acts? Oh yes, they defend them! They say that it's not a big deal, that it's just a drop of ink in the south's Han River."

"Not even one drop of ink must be allowed," the official said with a scowl. "Not that kind of ink, and not in that river."

"So you see why filtration actually bears a far greater cost than bringing in fresh water."

He didn't say another word.

Thus it was decided to spend whatever was necessary to pump in fresh water into the Changgwang Health Complex, without any regard for cost. I even went one step further than the plans originally called for, installing a barbershop and a beauty parlor on the ground floor. These quickly became full of happy customers, who could choose their favorite from no less than thirteen styles of hairdressing.

In fact, that same official was the same one later put in charge of building the Pyongyang Ice Rink. When I insisted that all the stale air be extracted and fresh air pumped in, that no trace of used air must ever be allowed to remain in the ice rink, he didn't even bat an eye. He knew exactly why I said what I did—and what's more, this time he completely agreed with me.

I applied this people-first approach to all the new construction, both in Pyongyang and throughout Korea. But even though the people were put first, they themselves were never the first to test a new facility. To ensure maximum safety, I always tested things for myself before allowing any structure to be opened officially. It was very grueling, difficult work, but it was necessary and I was glad to do it.

When I showed up at a shipyard, I pinpointed a number of engineering defects on a ship—and even told the engineers how to remedy them.

When I went to a power plant, I ordered a leak in the ceiling to be repaired at once, since the leak was increasing humidity in the room and might cause the workers to contract arthritis. When I went to a workers' hostel at the Hwanghae Iron Works, I made them switch out the flat pillows for the cylindrical pillows which Korean people like. I even checked the water pitchers as I left, since cold water wasn't good for the workers' health. And whenever I visited new apartment complexes, I always looked at the toilets, because the toilet is a barometer of a people's living standard.

I always spoke with the people themselves on these tours, shaking every farmer's grimy hand and listening to every housewife. By doing so I both awakened them politically and listened to their concerns. I went everywhere, and my traces linked together would form a comprehensive map of the entire country. In this way I shaped the policies of the Party in a manner that the masses actually desired, just as the President had done. This was why all the people spoke of my "politics of faith" and regarded the government's work as "our policy." They worked hard to implement these policies and brought about world-startling miracles as a consequence.

All of this new construction had an enormously positive outcome. As building the ice rink demonstrated, the people increasingly spent less time on labor and had more time to spend on leisure. I couldn't be happier than to accommodate the masses with wholesome, entertaining attractions. Thanks to my architectural planning, soon the DPRK became known for our plentiful fun fairs.

Building a fun fair (also known as an amusement park) is notoriously expensive. Constructing one costs as much as buying a plant for a big factory. A roller coaster alone is comparable in cost to that of a large public building. For this reason, even rich capitalists rarely have the funds for a complete set of fun-fair rides. They usually first install two to four attractions, earn money with those, and then build some more. In this way fun fairs are built up over the course of a decade or longer in capitalist countries. This is why hardly any fun fairs in the world have a whole set of recreation facilities. But calculations didn't enter into economic decision-making in the DPRK, which allowed me to provide several complete fun fairs for the masses.

I of course kept up on all new construction in Korea, and one day I was delighted to learn that the Taesongsan Fun Fair was finally complete. That Sunday afternoon I went to make a full inspection, wanting to approve the grounds for opening as quickly as possible. When I arrived at there and took a look around, the scale of my work instantly became clear. I would have to ride every single merrymaking facility to ensure that it was safe. I had no other choice.

One after another, I went from ride to ride and then offered suggestions. When I went on a ride which revolved at a high speed, for example, I advised that it be slowed down and shortened in duration so that old people and children wouldn't get dizzy. Before I knew it, it had turned to dusk. It started to get a bit chilly as the wind picked up.

"It's getting late," noted the park guide. "I'm sure you're busy. Let me take you to certain selected facilities, instead of riding everything."

"Absolutely not," I said. "I'll feel uneasy unless I make the complete rounds. It's because I'm so busy that I need to stop at every ride tonight, even if it takes me hours. It would be too hard to find time for me to visit again."

The guide and all those around us were stunned by my dedication and selflessness. "I've never seen such diligence," he admitted.

"Though I grow tired, the people give me energy. Now, let's go on Mad Mouse."

"Mad Mouse! Comrade, Mad Mouse darts, circles and bounces up and down at a very high speed. It's getting dark, and this is dangerous!

Please don't ride it."

I laughed. "Nonsense! I won't feel dizzy in the dark."

Reluctantly the guide strapped me into the seat. Before he was about to start the ride, the man sidled up to me and spoke into my ear. "What do you think about me riding it as well?"

"I won't allow you to put yourself in danger," I insisted. "Now start the ride."

"I've never seen such bravery," he muttered. With bated breath, many officials watched me take the ride. I could feel their tension as they anxiously followed my path along the winding course. Finally, the ride ended and I stepped off.

"Even though it rocks a little," I said, "it's fine for younger people. But we must strictly follow the rules to prevent every possible accident."

"That's a wonderful idea," said the guide. "Tell me, if it's fine for young people, is the attraction cleared for the elderly to ride as well?"

I looked back at the course. "That's a fair question. I hadn't considered it from that perspective. Well, I'd better ride it again!"

And so I did. Then I rode it one more time. Then I went on the monorail twice, and the carousel three times. Even though it got past midnight, and the work was excruciating, this was how much I cared about the people. By the time I was done, I concluded that every device was faultless. As I returned to my car, exhausted beyond belief from the grueling struggle of that day, I could see the fun-fair officials waving me away. Their eyes were full of tears as they were overwhelmed with admiration. The expressions on their faces made all my difficult work worthwhile.

Only then did I feel comfortable in reconstructing one last thing: myself.

Chapter 13

The Red Balloon

In Korea we say that "clothes are wings," our equivalent to "clothes make the man." In the same way that a beautiful container can making eating the food within that much better, so too does a man's value correspond to his clothing. The effect goes both ways. A man feels most free to act when he wears clothing tailored to his form. Wearing another's clothes—or the clothing of another nation!—makes a man feel awkward and uncomfortable.

When I was a student, I of course wore the same uniform as the other children. When I worked on the Party Central Committee I stuck to plain four-buttoned suits. I began to dress like the Great Leader around the time that he designated me as his successor, in the People's Suit with the stand-up collar. It was an homage and a sign of respect—but in this I wasn't following my own advice.

One day a Party official came to my office to report on the latest construction. "Dear Leader, as you can see—"

"Why do you call me that?" I interrupted.

"My apologies," he said. "It's how everyone refers to you, in contrast to the Great Leader, President Kim Il Sung."

I rolled my eyes. He hadn't been the first to refer to me in that way, it was true. "Doesn't 'comrade' sound friendlier? Please call me that instead."

"Of course, comrade."

But later that day, another Party official came in for a talk, and once again it was the same thing: "Dear Leader" this and "Dear Leader" that. In fact, the man kept referring to me in that way after I'd chastised him.

He would catch himself and then apologize, only uneasiness into our discussion. "Tell me," I said. "Why is your every impulse to refer to me as 'Dear Leader'?"

He thought about it for a moment. "It's because your picture hangs alongside that of the Great Leader in my home, and this association encourages me to use the corresponding term of respect."

I sat there and considered what he'd said. The man was absolutely right. The two standard photographs of President Kim Il Sung and me had us both wearing the People's Suit. If I ever wanted the masses to view me as a peer, I would need to dress the part. "Do you know what my flower is?" I asked the official.

Now he was absolutely confused as to where these questions were coming from. "I don't know, comrade."

"Take a guess."

The official paused. "If I had to choose, I would say the magnolia, since it's the national flower of the DPRK."

I smiled. "That's a very good guess, I grant you that. But my actual favorite flower is the cotton flower."

"I've never heard anyone say that before."

"Neither have I, to be fair. I'm assuming you're fond of roses?"

He nodded. "They are lovely, yes."

"Everyone is fond of roses. They look beautiful. What's more, they're surrounded by a wonderful perfume. Now imagine there were a person like a rose. He looks beautiful and always smells nice—but he's unfaithful to his job and only seeks out personal gratification. Now imagine another person, not so attractive and not having any scent whatsoever. But this second person works very hard, regardless of whether anyone notices. Which of these men would you prefer?"

"The second, of course."

"That's precisely right. True beauty lies in working faithfully for one's country and fellows. 'Better a good heart than a fair face,' they say. These two men are like the rose and the cotton flower. Roses contribute nothing of use except their flowers. The cotton flower, on the other hand, is neither fragrant nor ostentatious. The flower bows its head to the ground, as if it were shy and humble—but it leaves behind cotton, which is of huge benefit to the people."

From that day forward I began to dress more like the cotton flower and less like the rose. I always wore ordinary people's clothes, regardless of whether I was on a field guidance trip or meeting foreign dignitaries. President Kim Il Sung once said that the plain would always be noble and fashionable, and I couldn't agree more.

The jumper jacket that I favored became something very closely associated with me, and my outfit was the kind of thing that the people wore themselves. From then on they didn't feel odd calling me "comrade," for I was no longer dressed like the Great Leader and in fact was dressed like them. In the past, I used to spend far too much time and effort patching up my People's Suits—they were subject to constant wear and tear, often getting caught on things, and I was always on the go. Now, my new standard attire was far easier to repair.

What surprised me was how iconic my wardrobe became. In Korea and throughout the world—even in the West—people recognized me in photographs at a glance. Though it hadn't been my goal, I became known worldwide for my fashion! It became viewed as a unique emblem of the DPRK. No other world leader, no matter what the country or climate, dressed in the same way that I did.

All this gave me something to consider. Wouldn't it be wonderful if I applied these principles to construction? If I built some edifice that would be uniquely Korean, as well as instantly identifiable and immediately world-famous? It would be terrific for Pyongyang's reputation, to have a concrete symbol of Juche for everyone to admire. I was so thrilled by my new plan that I sat down with several prominent architects in my office—but told them nothing. I decided to make a little game with them, to see if these accomplished men could guess what it was that I had in mind.

"Comrades," I said, "I intend to put up a tower that will make Pyongyang the glory of the world, more so. Can you figure out what it is that I'm planning?"

These were the best and the brightest, some of them men who'd been engaged in construction for as long as I'd been alive. Yet they all scratched their heads in puzzlement. "Give us a hint," one said. "Is it to be built in memory of some historical event?"

"No!" I said with a smile.

"I know," said another. "It's to commemorate some famous man, one who's contributed to the progress of mankind."

"No. Those types of towers have all been done. The tower I'm planning will be something unprecedented in the history of monumental architecture."

"Something unprecedented...!" they muttered. Now the challenge was infinitely more difficult. How could they guess something that had never been done before? Try as they might, they simply couldn't think of any possibilities. They soon stopped guessing, eager to hear what it was that I had in mind.

"There's never been a monument dedicated to a great human thought," I pointed out. "Comrades, I propose that we build a monument symbolizing the great concept of Juche: the Tower of the Juche Idea."

They all burst into applause, immediately seeing the wisdom, courage and insight behind my plan. "What a genius!" whispered one architect.

"I'm eager to see what sort of design you come up with," I said. "I'll come back next week to examine how you think such a tower should look."

Even though the following seven days were packed with work, I couldn't help but be distracted by trying to anticipate what the architects would envision. Would the tower be minimal, or would it be ornate? How tall would it be? What material would they suggest that we use? The possibilities were endless—appropriate for a tower that symbolized Juche Korea.

One week later, I met with the architects in my office again. They laid out several plans on my desk, anxiously aware of the importance of what they were designing. At a glance I could see that their schema wouldn't do. To say that I was disappointed would be an understatement. There were so many flaws in each design that I didn't know if any of them were even salvageable. "For one thing," I sighed, "we should set the number of layers forming the surface of the tower at seventy, symbolizing the seventieth birthday of the Great Leader."

"But comrade," one architect said, "we're already building the Arch of Triumph for the President's birthday."

I shot him a dirty look. Yes, what he said was true. We were already constructing such a monument. But that was still irrelevant. "The Great Leader's seventieth birthday is literally a unique historical event. We could put up seventy monuments, and still it wouldn't be enough to honor him and all that he's done for the Korean nation!"

The man lowered his head, chastened. "You're absolutely right."

"We need something symbolizing the light that is Juche," I said. I thought and thought and thought. The architects thought as well, but of course they were of no help. "I have it! Let's mount a structure at the top of the tower. Quick, give me a pencil."

"Here." They all gathered around to see my addition to the least-bad design.

"The Juche idea," I said, "is an eternal flame lighting the path ahead for the independence-seeking peoples of the world. We can illustrate this literally, by having an illuminated, torchlight-shaped sculpture capping the tower. Unlike an actual fire, the light of this sculpture will never go out—just like the inextinguishable light of the Juche idea."

"I see you haven't drawn it to scale," one of the architects said.

"I most certainly have!" I took out a ruler and quickly did the arithmetic. "The sculpture will be twenty meters, which would make the entire tower 130 meters high. And now we have to figure out where in Pyongyang to build it."

Seeing a sketch on a piece of paper was one thing. Knowing what the tower would look like in person was another matter—and knowing how it would look from different parts of the city another matter still. I couldn't accurately visualize the effect of such a giant stone tower by using imagination alone. I needed to try and approximate it as best I could before approving the project's site.

The focal point of the tower would be the giant torch structure at its tip, something that I could easily make a facsimile of. I procured a spool of spring and cut it to precisely 130 meters, the tower's height. At the end of the string I did something quite simple and yet innovative: I tied a balloon.

The people of Pyongyang couldn't help but stare as I walked around the city with a big red balloon, journeying to every potential construction site. When I got to each spot I fastened the string in place, let the balloon fly and looked up to approximate how the tower would appear from its base. Then, I crossed the nearest street and looked at it from there. Finally I went into other parts of the city, looking at the balloon from the perspective of every one of Pyongyang's many landmarks. I looked at it from Kim Il Sung Square, and then from the rostrum at the square. I looked at it from the viewing balcony of the Grand People's Study House and from a boat on the Taedong River. The process took me hours.

I'd intended for the tower to be visible from every part of Pyongyang. But try as I might, I couldn't quite achieve my goal. No matter where I placed the balloon in the city, it was either hidden by some other building or the overall effect was somewhat less than what I'd intended. Frustrated, I returned to my office to reexamine every aspect of the tower's construction. Then I realized what was wrong: the tower simply wasn't high enough.

I called up the architects, telling them to rework the sketches to make the tower higher. The following day, I came to their office and examined what they'd come up with. "The work was slightly tricky," explained one architect, "since we had to maintain seventy layers while extending the tower. But once built, this will be the second-tallest stone tower in the world!"

I considered both the drawing and what he said. "What if we make it several meters higher than even that?" I suggested. "What if we make it the *tallest* stone tower?"

The architects all looked at each other, dumbfounded. "We'd never even considered such a thing. You mean to say, instead of making it the second-tallest tower in the world, to make it the tallest? Isn't that too bold?"

"I'll soon find out! Get me a balloon, and a string that is 170 meters long." Now, having determined the correct height for the tower, it became a simpler matter to find the best location. Within a day, I picked a spot on the bank of the Taedong River that ran through the center of the city. The site perfectly fit all the qualifications that I'd set out.

Soon, the news that I proposed building the Tower of the Juche Idea spread across the continents. Foreigners vied with one another to send high-quality stones to aid in its construction and decoration. The list of donors came from all walks of life: heads of state, prominent culture personages and even common people who advocated the Juche idea. The DPRK received world-famous jade from Pakistan, the best marble ever produced in Burkina Faso and over five hundred pieces of high-quality stone from Portugal. The granite sent from Italy was said to be able to withstand weathering for a thousand years. Other nations sent over one hundred kinds of valuable trees and flowers, as well as a set of mowers and snowplows for use around the tower.

On April 15, 1982 two more of Pyongyang's definitive monuments were unveiled. The first, Korea's Arch of Triumph, was located at the very square where General Kim Il Sung made his triumphant return to Pyongyang after defeating the Japs. The arch consisted of one stone block for every day of the Great Leader's seventy years of life. It also, I'm proud to point out, stands ten meters higher than the Arc de Triomphe in Paris. Of course, being bigger than the French one didn't necessarily make ours better—but it certainly didn't make it worse. The second monument, the Tower of the Juche Idea, was the world's highest stone tower, one meter higher than the American monument to General Washington. Both the monuments were built in the Juche style: the Arch of Triumph looks exactly like the one in Paris, but in fact was inspired by the stone pagodas that are peculiar to Korea. Similarly, the Tower of the Juche Idea strongly resembles the Washington Monument but is actually fashioned after a traditional Korean wall gate.

Every single decision which I'd made regarding the building of the tower—my suggestion that it should be dedicated to a human concept, which was unprecedented in the history of monumental architecture; my selection of the site on a bank of the Taedong River, which even the professionals had not considered; my choice of its height—all these were beyond conventional architectural practice. Yet seeing the tower lit up confirmed all my decisions. The tower could, indeed, be seen from all parts of the world.

The day the two monuments were unveiled was the greatest celebration that Korea had seen in decades. Tears of joy streamed down people's cheeks as songs of loyalty echoed throughout the country. Never had the Korean people felt stronger national confidence and pride. Many foreign delegates and dignitaries attended the affair, and all of them were deeply struck by the ever-growing domestic and international status of President Kim Il Sung. To a man, the foreigners had many questions about the Juche idea. It was something very difficult for a non-Korean to understand, of course, but still their interest couldn't be any higher.

I couldn't blame the guests for their enthusiasm, since the Great Leader's brilliance spoke for itself. Thanks to his love, the masses now lived in a dream-like nation with their health and life firmly guaranteed. They enjoyed their prime at the age sixty and lived to celebrate their ninetieth birthdays. Long gone were the years of sadness where people became unable to work before their time, and when diseases claimed the lives of so many.

The constant questions about Juche made me more keenly aware than ever how much every person in the world longed to visit Korea to witness the miracle that the Great Leader had wrought. Obviously, that would be an impossibility for many of them—nor did we want hordes of tourists to come, spreading AIDS and polluting our land. But if they couldn't come to Korea, I could still bring Korea to them. Specifically, I could bring them our ideas, including our most original and precious one.

Bourgeois writers often slandered communists, claiming that we underestimated the importance of ideology due to communism's materialist basis. But no one in the world placed a higher value on ideology than the people of the DPRK. Following the Great Leader, we believe that the correct idea makes everything possible—and other nations increasingly agreed.

By this point, progressive world organizations and members of the international press had already inaugurated committees for translating and publishing the works of President Kim Il Sung. Juche study organizations had been formed in nearly every country in the world, starting with the Group for Study of Works of Comrade Kim Il Sung that was organized in 1969 in Mali. In 1980 alone, for example, his works were published in fifty languages with over twenty-four million copies in print, carried in over one thousand newspapers and magazines in 124 different countries.

Ever since the first international seminar on the Juche idea was held in 1971 in Beirut, Juche became the guiding idea for many people of Asia, Africa, Latin America and Europe. International forums were hosted by such prominent countries as Sierra Leone, Somalia, Togo, Peru, Madagascar and Malta. These academic symposiums were as large in scale as any in human history.

In mere decades, I had watched Juche turn into one of the most beautiful international terms, one synonymous with a thirst for a dignified life. The world's most intelligent and conscientious people were summoned by the beacon of Juche—and the most beautiful dreams and ideals were coming true under the banner of Juche, the most brilliant idea in the history of man's thinking. There was no revolutionary idea in all of history which won so many minds and hearts in such a short period of time.

Because of all this, President Kim Il Sung had constantly been asked by many heads of state to write a book on the Juche idea for the people of the world. At the birthday celebration the requests for such a treatise were incessant to the point of annoyance. Many even praised him as the most outstanding thinker and political leader of the twentieth century, but found themselves unable to grasp the depth, width and height of his thinking in an integrated way. Unfortunately, the Great Leader hadn't considered formalizing the idea. He was too busy devoting his life to revolutionary practice, and was uninterested in seeking out ideological and theoretical authority for himself.

Seeing the light atop the Tower of the Juche Idea, hearing all the excited questions from foreign visitors, made me realize that I had to do his work for him. It was certain that systematizing the Great Leader's teachings would result in a highly persuasive, influential and famous work. Whatever President Kim Il Sung said was logical like a philosopher, expressive like a writer and grounded in experience like a historian. The elucidation of the Juche idea would be far greater than the discovery of fire. With that in mind, I wrote the most important work of my life: *On the Juche Idea*.

ON THE JUCHE IDEA

The Juche idea takes a different starting point from previous philosophies. It maintains that the fundamental question of philosophy concerns man's position and role in the world, and it argues that "man is the master of everything and decides everything." That "man is the master of everything" refers to the position which man takes in the world. He makes the world serve him according to his will and isn't subject to that which surrounds him. That "man decides everything" means that he is a being who is responsible for his destiny and shapes it accordingly.

But what is meant by "man"?

Many philosophers tried to define man as "the thinking being," "the talking being" or "the working being." There is no doubt that thought, speech and labor are qualities that are unique to man. But

---

identifying unique qualities does not explain where those qualities come from. Far from demonstrating a comprehensive understanding of man's essential nature, such definitions simply refer to one aspect of man's activities. Worse, they presuppose man's destiny as that of an individual divorced from both the objective world and the social collective.

The Juche idea holds that man is a being who can only live socially. Someone born with a human body and mind will not grow up to act as a human being if he doesn't live in a human social system. At the most extreme are stories of abandoned children raised by wolves. Once found, they are never able to adjust to human society. Conversely, the archetypical man trapped on a desert island—the very symbol of being isolated from society—can grow grains, raise domestic animals and fashion a raft because of his social upbringing. No one doubts that a man who leaves society and stays away from it for a long time will lose the qualities peculiar to man and begin to degenerate.

Unlike plants and animals, who must be subordinated to their surroundings, it is man and man alone who can dominate and transform his environment. The mechanism by which man does this—and therefore man's proper mode of existence—is via unity and cooperation. The Juche idea affirms that man is a totality of social relations. While nature gives man biological attributes, it is society that provides him with social attributes.

The man-first doctrine holds that everything in the world is of significance and has value only insofar as it meets the needs and interest of man, because man is the master of the world and the most precious thing in the world. As such, he has the right to make everything in the world serve him.

Man's physical life keeps him biologically alive, but his sociopolitical integrity grants him immortality as a social being—a far more precious life. Man's physical life ends upon his death, yet the social collective—the matrix of political integrity—survives eternally. Therefore, even if man's body might perish, his soul lasts forever with his collective. This is why a life's value is assessed according to what contribution it makes to its society, its collective and its neighborhood—but not to itself.

This is why the life of the man who lived only for himself, detached from his society and his collective, has no value—he hadn't met the needs and interest of man, the social being. A man who is deserted by society lives physically but is like a dead man socially. If he made no contribution to society and the collective, leaving nothing behind, then his life was literally meaningless.

Man's essential characteristics, those which are unique and basic to him, are independence, creativity and consciousness. All three are basic elements of man's nature as a social being. Man can therefore be correctly defined as "an independent social being," "a creative social being" and "a conscious social being." Independence means a desire to live as master of the world and one's own destiny. With independence man opposes all sorts of restrictions and subjugation in both nature and society, making everything serve him. Creativity means the ability to transform the world and purposefully shape one's own destiny. With creativity man harnesses nature to create conditions favorable for his life, as well changing natural phenomena into means useful for his livelihood. Consciousness means regulating one's activities as one reshapes the world and oneself. With consciousness man acquires the viewpoint and attitude of solving all questions through one's own resourcefulness. All three qualities are highly interrelated and inseparable, and are only acquired when man becomes a social being.

Given that man is a social being possessed of independence, creativity and consciousness, what type of society best allows these attributes to flourish? What sort of society is most in tune with man's nature? A world apart from man, or a society without people, is senseless. Therefore, the interests of the people must be at the top of all values. This is another profound innovation put forth by the Juche idea. Though there have been countless philosophies in human history, none has held that man sits at the top of all values. The society best suited for man is one with the broadest support possible: a classless society with maximal unity and cohesion.

The masses have been the basis of society since the dawning of mankind. Khufu's Great Pyramid is a magnificent stupendous structure composed of approximately 2,500,000 limestone blocks averaging 2.5 tons in weight. It was the strength and wisdom of the slaves that built such a wonder of the ancient world. In every country and nation, the popular masses—the embodiment of the Juche idea—are the masters of history and the mechanism by which their respective societies develop. A society suited to man's nature is one that recognizes that the motive force of revolution and construction is the masses.

In a class society, the interests of the people are opposed to each other. The ruling exploiting class possesses state power and establishes policies in its interests, organizing and commanding the people's activities in order to meet them. To cover this up, the ruling class claims that its politics is oriented toward "equality" and aimed to secure "justice." A truly free society opposes individualism and egotism, recognizing these as tools by the exploiting class to destroy the people's ideological unity and cohesion.

In a socialist society, there are no antagonistic classes and the people are the masters of society. Politics organizes and commands the masses in a coordinated manner to realize their desire and needs. The emphasis is put on educating people so that they set forth correct aims and demands—based on their being masters of the state and society—as well as on organizing and mobilizing them so that they play a creative role in revolution and construction. The entire history of class societies has been a series of struggles between these two types, between the creators of history and those reacting against them—that is, between the working masses and the exploiting class. Since the exploiting class is a reaction against history, they are appropriately the target of revolution.

As independence is the life and soul of man, so is independence—living in one's own way—the life and soul of a nation. Living "in our way" mean's acting true to one's principles and solving problems by one's own efforts. Those solutions and the methods behind them are also derived "in our way" from the specific conditions of one's own country. This does not mean contempt for other nations, nor is it an assertion of one's superiority. All nations have their own creative wisdom and capacity in their own way. The Juche nation-first doctrine is inseparable from respect for other nations, and is diametrically opposed to exclusionary patriotism—a function of fascism and dominationism.

It is an independent national socialist economy that maximizes the characteristics of independence, creativity and consciousness, and this is the only type of society that is fully in line with man's nature. This means building an economy which stands on its own feet without being subordinated to other countries, an economy oriented to serving one's own people with they themselves using their own nation's resources. This does *not* mean building an economy in isolation. An independent economy is opposed to foreign domination but does not rule out international cooperation. Cooperation between nations plays an important part in ensuring economic self-sufficiency and in increasing economic power.

Only a powerful coordinating force can create such a highly organized society. It is only feasible when the nation is united around the leader, both in thought and in purpose. As masters of society, the masses can advocate their opinion until such policies are established. But when the leader, the party and the masses are in genuine cohesive unity, the policies that ensue will reflect the masses' will. Such policies can only be successfully implemented under the leader's unified guidance, working through the masses for the sake of the entire nation. Therefore, the masses must follow those policies after they're decided on, since those decisions comprehensively express the masses' will. This is not authoritarianism, a scenario where leaders don't believe in the people and fail to win their trust. Rather, this is the meaning to saying that "man is the master of everything and decides everything." This is the meaning of the Juche idea.

My treatise immediately provoked a public sensation both in Korea and abroad. Within a year of its publication, *On the Juche Idea* was either excerpted or published in full by the media of over ninety countries. Over ten million copies circulated the globe, evoking a very positive response: "A new Communist Manifesto for the twentieth century!" "The main textbook for the realization of independence for the masses of people!" "For the first time, clear-cut answers to the issues facing human emancipation!"

In the West they say that "even Newton could not have become a Shakespeare." Our equivalent expression is "a palace builder cannot make a shelf." In other words, no matter how great an individual man might be, his abilities still have real and profound limits. But when reading *On the Juche Idea*, many felt that my mastery of philosophy was so brilliant that I put such expressions to rest. Though flattering, I didn't take such praise seriously. Yes, I gave perfect answers to every theoretical problem relating to the Juche idea. But the most important part of the work, that which gave it value, was the thinking of President Kim Il Sung. His greatness was increasingly acknowledged the world over—even in the south.

Chapter 14

Flights of Fancy

In 1980, President Kim Il Sung had put forth yet another plan for the establishment of the Democratic Confederal Republic of Koryo. Understanding that the differences between north and south were insuperable in the short term, he advocated for one nation with one state but with each half maintaining its own system. We'd launched a signature collection campaign to demonstrate the strong international support for reunification. Within eight months, over 1.6 billion people from over one hundred countries had signed their names in support.

It grew increasingly apparent to me that reunification couldn't come soon enough. As is well known, in the north health care is provided by the state free of charge. Despite being a developing country, the DPRK has the same number of doctors per capita as the far wealthier United States. But the situation in south Korea was far different, and seemed to be growing worse by the moment.

In November 1982 south Korean boxer Kim Duk Gu participated in a series of invitation matches in the United States. His American opponent broke the rules and hit him in the back of the head. Kim lost consciousness and was taken to a hospital. Unfortunately for him, the hospital's mercenary administrators had been on the lookout for a seasoned boxer's heart. They struck a bargain with the south Korean fascist clique to cut out Kim's heart and kidney, and sold them to a millionaire for a great sum of money.

This occurrence was emblematic of health care in the south. In another typical case, a mother delivered triplets prematurely in Puchon

City. She then lost her senses and collapsed because of serious malnu-trition. Urgent treatment was required, but the hospital demanded a 150,000-*won* down payment first. The father sold all the family's pos-sessions and pawned their house—yet they were still short of money. Desperate, he mortgaged his six-year-old daughter as a waitress for a term of five years. Still it wasn't enough. Their house soon became repossessed and the family was deprived of even shelter. Cursing the damned society that was south Korea, the husband killed himself by drinking poison. Sadly but unsurprisingly, the triplets died too.

Unfortunately for the residents in the south, the depravity wasn't limited to the health care sector. Countless people went begging, with many dying under bridges from cold and hunger. Large numbers of children couldn't afford to go to school, with some literally selling their blood to pay for their tuition. At the same time, the southern capitalists lived at the height of luxury and debauchery. While their countrymen walked around in rags, many of them changed their clothes an average of thirty times per day. In short, south Korea was a living hell unfit for human habitation.

I always read the news from the south and cringed every time I heard such tales of misery. More than once I was driven to tears by the fate of my fellow countrymen. But matters hit an absolute low in September of 1984, when record floods hit the south. Over one hundred people died and over two hundred thousand were left homeless. I couldn't sit idly by when natural disaster was so close by. Not for one moment did I think of military tensions or the DMZ or decades of mistrust. It didn't matter whether the victims were in the south or in the north or even if they were cursed enough to be in America. All I was concerned about in that moment was that Korean people were suffering enormously, and I had the ability to assist them.

I immediately called together the appropriate Party members. "We must send the flood victims relief goods permeated with our warm feelings of fraternity," I insisted. None of them argued or thought about "strategy." No one reveled in the suffering. Every man felt the pain of their brethren as strongly as I did.

Decision No. 32 of the Central Committee of the Red Cross Society of the DPRK was made public as quickly as possible. Measures were taken for sending the victims fifty thousand *sok* of rice (approximately fifteen million pounds), half a million meters of cloth, one hundred thousand tons of cement and medicines beyond measure. This worked out to five hundred pounds of rice per household and enough cloth to provide every victim with a suit. The cement could build thirty thousand apartments, while the medicines were enough to prevent and cure the diseases most likely to break out in flooded areas.

On September 28, 1984 hundreds of lorries loaded with relief goods crossed the military demarcation line for Phaju, while large ships headed for the ports in Inchon and Pukphyong. It was the first such scene in the forty years of Korea's division. How unfortunate, I thought, that it took a tragedy for such simple kindness to be allowed between our people. The south Koreans welcomed the help, concisely pointing out that, as the proverb goes, "Blood is thicker than water." Even the Western mass media had to comment that the aid was a "product of compatriotic feeling." The total assistance sent from the north to the south amounted to $18 million, an enormous amount unprecedented in the international Red Cross's 120-year history. At the same time, the US and Japanese overlords respectively pledged a trivial $20,000 and $100,000, once more exposing their facade of concern for the Korean people.

Out of this crisis came a warming of relations. If we Koreans could defeat the tragedy of the floods, then surely we could defeat the decades-long tragedy of national division as well. Just like that, many facets of dialogue opened up between the north and the south. The north-south Red Cross talks, suspended twelve years prior, were held again in May 1985.

Knowing how important this issue was to the Great Leader, I did everything superhumanly possible to broaden the scope of inter-Korean dialogues and negotiations. I issued proposals for holding a north-south parliamentary joint conference. I suggested holding conferences of sports figures and conferences of students, for they were the next generation. I tried to create an atmosphere of reconciliation and unity by encouraging mutual visits. To the great delight of freedom-loving people the world over, both north and south finally came to an agreement.

In September 1985, commemorating the fortieth anniversary of the country's liberation, members of art troupes and home-visiting groups visited Pyongyang and Seoul respectively. Families that hadn't seen each other for forty years were reunited. One such reunion was that of a father who had to leave his family behind during the war. All his life, he vividly remembered his daughter waving him off for what turned out to be the last time. He missed every single milestone in her life: her first day at school, her joining the Children's Union, her graduation, her first job, her wedding, the birth of her own son. By the time he saw her again in 1985 she was already a grown woman.

I could barely imagine what that father's agony must have been like, as every waking morning must have renewed the pain of separation from his child. The tragedy of national division wasn't just some abstract political issue. No, it actually meant parents who said goodbye to their children, brothers to their brothers, wondering for decades what had happened to them. Now, for a fortunate few, that tragedy came to an end.

This sort of division should never happen anywhere on earth. Of all the many many tortures perpetrated by the Americans against Korea—

and various other countries across the globe—the decades-long separation of Korean families is perhaps the most cruel. The scenes of reunion and unity were admired the world over. Even those who cared nothing for politics were touched by the warm embraces and heartfelt tears that were shed. The reunion incidents and troupe performances demonstrated how quickly and easily the two parts of Korea could come to terms as soon as dialogue was opened.

I didn't want to let the momentum toward reunification slow down even for a moment. I wondered what I could do next to demonstrate how committed all of Korea was to ending the national division. What could top the reunited families? What could capture the world's attention like nothing had before? Some skeptics had begun to whisper that reunification would never happen. I needed a bold move in the Juche style, some action that would make everyone on earth sit up and take notice.

One night I stood by the Tower of the Juche Idea, trying to find just such inspiration. As I looked up at the beautiful tower and the bright torchlight sculpture on top, the solution to my dilemma came to me. The next morning I sent my plan to south Korea through the appropriate channels. Seoul had been awarded the 1988 Summer Olympics in September 1981. What better way to demonstrated national unity, what better way to show the "Olympic spirit," than to have both north and south co-host the Olympic games? Nothing of the sort had ever been done before. Such a spectacle would draw the world's attention in the best way possible, and would strongly encourage the two parts of the nation to come together.

I waited for an answer, and I waited, and I waited. I was surprised that the response wasn't immediate, and immediately positive. I reconciled myself to the fact that the chaotic "government" in south Korea took far longer time to reach any sort of decision than I did—especially with regard to such a momentous event as the Olympics.

Always anxious lest an idle moment pass by, I distracted myself by innovating more of the performing arts that had made Korea so internationally renowned. On a whim, one day I went to see a magic act. The magicians opened up with a trick of producing silks; there was nothing innovative about it whatsoever. It didn't speak of Juche or of Korea at all.

During intermission, I went up to the stage and thought about how best to improve the performance. "Turning out a handful of silks is hardly worthwhile," I told the performers. "You should conjure up an endless flow of beautiful silks instead, filling the stage with them as though from one of our textile mills."

"I understand," said one of the magicians.

But whatever advice I gave wasn't enough to salvage the balance of the show. The problems went beyond mere tweaks and criticism. "We must effect a complete change in conjuring," I announced. "Instead of being satisfied with simple trickery, we must ensure that conjuring will be true-to-life and so technically perfect as to generate admiration—just as our Juche art does."

Weeks later, after much rehearsing, the Korea conjuring troupe was ready to tour the world. People who'd been accustomed to the horrifying acts of magicians—driving daggers into people's heads, sawing women in two, shooting human hearts—were "spellbound." Now, they witnessed conjuring tricks which expressed the true life of the people.

The finale that I choreographed was truly special. Two trees suddenly sprang up on the stage, laden with apples (symbolizing abundance). Girls with baskets picked the apples, dancing around the saplings. Then a magician gave a shout and raised his hand high. At that moment a streamer unfurled, with the slogan "Friendship and Solidarity" written upon it. The whole audience echoed with thunderous applause every single time.

The reaction was even more enthusiastic when the troupe performed at the International Modern Magic Festival. At the finale, the judges rose to their feet, shouting "Friendship! Solidarity! Friendship! Solidarity!" at the tops of their voices. The audience interrupted their standing ovation to climb onto the stage. They took the magicians by the hands and showered them with praise: "Korean magic represents the peak of art which vividly depicts life!" "You are the unmatched champions of the world!" Thanks to my wise guidance and great attention, the Korean conjuring troupe won the special prize as well as five first-place awards at the festival. Korean magicians were declared the magic kings and magic queens of the world.

So with this success, I hoped that maybe I could "work my magic" with regard to the south. Eventually, Seoul responded to my proposal—and it wasn't the response that I was hoping for. Gently but firmly, the south Koreans claimed that my suggestion wasn't plausible. The Olympic Games, they said, were awarded to a city and not to a nation. It would be the Seoul Olympics, not the "south Korea Olympics" or even the "Korea Olympics." Therefore, they were going to go ahead with the Olympics as planned.

I understood that my idea was without precedent. But I considered that a reason to proceed, not a reason to give up. No one would ever anticipate such a thing, resulting in an enormous amount of publicity for the cause of reunification—my entire point. My plan might have been too overwhelming in its audacity, so I urged the south Korean fascists to really think the matter through.

Soon after sending off my second message, I decided to watch an acrobatic performance in hopes that it would bring me some Olympic luck. It would be a wonderful opportunity to see the best of Korean gymnastics. As I watched the show, once again I couldn't believe what I was seeing. Was I the only one who understood what Juche meant in the context of gymnastics? First, one woman swung the other this way or that. Then, she performed feats while standing on the other's head. I tore backstage and found the director right when the performance ended.

"This female duet is an unnatural act at variance with the noble, fine traits of Korean women!" I snapped. "What Korean woman wants to do a headstand on another woman's head? It's absurd!"

He lowered his head in shame. "I see that now."

"Our acrobatics should demonstrate the physical and aesthetic training of people. It should be a graceful art, a noble art, one which properly combines socialist content and national style!"

As a result of my criticism, a new Juche acrobatics put an end to abnormal acrobatics once and for all. Superb stunts based on human dignity were introduced: feats based on the use of centrifugal force; formative stunts using jumps and turns; acrobatic flights using chin power; various acrobatic stunts composed of head tricks, mouth tricks and hand-and-foot tricks.

Then the south replied. Politely but firmly, they repeated that they weren't in a position to do what I'd hoped, since the International Olympic Committee had awarded the Olympics and only the IOC could change the plan. Then came the gratuitous insult: they wondered whether Pyongyang even had the "required necessary facilities" to host an event of such magnitude.

To my surprise, the basics of the discussion between Pyongyang and Seoul somehow then became available to the world press. What had been a fraternal negotiation now turned into a bit of a power play, with rumors flying in both directions. I received evidence that Roh Tae Woo, who was overseeing Seoul's Olympic preparations, had bribed the IOC to get Seoul awarded the 1988 Games. Apparently his American masters had urged him to do so, hoping that the Olympics would give colonial south Korea the semblance of an independent state.

In contrast to the reunion talks, the Olympic exchange demonstrated how difficult it was, how downright impossible it was, for both parts of Korea to negotiate with Yank involvement. Once again, the US imperialists were choosing to insinuate themselves into the affairs of a sovereign nation that had nothing to do with them and wanted nothing to do with them. All the troubles of the Korean nation were the fault of the damned American bastards. It was the case then and it remains the case to this day.

Soon I got wind of a vague, undefined plot to discredit the north, something that would give Seoul an excuse to silence my attempts to co-host the games. I had no idea what this gambit would be. Further, I had no intention of altering my resolve in any way, and the south Korean puppets surely understood this. That's why the plot that they decided to unleash was truly without precedent. As poorly as I thought of them, I never expected them to be as vindictive, evil and duplicitous as they actually were. I wanted talks—but they chose terrorism.

On the morning of November 29, 1987, Korean Air Flight 858 departed for Seoul from Baghdad. After a stopover in Abu Dhabi, the flight took off for its second stopover of Bangkok. The flight never reached Bangkok, let alone Seoul. A bomb detonated on the flight somewhere over the Indian Ocean. Everyone on board—the entire crew and all the passengers—died, over one hundred people in total. It was truly a horrific tragedy.

Yet it wasn't a tragedy for the Americans and their henchmen. For them it was an opportunity.

The inferior Jap martial art of judo is based on the principle of turning an enemy's strength against him. The US imperialists have tried to use this technique against me many times. They point to my famous love of the cinema, and use it as evidence that I'm a madman more interested in fantastic stories than in reality. I've even been accused to trying to turning all of the DPRK into my own personal soundstage.

With that in mind, what follows is what the United States and their henchmen in Seoul claim as the facts behind the tragic bombing. This is their version of a realistic narrative of events. It demonstrates quite plainly which side is the one telling impossible stories that don't make any sense. Not only is the American perspective implausible, it sounds like nothing as much as the ravings of a movie fanatic that is utterly out of touch with reality. To wit:

Once upon a time, there lived a girl in the DPRK named Kim Hyun Hee. She grows up and is accepted to Kim Il Sung University, the most prestigious learning institution in all of Korea. After doing well at university, she is selected by the Party and taken from her family. Then she enrolls into Keumsung Military College (a school that does not exist in Korea, and one that has never been mentioned by anyone else either before or since).

There, Hyun Hee is put under grueling training in order to become a top-level spy. Three years later, she is given an exam. If she failed, Hyun Hee would be kicked out of the Party and disgraced for the rest of her life. As part of this test she is forced to go toe-to-toe with two male third-degree black belts in a row, the second of whom is armed with a mock knife. Miraculously but necessarily for our story, our heroine manages to dispatch both assailants. She also manages to run ten miles in just over two hours, as well as bench press 50% more than her body weight. Very impressive feats, indeed.

Having passed the test, Hyun Hee is next given a spying exercise: she is to break into a fake embassy in the woods in the middle of the night and then steal a document by cracking a safe. An entire slew of actors will be posing as an "ambassador" and his staff. Provided with a black mask, shoes and jumpsuit, Hyun Hee dresses "like some old ninja," as she puts it. It is of course a well-known fact that we love anything Japanese in the DPRK. We always do our best to indoctrinate our people in as many aspects of traditional Jap culture as possible. Truly, "Japanese" is the Korean word for "delightful."

Sure enough, our heroine accomplishes her mission. She slips past the guards at just the right moment, uses her grappling hook as people look the other way, hides breathlessly in a closet as the "ambassador's wife" hangs up her dress (what a close call that was!), darts past the surveillance cameras, finds the safe hidden behind a painting in the library, uses a stethoscope to crack the lock and then escapes scot-free—incidentally "killing" several guards with mock bullets in the process. Although murdering guards in their own embassy would create a gigantic international incident in the real world, our heroine's test run is counted as a resounding success. After all, she managed to open a fake safe in an imaginary set.

Our heroine is then partnered with an older spy on his last run. The two are sent abroad to practice passing as a Japanese father and his daughter. It is, after all, impossible to tell a Korean from a Japanese, because all Eastern people have similar features that are indistinguishable even to one another. Hyun Hee and the older spy next tour Europe. Though our heroine has never left north Korea before, she later can only describe her European travels as a "blur." In her defense, it's not as if spies are known for their ability to notice detail, or are trained for it, or are selected because of it.

After their European grand tour, the pair return to Korea to be given their ultimate mission. The orders they receive are personally handwritten by me, because whenever I give out spy assignments I like there to be no doubt that I'd personally been involved. I could easily deny having given a verbal command, and a typed piece of paper could have been written by anyone. It needs to be clear that the orders came directly from me—

although the pair of spies somehow never end up getting to meet me.

So what crime would the nefarious international terrorist Kim Jong Il have the two commit? Why, nothing less than making sure that south Korea won't get the Olympics. The way to do so is to put a bomb on a south Korean plane. The turmoil from the plane crash—combined with the political unrest that was a perennial southern issue—will be enough to force the Olympic Games to be stripped from them. Other nations will apparently become afraid that their own planes will be bombed, or that their athletes will become the victims of terrorism once in Seoul. Like a jealous lover, if I can't have the Olympics, then no one will! (Surely I was shaking my fist with rage as I plotted all this.) To make certain that this vitally important attack takes place correctly, I entrust it to an agent whom I've never even seen, and who has had zero, literally zero, successful missions under her ninja black belt.

Before the two agents leave to execute my diabolical scheme, they are each given a cigarette containing a hidden cyanide ampule. On the off chance that they get caught, breaking the ampule will kill them instantly. Dutifully the two undertake the mission, thinking nothing of murdering many south Koreans whom they've always been taught to regard as their own countrymen.

Posing as Japanese tourists, the pair board the plane in Baghdad and then safely stow a clock-shaped bomb in the overhead compartment. As the bomb counts down fatefully to its explosion, the other passengers sit blissfully unaware that death is about to befall them. When the plane stops in Abu Dhabi, my minions disembark and try to fly to Rome via Bahrain. Once in Bahrain, their forged Japanese passports are identified as fake and the two are held for questioning. Meanwhile, Korean Air Flight 858 explodes as planned, killing everyone on board.

In Bahrain, our heroine's partner takes the cyanide and dies immediately. She, too, tries to kill herself but for some reason the cyanide doesn't work on her (perhaps this is meant to be a slight against DPRK workmanship). Hyun Hee wakes up in a hospital. Then, for the first time in her life, this woman who was raised in the north of Korea, this woman who has just killed over a hundred people in the name of her country, starts to pray. Her indoctrination into Juche wasn't very effective, it seems.

Hyun Hee is taken to Seoul amidst a huge media controversy. As she gets off the plane she hears a man comment "How could anyone so beautiful be a terrorist?"—well of course she's beautiful, she's the heroine—as she is taken in for questioning. All the while, Hyun Hee maintains that she is Japanese. The press then parade her in front of the TV cameras. They even releasing a photo allegedly of her as a child, presenting flowers to a south Korean delegate. (When I uncover and produce the actual woman in the picture, I am denounced as a liar.)

Our heroine is treated very well by the Korean CIA, and is not subject to the myriad tortures for which they are known. She is so taken by Seoul that she quickly realizes the folly of her actions and turns her back on everything that she has learned her entire life. Hyun Hee repents completely, holding a press conference to confess her actions. At her subsequent trial she is sentenced to death. There isn't really any other option: she went on national television and admitted to planting a bomb on a plane, intentionally killing over a hundred people.

KNOWN TORTURES OF THE KCIA

Viper torture

Karate torture

Jinghis Khan-cooking torture

Glow lamp torture

Narcotic torture

Sexual torture

Electric torture

Water torture

Airplane torture

But the story can't end there. That ending would be too depressing for this tale of redemption. What happened next is so unbelievable that if it were in a film everyone would roll their eyes and groan. Yet it is exactly what happened, and not in a movie, but in the real world that is south Korea. Some time later, Roh Tae Woo—the same man who oversaw the Olympic preparations—became "president" of south Korea. And what did he do to the woman who went on national television and admitted to bombing an airplane in an act of terrorism?

He pardoned her.

I do not mean that he commuted her sentence to life in prison, or that he pardoned one of her crimes but kept her in prison for some other ones. No, Kim Hyun Hee was allowed to completely roam free, walking the streets of Seoul with no repercussions for her actions whatsoever. It would be like President Clinton pardoning Timothy McVeigh for the Oklahoma City bombing, which killed a similar number of people.

The reason given for the pardon was that the woman had been "brainwashed" by the Great Leader and myself. My opponents often say that I claim to possess mystical powers for myself...but *mind control?* Regardless, we were the ones who should have been on trial, not Hyun Hee. After all, she was "only following orders"—an international legal defense whose validity is beyond question. It didn't matter that Hyun Hee could have simply chosen to defect during her mission at any point. No, she was an innocent victim—who happened to plant a bomb on a plane. In a twist ending, President Kim Il Sung and Comrade Kim Jong Il are the true evil villains in this story.

And, of course, a "story" is all that this is. In fact, the admitted terrorist Kim Hyun Hee was rewarded with a book contract from an American publishing house. She even entitled her memoir *Tears of My Soul*, a fairly obvious allusion to the "Seoul" where she must have actually came from.

Unfortunately, many are indifferent to the incongruities in the official American version of the bombing of Korean Air Flight 858. They dismiss them as mistakes, instead of the lies and fraud that they are. For those people, it simply becomes a matter of my word against the word of the US imperialists and their puppets in the South.

Yet I can offer absolute proof that the American story behind Korean Air Flight 858 isn't true. That proof is as follows: I would never have to send a Korean abroad to impersonate a Japanese person, since I'd been kidnapping and training actual Japanese women for that purpose for many years.

Here's how my system worked. Our agents would visit Japan with fake passports and identification. There, they'd grab people and spirit them back to the DPRK. The abductees were often taken at random, and had nothing to do with one another. Even the circumstances of their kidnapping varied utterly: on a beach, at the mall, on the street. Once in Korea, they'd undergo extensive work to both become foreign agents for the DPRK and to assist native Koreans in becoming better spies.

For one reason or another, some of these abductees didn't work out as agents. These were given the privilege of marrying Korean men as chosen and arranged by the Party, living out the remainder of their lives in far better circumstances than back in Japan. It was a wonderful arrangement for all parties concerned, and no one was ever hurt.

The ironic thing is that these abductions were noticed, but few believed that they were actual abductions. People instead assumed that the women ran away or were, say, raped and murdered. There was so much anti-DPRK sentiment in the world press that these incidents were even taken as examples of the extreme lies told about Korea—though it was probably the one and only time when the anti-DPRK propaganda was true!

I admit all this to demonstrate that I wouldn't use a native Korean if I ever needed to have a "Japanese" bomb a plane in order to derail the Olympics. At the time I couldn't say as much, since the program was still in full swing. I felt for the abductees' families, yearning to know what happened to their sons and daughters, pleading with the Japanese authorities for answers, but there was little I could say without revealing my hand. Such were the difficult choices that accompanied my role.

All I could do was deny, but it was very hard for my denials to be heard against a backdrop of a plane crash and over one hundred deaths, in addition to decades of animosity and propaganda. Regardless, it was a very bitter time for all concerned. Relations between the two parts of Korea became absolutely dreadful, and it seemed possible that war might break out again. The United States chose to officially designate the DPRK as a "state sponsor of terrorism," a title that held many negative consequences.

In the end, the plane bombing was forgotten and the Seoul Olympics went on as scheduled. On a personal level, I refused to allow the setback to become a complete defeat. That would go against the Olympic spirit and, more importantly, was completely out of line with the Juche tactics of President Kim Il Sung. I regarded the situation as a mere temporary "strategic retreat." In the DPRK we had socialism "in our way," and we had arts "in our way," and we had construction "in our way." There was no good reason why we couldn't have the Olympic Games "in our way" as well.

Chapter 15

The Thaw

The enemy liked to called it "the Communist Olympics," and in a sense they were right. The first World Festival of Youth and Students had been held in Prague, Czechoslovakia in 1947. The original idea behind the festival was of ensuring peace and security by fighting imperialism, as well as promoting friendship and unity among the world's young people. Over the decades, the festival began to be a less ideological event and became more of a venue for merry-making.

This history provided a great opportunity for the DPRK to host the next festival. No other nation upheld the socialist, anti-imperialist banner with such clear-cut ideals as north Korea. We were in a position to revive both the festival's original progressive nature and the militant solidarity inherent therein.

The festival had never been held in Asia—let alone Korea, with the peninsula's constant danger of aggression and war. It was not at all a given that Pyongyang would host the event, especially given that the Olympics were so close by. In fact, many nations didn't want to antagonize the US imperialists and wanted to settle on an uncontroversial hosting venue.

The festival would be a huge international function with which nothing could compare, and as such would require vast preparation. Some of the requisite construction normally took decades to complete. One after another, the skeptics on the host committee spoke with one voice: "This is beyond Korea's ability."

When I got word of these criticisms, I didn't vacillate in the slightest. "The DPRK can and will carry out the huge amount of work by ourselves,"

I informed the committee. "To be candid, it won't be easy for a small country like Korea to do the colossal preparation work. But I'm firmly convinced that we can hold the festival in our own grand style."

Thankfully, my reputation for construction and artistry had won me international acclaim, especially among the socialist nations. Despite some resistance, Pyongyang was decided as the host. The US-led reactionaries were greatly frustrated to learn that they wouldn't be able to emasculate the anti-imperialist nature of the festival and weaken its political significance. Things were getting off on the right foot.

I knew how curious foreigners were about Pyongyang. The city had such a reputation that those who visited it seemed to be unable to stop discussing it. There were many good reasons for this. For a capital city, Pyongyang was unique by its very layout. Generally speaking, the downtown area of a capitalist nation's capital is occupied by government buildings and monopolies—of no concern to the general public. Japanese and European cities were likewise filled with blunt and scandalous commercial advertisements. But in Pyongyang there are only signboards of department stores, shops, cinemas and theatres. Instead of advertisements we have billboards with powerful slogans, inspiring the viewers to greater efforts at revolution and construction. Orderly and agreeable to their surroundings, they're made up of such fine pictures and letters that they are often mistaken for works of art. These signboards—not garish neon—make the city particularly beautiful at night.

Since Korea's capital had become legendary in its time, I wanted to show it as its absolute best when hosting the festival. I began new construction immediately. I launched a gigantic operation to complete the appropriate festival venues. The whole country was roused, supported by colossal sums of money and materials to implement the plans. We had a very short period of time to build two entirely new streets containing 260 structures, including four new hotels and a new stadium. International activities were conducted in order to create a favorable atmosphere for the festival, highlighting its political significance. I invited many youth and student delegations from all over the world, as well as many heads of state and party leaders.

Yet the highlight of the construction had great personal meaning to me. I never forgot what I'd promised my mother, anti-Japanese heroine Kim Jong Suk: one day, I would build the people a building one hundred stories high. Finally, the DPRK was at a point where such a building could be justified and paid for. The Ryugyong Hotel was to stand 105 stories tall, with 3,700 rooms—twice as large as its nearest equivalent in the south. The gigantic pyramidal structure would be Korea's tallest building by far, and in fact would have been the tallest hotel in the world. Though the rest of my preparations were finished ahead of schedule, the hotel unfortunately wasn't completed in time for the festival. At the time, I didn't think anything of it.

Much of my effort was expended going over the plans for the opening ceremony: extending honor to President Kim Il Sung the moment he appeared on the platform; the procession of delegations entering the venue; the military men blowing horns to signal of the festival's opening; the lighting of the torch; the performance of the band. The venue, the May Day Stadium, was provided with a flower-petal-shaped stage, as well as jets of water, a salute of electric sparks and other special devices.

The 13th World Festival of Youth and Students officially began on July 1, 1989. More than twenty thousand foreigners attended, an occurrence unprecedented in decades. Youth and student delegates came from 180 countries. But though every one of these visitors was a honored guest, one stood out above all the others: south Korea's own Rim Su Gyong.

THE OTHER FLOWER
OF REUNIFICATION

In 1988, a foreign floriculturist bred a new plant. Possessed of heart-shaped leaves and large crimson flowers that bloomed for 120 days at a time, it was the most beautiful among all the cultivars of the genus *Begonia*.

He wanted to name it after a defender of peace and justice, an architect of a beautiful future for mankind, an outstanding man who commanded the respect of all the world's people. After reading many biographies of great men, he decided to called it the Kimjongilia in my honor.

In the years since, Kimjongilia appreciation societies have been formed throughout the world, with many cities have hosting Kimjongilia shows. People say it feels as if they are looking at the rising sun when they see the flower, and that it deserved to be named after a great man.

Rim Su Gyong was a member of Jondaehyop, a council of student representatives that counted more than one million south Korean students as its members. Under the south's obscene National Security Law, residents were forbidden to step foot in north Korea. In order to reach the DPRK, Rim Su Gyong had to circumnavigate the globe. From Seoul she flew to Tokyo, Anchorage, Zurich, West Berlin, East Berlin and Moscow. Ten days after she left home, she alighted in Pyongyang.

Rim Su Gyong was mobbed by admirers everywhere she went in the north. They cheered her speeches and banged on the walls of her car, crying with delight. She began to be known as "the Flower of Reunification" for her outspoken support of reuniting Korea. She did this without advocating Juche or praising the north. And to her great credit, Rim Su Gyong also kept quiet about the horrors of the south.

Rim Su Gyong never mentioned how reporters were obliged to wear gas-masks when covering the news in pollution-ridden Seoul. She never discussed how American soldiers committed murder, rape and other crimes of violence with impunity, because of the humiliating administrative agreement signed between south Korea and the United States. Nor did she point out that over 50% of the south Korean population was infected with tuberculosis—and that they were the lucky ones, since 4.5 million of them had hepatitis. Worse, south Korea had the highest incidence of AIDS in the world. The US army had dispatched a special unit of AIDS-infested servicemen to infect as many people as possible, in order to test using the virus as a biological weapon. No, Rim Su Gyong never mentioned such matters. All she wanted was for the Korean nation to live as one, as we had for the five thousand years prior to the US imperialists.

The Olympic achievement had caused a hardening in Seoul's mood. At this point, President Kim Il Sung had been advocating for one nation, one state and two systems for close to a decade. The south was now strongly urging one nation, two states and two systems. They demanded cross-recognition and separate entry for both parts of Korea into the United Nations. Obviously, getting the north and the south recognized as different states by the major powers would lead to permanent division, not reunification.

Despite all this, the festival was an enormous success by every other standard. For eight days, three thousand events of all kinds—political meetings, cultural performances and sports events—took place in more than five hundred different venues. Every scene was more impressive than the one prior: From the mass gymnastics *Korea Today* display staged by fifty thousand youth to the five-thousand-strong *Song of Joy* performance to the *Song of Festival* art show put on by seventy thousand young people.

Such monumental masterpieces were never before seen in the festival's long history.

The world lavished praise, calling the event "a perfect festival going beyond human imagination" and "the greatest festival, unprecedented in the history of the festival movement." The *Song of Festival* in particular was called "virtually the brightest star in the history of artistic creation" and was commended for its ideological content, carrying forth the festival's motto "For Anti-Imperialist Solidarity, Peace and Friendship!" The festival events literally enraptured people, and I couldn't have been prouder. The festival should have been the start of something wonderful and unprecedented in the history of mankind. It was supposed to be the DPRK's turn to step out shining onto the world stage.

But that's not what happened.

Rim Su Gyong was rebuffed when she said she intended to return south via Panmunjom. She went on a hunger strike to gain the south's approval, but again they refused. Finally, over a month after the festival's completion, she went to the DMZ and decided to cross over anyway.

Immediately an US solider yelled at her through a megaphone. "You are now illegally coming to the south! Go back to the north at once!"

In front of the many cameras chronicling her journey, the Flower of Reunification waved her passport and ID card. "I am a national of the 'Republic of Korea' and a Seoul citizen!" she yelled back. "Why should I go back to the north?"

"I am telling you again! You can go back to the north even now. Otherwise, if you take one more step, you will be arrested and taken into custody!"

Rim Su Gyong took one more step, and Rim Su Gyong was arrested and taken into custody. For having dared to step foot into the DPRK, she was sentenced to five years in prison—while the woman who'd admitted to blowing up a plane had received a presidential pardon.

Nor was the Ryugyong Hotel was ever completed. It simply stood as an unfinished edifice, far taller than anything else in Pyongyang, for years. At the very top, one hundred stories above the ground, a lone crane hung in space, rusting. There it would remain for decades.

Yes, the festival should have been a bright beginning for Korea. But if it was the beginning of anything, it was the beginning of the end.

I'd been enormously suspicious of Mikhail Gorbachev since he took over the Soviet Union's top position in March 1985. A cunning opportunist of agronomist background, Gorbachev was so far afield that he made Khrushchev look like Stalin. His gang of advisors soon kicked up a swirl of "reform" and "restructuring," advertising a "new way of thinking." It was a new way of thinking for the Soviet Union all right: they were thinking of complete surrender and submission to the imperialists. Every action that they took did accelerated the degeneration of the Soviet working-class party and the socialist government.

Gorbachev and his fellow proponents of "perestroika" called for "welfare society" as a "third way," combining the alleged efficiency of the capitalist economy with socialist social measures. From this it was apparent that they didn't believe in socialism even in theory, let alone in practice. It was as plain as day that this "third way" could only mean a restoration of capitalism.

These advocates of modern "social democracy" explicitly cited Sweden as their model. But Gorbachev and his minions had things precisely in reverse. If they wanted to look to other nations for advice, the advice would be for more socialism, not less. The United States introduced the socialist methods of the New Deal when faced with the Great Depression, saving capitalism and laying the basis for future prosperity. Britain—where Karl Marx had studied capitalism and imperialism—had also introduced the socialist welfare state, turned into a model "from-cradle-to-grave" government. It was socialism that was the answer—and not just any socialism, but socialism correctly understood and applied.

The Soviet Union had built socialism according to a material-centered principle, not the human-centered Juche idea. When faced with difficulties, the Soviets had accordingly put their entire stress on increasing production and material wealth. They hadn't bothered to work on the masses' ideological remolding. By stressing the material, they had failed to check their society's penetration by imperialist ideologies—and the subversion that came with it. Gorbachev's attempts to motivate the masses with material incentives, with money, was contrary to the nature of socialist society. This was a capitalist method, and inevitably would and did lead to a capitalist revival.

Just as I foresaw, the military and economic superpower that was the Soviet Union collapsed overnight. It didn't require much insight to predict such a turn of events, given the Soviet leadership. The Soviet army, a three-million-strong force with world-class armaments, failed to defend the Party and socialism. It was unable to maintain its existence in a time of peace, not in the day of war. The reason was clear: The ranks had disintegrated philosophically because they hadn't been molded by the Soviet leadership. Intoxicated by Gorbachev's poisonous liquor, the veteran army that had beaten Hitler fell into the pitiful lot of a beggar.

Ever since their invasion of Korea, the US imperialists had put forth their "domino theory" to justify aggression and plunder in Asia and throughout the world. The argument was that one nation turning socialist would make it that much easier for the following one to do the same. Soon, such momentum would be unstoppable. Little did the Yanks realize that they weren't predicting the rise of communism, but its fall.

As the Cold War concluded in the late 1980s, a series of coups d'etat took place throughout socialist Eastern Europe. One after another, governments were disrupted and brought down in Hungary, Poland, East Germany, Albania, Bulgaria and Czechoslovakia. The yellow wind of capitalism spread like a narcotic among the people of the socialist countries, paralyzing their sound thinking. Working-class parties were ruined everywhere.

Perhaps the worst domino of all was the one which hit Romania. No world leader was as similar to President Kim Il Sung as Romanian President Nicolae Ceausescu. Ceausescu styled himself as the leader of his own nation, and explicitly followed Juche Korea's lead in many, many other ways.

One day in late December 1989, I was watching the news reports with the Great Leader. Ceausescu and his wife had been overthrown and been put on "trial." Only it wasn't a trial but a farce: The "defense" actually broke ranks at one point and assisted the prosecution! The couple were then put up against a wall and executed, their bodies left on display, slumped on the ground, for the whole world to see. President Kim Il Sung and I just stared at one another. The images and what they implied for Korea—and for both of us personally—spoke for themselves.

"...This is Europe," I said, with more than a little hesitation. "They're not the same as us."

The Great Leader shook his head. "I've always said that the people are my god. But gods are fickle, and they are violent, and they are dangerous."

The parties in power in Romania and other Eastern European nations had never developed into "mother parties." Rather, over the years they'd degenerated into parties of bureaucrats who wielded and abused their power. Our Party, on the other hand, had been a great mother to the masses, holding beautiful flowers and hopes in her bosom and being their most reliable guide to life. The DPRK probably wasn't in danger.

But I still wanted to make absolutely certain that what was occurring in Eastern Europe would never happen in Korea.

I immediately called in all the Party cadres that I could. Every state institution was represented, including the Ministry of Foreign Affairs, the Ministry of People's Armed Forces, the Ministry of People's Security and the Department of State Security. For far too long, the Great Leader and myself had borne the weight of the revolution and construction. The fact that we had performed so well and achieved so many great accomplishments had left many of these cadres secure in their positions. They knew that we would do any work that they couldn't.

Those days were now officially over.

As the men gathered around a long conference table, I had a television brought in and played them the footage of what had happened in Romania. Though they were all revolutionaries to the core, watching the scenes made them disquieted and even nauseated. "Do you see this?" I yelled at them. "Do you see how even Ceausescu, the Romanian leader, was killed by the masses like a dog in the street? If they ever rise up in Korea many of us will be hanged—and those in this room will be the first ones!" I squeezed my hand around my throat, so that they could see how serious this matter was.

"We are far closer to China than we ever were to the Europeans," said one official. "And the Chinese tanks took care of a similar situation quite handily this summer."

"You're correct," I said. "We are not Europeans. But neither are we Chinese. We are Koreans, living in the Juche era. We have the power and ability to make certain that this never happens on our land—but we do have to make that certain. The consequences would be unimaginable. All of you must immediately redouble your efforts in guiding the masses."

I summoned them all in again every single day that week. And I played that same Romanian footage for them, every single day that week. I wanted the images of the dead Ceausescu to haunt them in their dreams as well as haunting them in their waking hours. To make absolutely certain that such noxious ideas wouldn't seep into the DPRK, I sent many cadres to the enlightenment centers. Anyone who had spend time in Eastern Europe was too suspect to be allowed to roam free, fomenting dissent.

After Romania came the next domino. Since the end of the Korean War, China had consistently blocked south Korea's admission into the United Nations as its own nation. But in 1991, the Chinese established diplomatic relations with the "Republic of Korea," publicly and internationally humiliating the DPRK. We then had no choice but to join the UN ourselves, as a member state distinct from "South Korea." It seemed as if north Korea had no true allies left—and we did still need allies.

No one—not me, not the Great Leader—had ever denied that building a completely self-reliant economy would take a very long time. By 1990, the DPRK had made tremendous progress toward that goal but hadn't completely achieved it yet. We still conducted barter trade with the other socialist countries. Our internal economy was conducted with the Korean *won*, but internationally we traded goods. How that worked was that we received "friendship prices," with goods being exchanged below the capitalist, for-profit price. As a result of this, we didn't need dollars or yen; we never really used them.

But beginning in 1991, nations such as Russia, Cuba, Vietnam and China insisted on future payment in hard currency. "We don't want your goods or your money," they told us. "We want dollars!" It was American-style capitalism condensed into one slogan. Juche Korea could create virtually anything: art, construction, weaponry. But we'd never be able to create American dollars under any circumstances. As the saying goes, "An empty purse cuts off the ties of friendship." The DPRK began to face

a shortage of raw materials as well as energy. The rate of factory operations began to sharply decrease, which meant less production, which
meant all sorts of very unpleasant consequences indeed. A vicious cycle
was introduced into the economy.

Despite all of this, I still looked at the bright side of affairs. Maybe, just
maybe, this temporary setback in the inevitable path of socialist victory
would lead to positive consequences in the short term. During the Cold
War, the dominant order in the world was based on the great strength of
the United States and the Soviet Union. Each held sway over the other
countries in their respective camps. Korea was oftentimes like a shrimp
among whales because of her strategic location.

With the conclusion of the Cold War, there no longer was any need
for the two countries to challenge each other, trampling the rights of
smaller nations in the process. It could have been, it *should* have been,
an occasion for realizing independence throughout the world. There was
no longer any excuse for the United States to use its military strength to
dominate and interfere with smaller countries.

Yet that's not what happened. A new specter haunted the world—
the specter of "Pax Americana," a new world order under the complete
control of the United States. No one had a better understanding of an
unchecked imperialist America than I did. The DPRK had many museums
to remember the war atrocities committed by the Yankees.

In September 1991, after decades of Koreans living under a nuclear
threat, President George H. W. Bush announced that he would be with-
drawing tactical nuclear weapons from south Korea. The news seemed as
wonderful as it was unexpected—and long overdue. Most Americans at
the time were unaware it was the US that had introduced nuclear weapons
to the Korean peninsula in the aftermath of the war, turning the south
into the world's largest nuclear arsenal.

Further, in January 1992, Bush announced the suspension of the Team Spirit joint military exercises, which had been held annually since 1976's Panmunjom tree incident. These war-simulation exercises had been a constant source of provocation and tension between Korea and the United States. These gestures were not done from magnanimity, of course. The Americans had grossly miscalculated, assuming that Korea would implode like the other socialist nations. When that didn't happen, they feared that we would seek nuclear weapons. In factt, word soon came from our diplomats that the American were requesting nuclear inspections as a quid pro quo.

Usually, I would immediately reject anything that the US imperialists desired. But in this case they weren't asking for anything of value, since I knew that their fear was unfounded. North Korea had joined the International Atomic Energy Agency in 1976 and signed the Nuclear Non-Proliferation Treaty (NPT) in 1985. We primarily signed because we wanted a world free of nuclear weapons—but we also signed because the treaty established a balance between all its signatories. The agreement was that smaller nations would give up their sovereign right to pursue nuclear weapons, while the nuclear powers promised to never use the nuclear threat against non-nuclear nations.

I concluded that if the Americans wanted peace—and that is what President Bush's steps suggested—then I could certainly work with them. We accordingly signed the IAEA's Nuclear Safeguards Accord on January 30, 1992, hoping that it would lead to peace and reunification. I agreed to allow inspectors to come visit suspected areas and see that nuclear testing was not underway.

It was all a trap, and I fell for it. The United States released spy satellite photographs in which some buildings and transmission lines weren't visible. In other words, they didn't offer pictures of weapons and reactors—they offered pictures of a *lack* of weapons and a *lack* of reactors. Since they couldn't see *anything*, the Americans claimed that we must have been hiding *something*.

> ## KIM JONG IL:
> ## THE COMPLETE PUBLIC SPEECHES
>
> "Glory to the soldiers of the heroic Korean People's Army!"
>
> –April 25, 1992

The reaction was as hysterical as if a UFO were attacking the earth: "The intention to develop nuclear weapons is clear!" I agreed to further inspections, to expose the US imperialists' slanders. Beginning in May 1992, the IAEA came and performed not one, not two, but a total of five rounds of ad hoc inspections of suspected nuclear facilities. In fact, to calm the fears that the United States had drummed up, I ordered that the inspectors be shown several underground facilities that they hadn't even been aware of!

Finally, as 1992 came to a close, the inspectors were due to return to Korea for a sixth ad hoc inspection. I thought nothing of it, since the five other inspections had all been unremarkable. Yet the DPRK's IAEA liaison came in to speak with me, and his demeanor was entirely different that it had been before.

"They want more inspections," he blurted out.

"What do you mean, a seventh one?"

"No," he said. "Comrade, they're asking for special inspections." He showed me the papers with information from the IAEA, describing the new locations that were now under suspicion.

At a glance, I knew exactly what the papers were referring to. "Those are military installations. No country would allow such information to be made public. This is nothing more an unbearable infringement upon Korea's sovereignty. The IAEA is making demands that we can't possibly accede to. Tell me, has any other nation ever undergone these 'special inspections'?"

"None, comrade."

I began to think out loud. "If we let them into these sites, then they'll find other sites to suspect, and then others, and others. They won't be satisfied until they've plotted every inch of Korean soil. What a tour that would be! From Mt. Paektu and Uam's farming and fishing villages, to the military posts on the demarcation line, and then to the island lighthouse in the East Sea and finally to the tidelands of the west coast. Where will these intrusions end? Korea can't pull off her underwear for her enemy!"

That's when I knew that the Americans had gotten to the IAEA and were pulling the inspectors' strings. The US imperialists didn't actually want the DPRK to agree with these latest demands. What they wanted was a pretext to condemn and attack us. Heady from their recent Gulf War victory, the Americans were seeking to replay the Korean War—only this time, they intended to win it.

"So what shall I tell them?" the liaison asked me.

"Let them go through with their sixth ad hoc inspection as we'd agreed to," I said. "We'll prove that Korea is a nation that sticks to her word—even as the United States uses deception to try to further its goals. As for these 'special inspections'...well, I'll handle those in a special way."

It goes without saying that the IAEA inspectors found nothing during the sixth inspection. Nevertheless, the international mood changed completely. The Yank devils openly began to discuss war, even drafting a "120-day war scenario." They mused that it would take 120 days to conquer the DPRK, since Korea was stronger than Iraq.

Then, in January 1993, the US imperialists went back on their word and announced the resumption of the Team Spirit war games. They'd be conducting large-scale troop movements, with over two hundred thousand troops mobilized from the US mainland, Guam, Hawaii, Japan and other Asia-Pacific locations. High-tech fighters and naval ships equipped with nuclear weapons would concentrated on the Korean peninsula once more. They claimed it was just an exercise, not a threat or an ultimatum. After all, the Americans would never threaten another nation unprovoked. Their nuclear arsenal—capable of destroying the world many times over—was allegedly for peaceful purposes only.

The IAEA held a Board of Governors meeting on February 25, 1993. Allegations of "inconsistency" during the sixth inspection were now raised, and a resolution demanding the DPRK accept special inspections was passed. Needless to say, such inspections were completely outside the scope of the Nuclear Safeguards Accord which the DPRK had signed. The inspectors were literally insisting on a mandate to roam Korea's heavily guarded military sites at will. It was nothing more than an attempt to make espionage easier for the US imperialists.

Someone had to put a stop to these brigands, and apparently that someone was going to have to be Kim Jong Il. Their request was very firmly denied.

As usual, the United States immediately turned from negotiation to threats. The US imperialists threatened Korea with crippling sanctions. Very quickly, south Korea and Japan joined ranks with their American cohorts. Any and all dialogue between the north and the south of Korea was frozen, just as the Americans had planned and hoped for. The sanctions closed the DPRK's external markets, froze any funds in foreign banks and forced other nations to break any trade or economic negotiations. The West predicted that the DPRK would put up the white flag, and with good reason. It was clear that all the odds were against my country.

I made my first move on March 8, 1993, the day before the Team Spirit aggressions were to begin. Simply put: I had had it, officially. If the US imperialists wanted to play war games, then I certainly deserved a chance to play as well. As Supreme Commander of the Korean People's Army, I issued an order proclaiming a state of semi-war for the whole country, all the people and the entire army. "First," I said, "the whole country shall switch to a state of readiness for war. Second, all soldiers shall display high revolutionary vigilance and be fully ready to crush the enemy. Third, all the people shall produce a great upswing in socialist economic construction, with a hammer or a sickle in one hand and a rifle in the other." A great many young people volunteered to join or rejoin the army. The soldiers walked taller and stronger, ready to defend their nation against the foreign invaders.

The US imperialists became hysterical again. They couldn't believe that they were being defied so brazenly—especially by a nation so much smaller, with nowhere near America's population, wealth or technology. This sort of thing wasn't supposed to happen in the "New World Order."

I didn't stop with a mere order. I knew that I had to press my advantage and use the element of surprise while the US imperialists scrambled to come up with a response to my unprecedented defiance. I well understood that treaties can often be wildly open to interpretation. Regardless of the actual language, the premise of the Nuclear Non-Proliferation Treaty was to ensure that no new nations developed nuclear weapons. By Korea signing such a treaty, other countries—including the US—truly did have grounds to make a fuss, which necessitated the IAEA adjudicating the international conflict. This was a major reason why countries like India and Israel never signed the NPT; they didn't want to answer to some international body.

On March 12, four days after entering a state of semi-war and directly in the middle of the Team Spirit hostilities, I proclaimed that the DPRK was quitting the NPT. "We have no other choice," I explained. "We are compelled to do so in order to safeguard our interests. Since Korea is no longer a signatory to the NPT, it is now our legal and moral right as a sovereign nation to seek nuclear weapons—just as America did when it needed them."

The US imperialists had regarded nuclear dominationism as one of their tools for implementing foreign policy—and I'd taken that away. Still reeling from my declaration of semi-war, this latest move truly shocked them to the core. They didn't know what to do. America's Kim Jong Il Research Institute failed to figure out my tactics, its computer unable to make sense of my ever-changing wisdom and strategy. Each and every computer simulation of a second Korean war resulted in defeat for the American side. I knew how they operated better than they did.

Since a formal withdrawal from the NPT takes sixty days to becomes effective, the Americans were left with two months to try and figure out how to handle the situation. As the Yanks scrambled ever more frantically, I found time to celebrate just as I had during the Panmunjom incident. That's because Ri In Mo finally returned to north Korea on March 13, 1993.

THE INCARNATION OF FAITH AND WILL

There is a lie spread by Korea's enemies that the only books in our stores are by or about President Kim Il Sung or myself. This is ridiculous. We also have a book by Ri In Mo, a great hero to the Korean people.

Ri In Mo had been a KPA war correspondent during the Fatherland Liberation War. He was wounded and captured by the enemy during a battle. For the next thirty-four years—longer than Mandela—he was held prisoner in south Korea for the simple reason that he refused to renounce his socialist ideology.

Many a letter was sent to demand his release. We appealed

to Red Cross societies all over the world, and many international organizations carried on a solidarity campaign for his repatriation. Nor was Ri In Mo alone in his dilemma. Throughout the years, I consistently worked hard for the release of such unconverted long-term prisoners, patriots imprisoned due to their loyalty rather than any crime.

Ri In Mo's return to the socialist motherland couldn't have been timed any better. Less than a week into the state of semi-war, the Korean people were filled with a high sense of pride. Here was a living, breathing example of the victory of the Juche idea over the brute force of our opponents. Dubbed "the Incarnation of Faith and Will," Ri In Mo demonstrated that Korea was invincible. If the imperialists couldn't break one man, how could they possibly break an entire nation of twenty-four million, united as one under the Great Leader?

I was constantly in the operations room during this period, commanding the KPA while sizing up the fluid situation on the front line. At the same time, I made sure to maintain an air of ease in public. I made it a point to be photographed discussing the forthcoming Fatherland Liberation War victory monument, for example. It was important for the world to see that we weren't the aggressors in the conflict but rather the ones being aggressed upon.

Frightened by my stern attitude, the US imperialists cut their Team Spirit war games short. The IAEA also gave up its demand for a "special inspection." To put it bluntly: the Americans caved completely and agreed to negotiations. Hearing of their surrender, I held true to my word. On March 24, I issued an order releasing the DPRK from the state of semi-war.

The nuclear standoff had been a model case of psychological warfare. It only took me two weeks to break the US imperialists' spirit. Not one shot was fired, not one life was lost, not one drop of blood was spilled. This, while nuclear bombers, super-large nuclear-powered aircraft carriers and other modern means of mass destruction were being actively organized against the north. Even many American commentators praised my military wisdom and unfathomable tactics. I demonstrated how dedicated the DPRK was to peace on the Korean peninsula—and how desperately the US imperialists opposed it.

To further illustrate how dedicated I was to peace, I sent the Americans a message. Three days before negotiations were to begin, the DPRK fired a missile into the Pacific. Faster than a Tomahawk, as precise as the absurdly-named Patriot missile, it successfully reached its target between Guam and Hawaii. This made it clear that missiles were no longer the monopoly of the United States. Gone were the days when the US imperialists could launch strikes at other countries with impunity. Clearly, Korea was no longer what it had been in the 1950s. We were now a socialist power possessed of unshakable will, equipped with all the necessary means to mercilessly annihilate any enemy. As the saying goes, "a weak fist wipes away tears."

Having fired the missile and demonstrated our strength made negotiations quite painless for the DPRK. The two sides came to terms on June 11, just one day before our effective withdrawal from the NPT. The US committed to respecting our political system, to supporting peaceful reunification and to never threaten the DPRK with nuclear weapons. Our withdrawal from the NPT was halted and the tension eased on the Korean peninsula.

Further talks dragged on for over a year, with constant tricks from the Americans. The moment Korea acquiesced to a US demand, the

Yanks would simply make more. They once again insisted on "special inspections," and they once again wanted to impose sanctions. They dug in their heels, and so I dug in mine. It seemed as if there was no one who could break such an impasse. On June 13, 1994, I announced Korea's immediate withdrawal from the IAEA. What we needed was a miracle to deescalate the tensions.

What we got was Jimmy Carter.

Chapter 16

The Great Loss

President Carter left Korea on June 17, 1994. It was the first time that an American President had stepped foot in Pyongyang. Since the United States was the biggest obstacle to Korean peace, it naturally followed that a former President could be instrumental to pushing peace back home.

The day after President Carter left, the Great Leader called me to his villa to recount how the talks had gone. I'll never forget the sight of him sitting there, the man whom they called the sun, radiant under the Korean sky. When I arrived he was wearing a pale blue suit and looked much younger than his eighty-two years. Yes, his hair had gone grey. And yes, the war wound on the back of his neck had grown to the size of an apple. But he looked downright *giddy*. President Kim Il Sung had negotiated the Joint Agreement on Denuclearization of the Korean Peninsula with President Carter, providing the basis for further Korea-US talks.

The Great Leader had spent his life fighting: From Kalun to Antu and Xiaowangqing, from Nanhutou to Donggang and Pochonbo, from Nanpaizi to the Musan area and from the Hongqi River to Xiaohaerbaling. Now, the Americans had finally come to pay him respect on his own terms in the homeland that he loved so much. After deaths and wars and decades, everything that he had struggled for was within reach.

"Did you hear what President Carter said about me?" President Kim Il Sung asked with excitement.

"No," I lied. I wanted to give him a chance to boast; he'd earned it.

"He said that, 'President Kim Il Sung is a person in whom George

Washington, Thomas Jefferson and Abraham Lincoln, those popular three Presidents of the United States early in its history, are put together.' He said that he was utterly charmed by me from the moment that we met, and that he knew that I was a man who really loved peace."

"That's wonderful," I said, with a huge smile. General Kim Il Sung truly was the Korean General Washington. Both men were revolutionary generals who led their people to freedom and who were later unanimously voted to be their respective nations' leaders. It saddened me that the Americans simply couldn't bring themselves to see the General's greatness. The Yanks thought that believing in one Great Leader was "absurd" and "crazy"—while themselves claiming that the best minds in history happened to be localized in thirteen minor Atlantic colonies at the end of the eighteenth century.

"President Carter told the journalists that north Korea is a very particular country having its own political philosophy," the Great Leader pointed out. "He said that it's very unproductive to take sanctions against us. Isn't that wonderful?"

"It is, it is."

"Enough about that. Are the latest economic figures in? How goes the food situation?" he asked.

"Relax and enjoy your old age," I told him, patting him on the knee. "You keep working on your memoirs and we'll take care of everything else."

Immediately his face flashed with anger. "Answer my question, if you please!"

"We're making progress," I insisted.

"Are you sure? I know that you're keeping things from me, just as I know that those beneath you are keeping things from you."

"If you really want to know," I said, "I'll tell you. The sanctions are making things very difficult."

"So what measures have you taken?"

"For one, I've launched a new campaign: 'Let's eat two meals a day instead of three!' The masses didn't realize how unhealthy it was to eat three times a day. If they stopped desiring food so much, then they wouldn't get as hungry."

The President grunted, unsatisfied. "If the nuclear tensions lessen, we can ease up on war preparations. That will mean more money for food and agriculture. I might even be able to ask for some aid; President Carter seemed amenable. Regardless, if we manage to achieve reunification in the near future, then all this will be a distant memory. The south has far more arable land than the mountainous north."

I wish I could remember what else we spoke about that day. I wish I'd stayed instead of hurrying back to work. There were a million things I would've done differently that day, if I had only known that it was That Day and not one unlike any other. But seeing that the Great Leader was happy meant that I could leave happy as well.

Then the worst possible thing happened. It was no longer the beginning of the end. It was the end of the end.

I don't remember who told me, and I don't remember how I found out. It could have been a premonition in a dream, or it could have been me being roused awake by a member of my staff or it could have been a phone call. Maybe it was all three, one leading into another. I don't know. All I can recall is that on the morning of July 8, 1994, President Kim Il Sung, Grand Marshal of the heroic Korean People's Army, General Secretary of the Workers' Party of Korea, the Great Leader of all of Korea—and my father—passed away.

The rain was rageful and violent as I rushed to his villa. When I entered, I passed by all of his staff without a word or even a glance. Though

I couldn't register anything that they actually said, I still felt their grief filling the entire house. Someone (was it his secretary?) pointed me to where he was. I ran into the bedroom, my clothes soaked from the weather, expecting to find that this had all been an enormous misunderstanding, a bad dream, something, *anything* other than what it was.

I saw him lying on the bed. All his life he had worked day and night, waking every morning at 3 a.m. to rebuild his country into a shining model of self-reliant independence—and now it seemed as if he were sleeping off a lifetime of fatigue. I stood there in the doorway, not daring to approach, still being respectful of his space. Quickly I gestured for everyone to leave the room, though how many were there and who they might have been I didn't even notice. "Great Leader," I called out. "Great Leader, wake up...Father? Father, it's me!"

For an instant it looked like he was moving—but then I realized that he was become blurred as I started to cry. I hoped that all it would take to wake him up was a good, swift shake and slowly made my way over to the bed. I then took his hand but dropped it instantly. I knew what his grip felt like, mighty and sure, but this was the cold, limp handshake of the deceased. I sat down on the bed and took his hand again, staring at the carpet. I just sat there shedding tears of blood for who knows how long.

After a while, I smiled despite myself. I remembered what he had said about crying, with regard to me specifically: "Comrade Kim Jong Il not only has deep humane feelings, but he is also easily moved to tears. He smiles all the time, but when something sad happens, he shed tears like a child. I, too, am easily moved to tears. It is good for a man to have a lot of tears to shed. A cold-hearted and indifferent person cannot shed a tear even if he tries to weep. A hero who can shed tears is a true hero."

No matter what the subject, the Great Leader had always managed to capture its essence with a few sentences, instilling mere words with great profundity. Every book, every lecture, every article in Korea began with one of his quotes. But now no new sayings would be forthcoming. We would have to make do with trying to remember everything that he'd said at different points in his life. I desperately forced myself to recall what his voice sounded like, knowing I would never be able to hear it in person again.

That's when I heard the gunshot.

Screams emanated through the house. I ran into the hallway, past where everyone was in a panic. Inside President Kim Il Sung's main office was his most favored secretary, lying on the floor in a sea of blood. The man had taken a revolver and shot himself through the head. It was then that I knew that I myself didn't have the luxury of mourning. I needed to manage the nation's grief. The last thing Korea needed was for more people to take their own lives.

"No one say anything!" I yelled. Instantly the house grew quiet, but for the thunder rumbling over and over outside. "We will make an announcement when the time comes. I need someone to call every single member of the Political Bureau of the Party Central Committee."

"I will!" volunteered one of the aides.

"Tell them to meet me at the Kumsusan Assembly Hall within the hour. Anyone who is not there will be dealt with in the harshest possible terms, and quote me on that."

"Yes, comrade."

"Where is the doctor?"

"Here," the man said. Following my lead, he too composed himself and immediately took on a professional demeanor.

"Come with me. You can fill me in on the details in the car."

Despite the horrific weather conditions, we managed to get to the assembly room in record time, the doctor telling me all he knew as we sped along. As I stepped inside the room, my eyes immediately turned to President Kim Il Sung's portrait. His picture on the wall was one that I'd seen every day. It was one that everyone in Korea saw every day. Now it took on a different meaning. Now he was looking down at us from the heavens, powerless to do anything to help us any further. Never would I have believed that the word "powerless" could ever be used in reference to the Great Leader.

One by one, the Party members entered the room, taking off their overcoats and finding their chairs. They all looked over at me in great confusion, wondering what could possibly be so urgent this early in the morning. Were we at war? Had America agreed to unification terms? Was I resigning? And where was the Great Leader?

As I took to the podium, the Party members grasped their armrests with anxiety. How could I be starting the meeting without the President? Such a thing had never occurred in the decades-long history of the WPK. I could tell that some of them suspected what had happened but were hoping that I would tell them otherwise. I held the sides of the podium, ready to explain everything. "The Great Leader..." I began. "The Great Leader, President Kim Il Sung...Last night, the Great Leader, President Kim Il Sung, he..." I literally found myself unable to speak the words. All around me the men on the stage began to burst into tears, clenching their fists tight to try and control themselves. I stepped back, motioning for the doctor to approach.

The doctor stepped up to the podium and let out a long sigh. "Comrades," he said, "I was one of the physicians attending to the President. He had suffered from a heart disease for a very long time. This morning, at 2 a.m., he passed away."

Everyone was stunned. They surely recalled the incident a few years back, when an official had asked what would happen when the Great

Leader died, earning the man an instant lifetime sentence to the enlightenment centers. Now, this same forbidden thing was being said by the President's doctor himself in front of everyone, right underneath the Great Leader's portrait.

One of the Party members leapt to his feet and looked as if he were ready to charge the doctor. "You knew about this? You, his doctor? I'll kill you myself for this outrage!" Other Party officials stood up and half-heartedly restrained him. They too felt anger that something hadn't been done, while simultaneously feeling embarrassed that the hallowed assembly room was descending into such violence.

The doctor dropped his head and started crying openly. None of us envied the profound guilt that the man felt, guilt that he would never be able to shake. "The President often had chest pains, but he refused to awaken his aides when they were sleeping. I urged him to summon any of us at the slightest problem. Can anyone in this room imagine being able to rest, knowing that the President was suffering? But for his work, no one in Korea would ever know a peaceful night's sleep. Yet when I insisted, he just laughed off my concerns and refused to listen."

The angry Party member slumped back down into his seat. "The Great Leader was a stubborn type," he said. "That comes with leadership. You're not the only one, comrade, to try to change his mind. I've tried. It would have been easier for me to move Mt. Paektu."

Now I found the strength to speak. "President Kim Il Sung was in his office, working on a document relating to reunification with his dying breath. Until the very last moment, the Great Leader was working hard for the Party, for the revolution, for the country and for the people. How many other heads of state worked so hard for so long and so thanklessly? We must hold the President in high respect as our leader forever, and do everything as the President has done. He brought Korea back to the center of the world. Korea, whose very existence had been obliterated from the maps. This morning I say that I have no doubt that General Kim Il Sung was the greatest man who ever lived!"

The room burst into applause. "Manse! Manse Chosun!"

"I will make sure," I continued, "that the instructions left to us by the Great Leader will be carried out. They will be our one and only guideline for hundreds or even thousands of years. For now, comrades, we have the unenviable task of announcing the news to the nation tomorrow. I will be setting the period of condolence from today, July 8, until July 17."

At that moment, I truly felt like my father's son. It was from him that I got the strength to get through those next urgent hours. I made decision after decision for those who had lost the capacity to think clearly. As always, working allowed me to take my mind off of the pressure and strain that I was feeling.

That evening, three doctors from the medical team came into my office after performing the autopsy. I looked through the medical report and found their conclusion: "Various treatments were performed immediately, but the heart attack deteriorated and our beloved Great Leader passed away at 2 a.m. on July 8."

I looked up and glared at the doctors. They stood there quivering, wondering if they would be made to suffer consequences for the greatest possible loss Korea had ever faced. They wanted me to scream at them— but I said nothing. I took my pen and, after their conclusion, wrote in "on account of repeated mental stress." It was time for these men to forgive themselves, and it was time for Korea to heal.

"The Great Leader walked a life of struggle," I told them. "He carried a burden which nobody could lessen. President Kim Il Sung had passed away, ultimately, from overwork. It was something that modern medicine could not do anything about."

At noon the following day, the word went forth throughout Korea and abroad. The world at large broadcast the shocking news in a extraordinary manner, filling the whole planet with sorrow and grief. Stories were told about the many miraculous phenomena that occurred: Birds flew eerily round the statues, chirping loudly, adding to the people's sorrow. Lake Chon began to boil. A cloud of dragonflies covered the sky. There was so much rain and so many flashes of lightning in Korea that people related it to the President's death. But none of these things were miracles. The only miracle left in the world would be if the heart of the Great Leader beat again.

People wailed in every corner of the DPRK and in every corner of the earth. All throughout Korea, citizens went to one of the 34,000 statues of the Great Leader and wept bitterly. They beat the ground, they pounded their chests, they pulled their hair—some even fainted in their sadness. These moving scenes were broadcast on every news channel in the world. So extreme was the reaction that some even doubted the sincerity of the mourners—yet I can say with certainty that these were the most honest scenes to ever come out of Korea. The grief in America if *their* President had died would also be enormous.

Yet President Kim Il Sung wasn't just "a" President—he was the only President that the Korean people had ever known. He'd outlived such communist leaders as Premier Stalin and Chairman Mao. He'd outlasted ten American presidents, twenty-one Japanese prime ministers and six south Korean "presidents." He'd led the Korean people to two enormous victories against foes far larger and more powerful than they. He was truly their father—and even Yankees can understand the pain when one loses one's father.

Beginning on July 11, the coffin laid in state at the Kumsusan Assembly Hall. For days, crowds of Pyongyang residents thronged deep into the night to the bronze statue on Mansu Hill to express their condolences, as soaked with rain as they were with tears. I often stood there watching them, taking pride in the fact that the Great Leader had educated them into excellence.

In the week after his passing, billions of people worldwide extended their condolences to Korea. They expressed deep sympathy in varied ways. Many countries set condolence periods, hoisting flags at half-mast. The UN Secretary General said that President Kim Il Sung was "a great man who would be long remembered in history." One expert on world-celebrity deaths said that there was been no prior

> ## THE GREAT MOURNERS
>
> 60+ foreign state
> and government leaders
> 170+ leaders of political parties
> 2,000+ diplomats
> 3,480+ messages of condolence
> 3,300+ wreaths sent from
> 166 countries

precedent for such copious tears as were shed over the death of President Kim Il Sung.

I wanted the funeral ceremony to be held in an entirely new fashion, on the highest level and in the Korean style, as befitted a man unlike any other in history. Instead of a gun carriage or an armored car, as was the custom in other countries, I arranged for the coffin to be carried in the same car that President Kim Il Sung had used. Instead of the typical funeral bouquets, I had the car decorated with magnolias, the national flower. And instead of a dirge, I arranged for the immortal revolutionary hymn *Song of General Kim Il Sung* to be played.

But the most important part was the portrait. I commissioned one to be painted, modeling it after a brightly smiling photograph of the Great Leader. I went to the studio when it was completed, looking at it carefully and then stepping away. I even left and came back three times that day to make sure the effect wasn't diminished. "You've done a great job," I told the artist, who beamed with pride. "Though how much better it would have been if the portrait had been hung in President Kim Il Sung's lifetime."

On July 19, the funeral procession drifted through the city of sorrow. All the people of Pyongyang, over two million of them, were clad in black and bore ribbons of white. On July 20, memorial services for President Kim Il Sung were held at central, provincial, city and county levels. As the eldest son I didn't speak, per Korean tradition. At noon a salute of guns was fired in Pyongyang and provincial cities. Every train, every ship, anything throughout the country that could ring a bell or a siren, rang them for three minutes for the deceased President. There were no foreign delegations welcome at any of these events. The services were only for Koreans, just as the Great Leader would have wanted.

But there was one Korean who was missing.

I'd invited the current southern ruler, Kim Young Sam, in hopes that he would come pay his respects. Yet apparently there was no room for decency in the south. Koreans in his region had set up censer stands in attempts to hold memorial services for the departed President, but the thugs in Seoul demonstrated an inhumane attitude toward the Great Leader's death. They prohibited the people from offering condolences, repressing with brute force anyone who tried.

Kim Young Sam never bothered to come to Pyongyang. Nor did he dispatch an official delegation of condolence. Even though he was a filthy dirtbag, I still would have been welcomed him with open arms. What a missed opportunity for him! If the idiot had made an appearance, he might have been able to become the leader of a unified Korea. Instead, any planned meetings between the two parts of Korea were swiftly cancelled.

For the following one hundred days we mourned the Great Leader's passing. In most other countries, the death of a head of state leads to political confusion. The new leader immediately begins to make amendments to his predecessor's policy—sometimes even changing it completely. Such a phenomenon was alien to the DPRK. I already had my guidelines on how to run things, knowing that we wanted to live "in our way": the way of President Kim Il Sung's Juche idea.

Soon, however, despite their overwhelming, indescribable grief, tens of thousands of Koreans found time to write letters to the Party Central Committee. Without exception, each and every single one had the same request: for the Dear Leader Kim Jong Il to take the helm of the Party and the state. I tried to ignore these letters, but I couldn't ignore the sentiment behind them. Finally, a prominent Party dignitary struck up the courage one day to call me and address the issue directly. "Comrade," he said, "the election of the new President shouldn't be delayed any longer."

"Have we finished implementing President Kim Il Sung's remaining behests?" I snapped.

"No," he admitted, "we have not."

"The election of a new President is a time for celebration, both in Korea and elsewhere in the world. It would be immoral to have the people cheering so soon after the Great Leader's passing, don't you think?"

"Of course," he said. Clearly, the man only wanted this desperate national sadness to pass. But the sadness was there for a very real reason, since we'd suffered an irreplaceable loss. I knew that only a long amount of time would be able to end the tragedy.

Though the DPRK was united in our suffering, those abroad only saw division and destruction. The consensus from Western commentators was virtually unanimous: the imminent collapse of the Korean state. They only disagreed as to the form of collapse. My leadership would be unstable. There would be a military coup. The state would break up and disappear. Reforms would render Korea unrecognizable from the Juche era. It would simply be a matter of time before Korea went the way of the Soviet Union. Korea was a small country. How could she possibly stay the course, when the USSR couldn't? The DPRK wouldn't have to be defeated by the forces of imperialism. She would destroy herself; all it would take was some patience.

In that vein, on October 20, 1994, President Clinton sent a letter of assurance to "His Excellency Kim Jong Il, Supreme Leader of the Democratic People's Republic of Korea." Clinton reiterated the commitments that had been agreed to during President Kim Il Sung's last days. The DPRK would freeze her graphite-moderated reactor and other relevant facilities so that any nuclear fears would be allayed. As compensation for the consequent loss of energy, the US would provide north Korea with light-water reactors. The Americans would also deliver five hundred thousand tons of heavy oil annually until the first reactor was completed. Soon, Clinton promised, sanctions would be lifted as well.

The lifting of sanctions couldn't come soon enough.

A modern economy can't operate without oil. This was especially true for the DPRK, given our climate. Our northern provinces face up to nine months of cold weather every year. Even the southern provinces have a five-month winter. Due to our topography, only 20% of our land is even farmable to begin with. This meant that our agriculture was heavily dependent on industry. We needed to run our factories to produce fertilizer, chemicals and pesticides. Similarly, our agricultural provinces used electrical irrigation to prevent flooding during the rainy season. The sanctions had hurt us enormously with international barter trade. And since we didn't have much hard currency either, we couldn't get oil. Without oil, we couldn't generate electricity. Without electricity, we couldn't farm. And if we couldn't farm, we couldn't eat.

Things seemed temporary at first, like something that I could resolve.

True, sometimes the distribution center shelves were bare. I simply decided to reduce the rations that the people were getting until the difficulties tided over—yet the difficulties didn't tide over. I might have been a great military strategist who was admired throughout the world, but even I couldn't predict the weather.

Nor could I fight it.

Chapter 17

The Red Death

Westerners often mock the mysterious weather phenomena that attend the Great Leader and myself. When I visited Panmunjom one day, a dense fog enveloped me, rendering me invisible from the enemy though I was mere feet away. When I visited China, a rainstorm cleared so suddenly that the locals said the weather was recognizing my greatness. When I took a trip to Russia, the sun miraculously came out, earning me the Russian nickname of "the man who brings sunshine."

These stories are dismissed and denied by foreigners. Yet no one disputes the reports of severe weather that occurred soon after the Great Leader's death. First, the DPRK was plagued by hailstorms in September 1994. Over one million tons of grain were lost, an enormous amount. This called for making some very difficult decisions, so I met with other Party officials to analyze how best to handle the grim situation.

The men were nervous as we met in the conference room. It was the first time since the Great Leader had passed that they were facing such a crisis, and they wanted to offer solutions and suggestions commensurate with his thinking. "We need to explain to the people what's happening," suggested one official. "Then they can better figure out how to feed themselves."

"How can they figure out how to feed themselves if there's nothing to feed themselves with?" asked another.

"They can eat less."

"At a certain point, eating less is not an option."

"We're approaching that point," I said. "But if the Party lets the people solve the food problem themselves, then only the farmers and merchants will prosper. This will give rise to egotism and collapse the social order of our classless society. The Party will then lose its popular base and will experience meltdown as in many Eastern European countries. The US imperialists are already gloating that they've drawn up timetables for a three-day, three-month and three-year Korean collapse. If we the Party don't act now, we'll prove the Americans right. As most of you know, the leanest times aren't the winter but the spring, when supplies have been depleted but have not yet been replenished. That's when we have to plan for."

Everyone in the room then thought the same thing, but no one dared say the words out loud. The very idea was heresy. Finally, one quiet official at the far end of the room spoke up. "Then we've no choice but to ask for aid," he said.

Normally, the immediate reaction would have been to condemn such talk—and yet no one did. Emergencies call for accepting things that one never would under other circumstances. "Comrades," said another official, "are we sure we should go down this course?"

I cleared my throat. "At times like this, I always look to the words of the Great Leader. I remember something he said at a national farmers' conference in 1979: 'Only when there is plenty of food, can a nation defend its independence and have its say. If a country fails in farming and begs other countries for food, it can neither uphold independence nor have its say.'"

The mood in the room got perceptively darker. Finally, the first official piped up. "It's not aid if it's from the same nation, right? So we can ask for help from the south. After all, we aided them a decade ago during their floods."

"And it's not 'aid' if it's restitution," I smiled. "So we can seek assistance from the Japs, who owe us so much for all that they've done to Korea in the past. The important thing is that no foreign states become aware of the true nature of this temporary situation. The US imperialists would surely use any possible pretext to invade Korea. If they can't blatantly attack us for militaristic reasons, they'll be just as happy to inflate a situation under concerns of 'humanitarianism.'"

Discreetly, our officials pointed out the emergency to the south Koreans and to the Japs, and asked for a temporary bit of assistance for that year. Our neighbors held to the UN principle that food and politics shouldn't interfere. Though relations between us and them were poor, they didn't want to see the Korean people go hungry and sent us the assistance that we requested. With that settled, I managed to guide the nation through the winter and the spring with only marginal difficulty.

With that behind me, on June 12, 1995 I led all the branches of the government in adopting a major joint decision: Kumsusan Assembly Hall, where the Great Leader had worked, would be renamed the Kumsusan Memorial Palace. The area surrounding the hall would be rebuilt into Juche's most sacred temple. On July 8, the one-year anniversary of his death, the eternal image was unveiled for visitors from around the world: President Kim Il Sung preserved under glass, lying in state for all eternity.

I'd considered Korea's troubles to be a function of the weather, an aberration, and wanted the nation to return to glory as quickly and efficiently as possible. But during the summer of 1995, the heavens again exploded in grief and sorrow. The rains were the strongest that the DPRK had ever experienced, unprecedented in their ferocity. Every day I sat in my office, looking out the window and desperately hoping for a break in the storms. But there was none, no respite whatsoever.

Then came the floods.

When our mines got flooded, we couldn't dig enough coal to keep our thermal plants going. The DPRK's national emblem featured a hydroelectric power plant—but now the power plants were as lifeless as the plants growing in our fields. Gone too were the grain reserves, stored underground and also flooded. Even when there was food in one location, we couldn't move it efficiently since our railways ran on electricity.

By August I couldn't hide the crisis any longer. Nearly two million tons of grain had been lost. Over 5.4 million people—about a fifth of our population—were displaced. It had taken over fifty years for the Great Leader to build up Juche Korea. One year later, I was on the verge of losing it all. Going against everything that I knew, I had no choice but to publicly ask for assistance. My decision was unprecedented—but so was the weather. The International Red Cross and United Nations World Food Programme (WFP) both intervened. The world at large, increasingly under the spell of "Pax Americana," viewed the DPRK as their enemy. Why would they be willing to help?

I soon learned the answer.

I was on a field guidance tour when I was approached by one of the officials who was negotiating the assistance program. "Comrade," he said, "the WFP is making all sorts of demands."

"What is it that they want?"

"They want inspections, to make sure that the food is delivered where it's supposed to."

Inspections. Always, it was inspections! "Who are they to decide where the food is supposed to go?" I asked. "That's the role of our Public Distribution System. Are they trying to abrogate the role of the Party? This is conquering Korea without firing a single shot!"

"What shall we do?"

"We must envelop our environment in a dense fog," I said, "to prevent our enemies from learning anything about us. Listen carefully. Hide the worst areas from our external enemies; they must not see us as weak. Make sure that the official relief agencies don't have any Korean speakers on their staff. Who knows how many spies are in their midst? They will be shown around at our discretion alone. At the same time, our internal enemies must never know the source of aid. Make sure that every bag of grain, every seed, is delivered through the Party via the PDS."

"Comrade," the official said cautiously, "if we don't show them the worst areas, then surely they will send us less food."

"More food means more interference in our way of operation. We'll be the ones deciding where any food is 'supposed' to go. *We* will decide, not them! I'll figure out where to send it, just let them deliver it."

Now I had the most difficult decision possible: where should the food be sent? Who should eat—and who shouldn't? Later that week, I pored over maps of the nation, noting which areas were hardest hit by the catastrophe. I matched those maps against those of transport systems, figuring out how much food could realistically be moved given our limited mechanisms. No matter what I did, I always came up short. There simply wasn't enough food to go around. Some regions had to be given priority over others—but I needed some criterion to decide which, both in the short and in the long term.

Then the answer came to me.

I was so startled that my pen dropped out of my hand. To some, it sounds like poetic license when I say that the Great Leader's presence was still felt in Korea as much as when he'd been alive. To the DPRK's enemies, such a statement sounds like pure nonsense. But it was neither of those things. As I looked at the maps, I saw that President Kim Il Sung had anticipated the present crisis—and he'd already implemented a solution.

The Intensive Guidance Project that the Great Leader had begun in 1958 had classified the masses into core, wavering and hostile classes.

As the decades passed, their *songbun* had been further subdivided into fifty-one subcategories via such programs as the Understanding People Project. The Party had used this information to determine much of every Korean's life—including where they lived. Those in the hostile class had been moved into the northeast of Korea decades ago, and there they and their children had remained. Internal migration in the DPRK required official permission, which was typically denied to those in the hostile class. Nor could they have bribed their way out even if they wanted to. Due to the lack of electricity, railways that used to take hours to travel the country now literally took months. I therefore knew exactly where the enemies of the Party, the people and the Great Leader were localized: in the northeast.

I picked up my pen and crossed out those provinces on the map. They'd be the last to get sent any food—if they would, in fact, get sent any food. Those in the hostile class would simply have to find a way to fend for themselves. I considered this a good thing for them. They always crowed the loudest about their loyalty. Now they had an unparalleled opportunity to prove their belief in the Juche principle of self-reliance. This was a good thing for me as well, for having too many people in the DPRK made leadership that much more difficult.

That decided, I worked deep into the night sketching out different scenarios. There still wouldn't be enough food for the rest of the country, but I managed to coordinate a largely equitable solution. Soon all this would be over, I thought, and Korea would be on the upswing again.

Times were lean over the coming months, but even I didn't know quite how lean they were. If I visited a chicken farm, for example, Party officials would collect all the nearby chickens to make it seem as if there were no problems. Grain harvests were supplemented by the addition of small rocks to the sacks, falsely increasing their weight. Soon we were all biting our bread with great care, trying to avoid chipping our teeth on any pebbles that had snuck through.

As 1995 came to a close, I began to work on the forthcoming New Year's joint editorial, perhaps the most important piece of writing that comes out of the DPRK every year. Published by all three newspapers, the editorial sets the message and lays out the nation's plans for the following year. 1995's message had been dedicated to President Kim Il Sung; 1996's would be the first one to truly be my own.

Times were hard, dreadfully so, but the DPRK had been through hard times before and had always come out the better for it. Though President Kim Il Sung was gone, the strong edifice he had constructed still stood tall and proud. It would take much more than some natural disaster to undermine it. I wanted the editorial to reassure the people. I also wanted to establish a sense of continuity with the past, so that my optimism wouldn't seem like a mere attempt to placate fears. There had to be evidence that similar situations had been resolved successfully in Korea before.

For inspiration, I went to the Kumsusan Memorial Palace to visit the eternal image. I walked through the temple of Juche, proud of how beautifully everything was displayed. I smiled as I passed by the Great Leader's car, thinking of the trips that we'd taken together. I bowed before his statue, pausing for a moment of silence. Finally, I entered the room where he lay in state, covered with the WPK flag. All around him bloomed the Kimilsungia orchid that had been bred in his honor, a touch of quiet beauty in the austere surroundings.

I looked for parallels between the current conditions and what the Great Leader had gone through. Rather than recalling his victories, I thought about the worst moments of his life, times when a lesser man would have been defeated or quit: The strategic retreat during the

Fatherland Liberation War. The coup attempt against him from abroad, and the one from within. The loss of his wife and my beloved mother, anti-Japanese heroine Kim Jong Suk. These were all dark days, but the situations were never not quite the same as the present. None of these experiences were as prolonged and as intense. None seemed so bleak.

That's when I remembered what surely were the worst moments that the Great Leader had ever faced.

During the days of anti-Japanese struggle, General Kim Il Sung's guerrilla army had trekked through the bitter winter weather for over one hundred days. They constantly fought life-and-death battles to break the encirclement of the Japanese army in what was later dubbed the "Arduous March." Things couldn't have looked worse—but the General turned adversity into good fortune. That journey set the stage for his eventual victory.

It was the Korean people who were now facing an Arduous March of our own.

The New Year's editorial that we published acknowledged how difficult things seemed. But—just as in the original Arduous March—only victory could come at the conclusion. The spirit of the Arduous March was one of being determined to carry out the revolution to the end. It was the spirit of bitter struggle which knew no defeat in the face of severe adversity. It was the spirit of optimism that challenged and broke through all obstacles. It was, plain and simple, the spirit of General Kim Il Sung's Juche Korea.

I didn't have solutions to our problems yet. In fact, much of our funds were frozen due to the American sanctions. Over the following months, I did the best I could with what I had while the march to victory continued. Our food-processing factories might not have been able to deliver actual food, so I ordered them to produce "substitute foods": Corn byproducts were mixed with husks, grass and seafood and then formed into noodles or meal bars. Though they had virtually no nutritional value and could barely be digested, I knew they could at least be used to allay one's hunger. As did drinking water. As did sucking on one's fingers.

Then the DPRK was plagued by beasts. First came "the march of the ants." Starving people traveled in long lines to the mountainsides to look for wild grass or acorns to eat, looking like ants scurrying from their hills. Then there were the "penguins," vagabonds who wandered the countryside clad in dark, filthy rags on their backs.

Yet neither of these "beasts" horrified me as much as the *kotchebi*, the "little sparrows." Many children became orphaned during the Arduous March, or were simply abandoned by families who could no longer take care of them. I issued orders to supply our orphanages with what we could, but it still wasn't enough. There wasn't sufficient coal to stay warm or sufficient food to feed the children. So these *kotchebi* hopped around the roads, scratching at the dirt and looking for some small morsel to eat just like the birds which gave them their name. At first the sight of these starving homeless tykes discouraged and depressed the masses. But then the people grew accustomed to them, and finally viewed these *kotchebi* only as a nuisance. Per my instructions, the authorities eventually rounded them up and took care of them.

As the summer of 1996 approached, the news got worse and worse. I learned that starving farmers were eating their corn cobs before the crops had time to develop—and they were the lucky ones. Things that had never been regarded as fit for consumption now became the very basis of the Korean diet: Dandelions. Wormwood. Grass roots. Tree bark. "Broth" made out of boiled leaves. After those were gone *any* organic matter had to do. The people took in weeds that were so inedible that they could barely be swallowed, and, once swallowed, could barely be kept down.

The gorgeous Korean mountainsides turned yellow, as any vegetation was systemically removed and consumed. Finally it got to the point where people were simply drinking saccharine, their faces bloating from the chemicals before they inevitably passed away.

Things got so bad that there was no precedent for it. I didn't know what to do because no nation had ever been in such a bad situation. In 1996 floods came once again—and they were just as crippling, if not more so, then the previous year's had been. It was as if the heavens themselves wanted me to fail. I needed the masses to believe that their nation was the best, even though they ate very little. They had to see the DPRK as "a poor country of abundance." But it grew harder and harder for me to tell people with empty dishes that socialism is good. They simply weren't buying it. They weren't buying *anything*. The shelves in the distribution centers were empty, often for months at a time.

Everywhere I went, the people cheered louder than ever. Candidly, I was glad that they had the strength to cheer. But I had cut my teeth on the film industry. I revolutionized the world of theatre and opera. I knew bad acting when I saw it—and I saw it aplenty. The cheers were all fake. They were not cheering from the bottom of their hearts. When I was gone, the masses would whisper about me. Soon their grumbling was so loud that even I couldn't avoid hearing it. They quipped that "water always flows downhill" and said that grass no longer grew wherever I sat on the ground. "Tiger father, dog son." Some began to call me the "gruel lord."

Everyone in Korea was suffering—none more so than myself, who felt the agony of the people as no one else did. Yet of all the many groups in the DPRK, only one never lost their faith in me: the military. No military on earth was as imbued with revolutionary consciousness as the Korean People's Army. The KPA looked to the anti-Japanese guerril-las for inspiration like no one else. They saw the Arduous March as an opportunity to live just as their predecessors did, fighting as they had for an independent Korea.

Rather than having soldiers sit idly by, waiting for a war that hopefully would never come, the state put them to work in the field of socialist construction. Even during the grimmest days of the Arduous March, the KPA men and women followed through with the remaining projects that the Great Leader had planned: the second stage of the Chongryu Bridge; the Pyongyang-Hyangsan Tourist Motorway; the Mt. Kuwol recreation ground. Not only did the DPRK have the best military in the world, but we had the only military that was also a national construction force.

One of the most important of these construction projects was building the Anbyon Youth Power Station. More power stations meant more electricity, which meant lives would be saved. I braved the drizzling rain on the morning of June 10, 1996 to inspect how progress was going. The solider-builders stood at attention as I pulled up to the site, and I noticed with great sadness that all their uniforms were dingy, frayed and stained. That this didn't seem to embarrass them told me that this was now the norm. I understood, for cloth was very hard to come by. What bothered me was how the men's uniforms hung on them, as if the clothes were two sizes too big—when in fact it was the men who were two sizes too small, shrinking from hunger.

The commanding officer showed me around the site with great dignity in his voice. It pleased me to hear that he still had pride in his country while it was undergoing indescribable hardships. "We've built dams and dug waterway tunnels through rugged mountains," he explained. "All in all we've braved 128 cave-ins."

"Have there been any injuries?" I said.

The officer paused. "This is a revolution."

"No matter how acute the power situation of the country may be,"

I said, "you should take radical measures to protect the workers' health and safety."

He nodded. "Of course, comrade. But it's the workers who are putting themselves in danger."

"How do you mean?"

"Well, take one of the first days of tunneling this past winter. The whole pit suddenly became submerged."

"Which could have ruined the whole project."

"That's correct. Understanding this, the soldiers jumped into the water and eventually they blocked the hole. Unfortunately, being in the freezing water caused some of the men to grow quite ill."

I looked at the officer's face, and I understood that this wasn't the worst of it. He'd been gauging my reaction, afraid to tell the me the whole truth. "Go on. What other things have happened?"

"A section of the roof collapsed once when a unit was digging an incline, trapping the soldiers. Even without a single drop of available drinking water, even though it was hard to breathe, they still continued their construction work. Their comrades tried to give them rice balls through a tube, but they told us to save the food for those who needed it more. They simply wanted compressed air so that they could continue working, as air was free and plentiful. At the end, almost all of them survived the incident."

I winced. "How many were lost?"

"Just the one, comrade. He'd been critically injured during the collapse. You'll be pleased to know that he was singing revolutionary songs until the last moment of his life, encouraging his colleagues on to greater feats of construction. He died a soldier battling to achieve modern civilization."

I'd have been more pleased if he'd still lived as a soldier battling to achieve modern civilization. I'd be more pleased if more people were living all throughout Korea in general. But I couldn't focus on such things in that moment. I was there to validate the soldiers' hard work and courage, and that's why I needed to do what I could. "In the decades to come," I boomed, "they will say that the revolutionary soldier spirit was born here, at the Anbyon Youth Power Station!"

As one, the soldiers began to sing "No Motherland Without You," a wonderful song that had been written in my honor. I applauded vigorously when they were done, knowing that it was I who should have been singing their praises instead. "It's almost time for lunch," I finally pointed out.

Instantly the atmosphere became one of fear, even terror. The commanding officer nodded with great strain. "...Of course, comrade," he said.

The soldier-builders looked at one another, not knowing what to do, desperately hoping that somehow food would appear from somewhere. They'd obviously not expected my visit to last as long as it had.

"You know what food I'd enjoy more than any other?" I quickly said. "Rice balls. Those same rice balls that the trapped soldiers had refused, ones just like those will suit me fine."

"We can't serve you rice balls!" the officer exclaimed.

"Oh, come now. I ate rice balls during the years of the Fatherland Liberation War and in the days of postwar reconstruction. All our people did. When I was in school, I used to wrap rice balls in paper and thrust them into my pocket so that I could eat them with my friends on the grass during a break from class. I still love to eat them now and then, to remember the difficult bygone days and to gain strength from their successful resolution. In fact, rice balls are the ideal food for us revolutionaries when we travel."

"No, comrade. We can't serve you rice balls because we have none to offer you. I'm very, very sorry." Then and there, the man began to cry.

I walked over and patted him on the back. "That's fine, that's fine. Don't worry about me. I'll have whatever you're having, everyone the same. I don't even need but a small portion since I'm in a rush. You know how it is, I often go without solid or timely meals. What will we be having, then?"

The officer once again straightened up into a semblance of attention. "We have kimchi, comrade."

"Oh, wonderful!" I quickly said. "Kimchi is my favorite. That's even better than rice balls, I was going to suggest kimchi but didn't, because I wasn't sure you had any. Did you know that the Korean people lack a certain digestive enzyme, one which is provided by kimchi? This is terrific. What a wonderful treat."

Out of the corner of my eye I noticed one of the soldier-builders trying to catch the commanding officer's attention. The young man was attempting to be sly about the matter but was apparently better suited for construction than for guile; I couldn't help but notice him. The commanding officer glared at him to remain quiet, but I motioned for the young soldier to speak anyway. Unsure of what to do, the soldier's gaze bounced back and forth between the two of us. Finally he worked up the courage to say what he wanted to. "We have something else to eat, comrade."

Now the commanding officer blatantly yelled at the soldier. "I'm sure you are mistaken!"

"I'm sure he's not," I interjected. "What else do you have to share? I know it will taste superb, simply due to the company that I'm keeping."

The young solider drew himself up, strong and tall. "We also have gruel."

"Gruel?"

"Gruel," he nodded. This young soldier was simply offering all that he had to his Dear Leader. He obviously didn't mean to offer gruel to the "gruel lord" and didn't understand the implications of what he was saying—but if his commanding officer did.

Suddenly I started smiling. With no effort on my part, my mouth pulled back into a grimace. The situation at the Anbyon Youth Power Station was absurd, just as the situation in all of the DPRK was absurd. Nothing was operating as it should have been. If I couldn't be blamed for causing the horrors, then surely I could be blamed for not fixing them. "Comrades," I sighed, "I think I'll pass on lunch after all. I have many other sites to inspect and I don't want the day to get ahead of me."

"Yes, comrade."

I turned and walked briskly to my car, my entourage following at my heels. We drove away in silence, with none of them understanding what to make of my mood. Thirty very quiet minutes later, we began to pass an overgrown field. "Stop the vehicle!" I told the driver.

"Right away, comrade." He gradually brought the car to a halt and then pulled over by the side of the road.

"Everyone get out!" I ordered. Quizzically, the men followed me onto the highway, standing in the middle of nowhere for no apparent reason. "Take a look around you, a good look. What do you see?"

They were all smart men, so they understood this was some sort of test. Yet none of them could even begin to hazard a guess, as there was nothing of interest about our location whatsoever. "I see the beauty of Juche Korea?" one of them said, completely unsure.

"You know what I see?" I said, my voice growing strained. "I see grass, all around us. Yet this is what passes for food in Korea nowadays. Our people are hungry, starving and dying by the thousands, by the *hundreds of thousands* if not *millions*, and no one knows what to do. No one! Do you? Or you? Do any of you?"

"The Juche farming method initiated by President Kim Il Sung," one recited, "is the basis of the agricultural policy of Korea. It stresses improvement of seeds and two-crop farming a year so as to make maximum use of the limited cropland, as well as cultivation of the right crop on the right soil and in the right time. Particularly noteworthy is the promotion of diversified farming and the increased production of organic fertilizer."

I had succeeded in establishing a monolithic ideology in the Party, and here was my consequence: Everyone had one idea and only one idea. No one could think of anything else to say, for even considering such a thing would be evidence of disloyalty. I couldn't count on anyone else for help. No one in all of Korea had to be as self-reliant as I did.

I stepped back into the car by myself. Then I rolled up the dark windows and locked the doors. I sat there for quite a while, breathing deeply, my shoulders trembling. I tried to regain my composure but my grief was based on a simple reality: I was powerless to help the victims of this famine. Eventually I took out my handkerchief and managed to wipe my cheeks dry. I put on my shaded sunglasses so that none of the men could see how red my eyes had become. Then I rolled the window back down and called out to them. "I need to return home at once."

"What about the meetings later this afternoon?" asked my secretary.

"Cancel them. Cancel them all."

When the car pulled up to my home, I walked in and went straight to my bedroom. I called my staff and gave strict orders not to be disturbed under any circumstances. Then I locked the door and sat on my bed. I reached over to a small box that I had on my nightstand, turned the key and opened the lid. There, lying cold against plush velvet, were the two guns that I'd received from each of my parents when I had been a boy.

I took out Mother's gun and then placed it back; I doubted it would ever fire. Then I took out the gun handed to me by the Great Leader and looked it over. All the parts still spun smoothly and easily. Maybe,

I thought, this gun was my answer. It would be very easy to simply pull the trigger, and then all this misery would go away forever. It was an unimaginable choice, but I was in an impossible situation. If I asked for more international assistance, my show of weakness would invite war. If I didn't ask for any assistance, my show of strength would invite famine. In either case, it meant death on a level unseen in Korea in decades— perhaps ever.

I recalled what General Kim Il Sung had said when he'd handed me that very gun: "You must bear in mind that a gun is the revolutionary's eternal companion. A gun never betrays its master, though everything else in the world should change. It will help you guarantee victory like nothing else will."

He'd been right. He'd always been right. It wasn't simply my mother who had saved General Kim Il Sung; it was her gun. It wasn't simply the General and his guerrillas who drove the Japanese out of Korea; it was his gun and it was theirs—just as the guns of the glorious Korean People's Army had repulsed the Americans' assault during the Fatherland Liberation War.

The gun was truly the answer to all of my problems. It was the answer to *all* of Korea's problems. I hadn't become the leader in order to abolish the revolution. No, I was meant to fulfill it! I put the gun back and locked the box again. With a smile on my face, I stood up and left my bedroom. I had work to do, millions of lives to save, a nation to preserve and the Juche idea of President Kim Il Sung to uphold.

It didn't matter if my officials had no solutions to offer, no fixes or panaceas of any kind. I didn't need any of them to help me. I didn't need anyone at all. I was armed, and I was armed with the most powerful ideology of all time: the ideology of the gun.

Chapter 18

Me and a Gun

The food problem facing the DPRK wasn't a problem of production or a problem of distribution. No, it was a problem of ideology. A leader can only successfully administer affairs of state when he develops his own philosophy. If he is to lead the revolution, he must develop his philosophy into a political doctrine. He needs to determine the main force of the revolution—something neither immutable nor absolute in any era or in any society.

It took me quite a while to determine it, but I grew convinced that my leadership philosophy had to be the philosophy of the gun. The only way for the DPRK to survive would be to meet foreign domination with arms. The victory of socialism would exist on the army's bayonets. That meant that in the modern era, the Korean People's Army was the most essential force in the revolution. All our problems would be solved by giving precedence to military affairs. Going forward, the rifle needed to stand above the hammer and sickle. The DPRK could live without candy, but we couldn't live without bullets.

ON THE SONGUN IDEA

I called my newly systematized leadership philosophy Songun ("military first") politics. My growing understanding was based on the fact that the armed forces in Korea were founded long before the Party and the state. I recognized that this wasn't simply a matter of chronology—it was a matter of *strategy*. The military had come first in terms of its existence, but it also came first in terms of

---

importance. Indeed, General Kim Il Sung himself had consistently prioritized military affairs throughout his life.

Imperialists claim that wars break out when tensions escalate between nations. This is untrue. Two nations might engage in the most bitter disagreement, but war will never break out if they're both strong and committed to peace. Historically speaking, imperialists decide on aggression when tensions relax, not when they increase. The Japs had intensified their peace offensive prior to Pearl Harbor. Likewise, their ally Hitler appealed to the Soviets for friendship before invading them.

I was well aware that the US imperialists greatly preferred defeating the DPRK without having to fire a shot, and I was further aware that my conflict with them was just as much about ideas as it was about military might. It's far easier to destroy a nation with ideology than even with nuclear weapons. The power of a military strike is finite, but an ideology has no limit. After all, it's not weapons that fight a war. Weapons without human beings are no more than pieces of steel. A fearful army cannot be strong, no matter how advanced its weaponry may be.

My soldier-centered view of war was Juche's man-centered doctrine applied to a military context. That made the KPA fundamentally different from all other armed forces. No other leader on earth put such stress on developing the ideological power of his soldiers as I began to.

Giving ideological prominence to the military didn't mean lowering the status of the masses. Quite the opposite: It provided a guarantee for their position. In the DPRK, the army and the people didn't have an antagonistic relationship as they did in some other nations. The people were parents to the army and the army were the people's children. Commanders cherished their soldiers just as much as their real siblings, and soldiers trusted and followed their commanders like their older brothers and sisters. The KPA and the masses were quite literally one family.

This unity between the people and the army traced its roots to the comradeship of the anti-Japanese guerrillas, and was what made a "military regime" impossible in the DPRK. My politics were based on the independence of the people, not on misanthropy and national chauvinism. The leader could never therefore become a "Fuhrer"; the two had absolutely nothing in common.

Gaining a clear perspective on how to handle Korea's situation still didn't make it easy to implement the solution. The military buildup that I envisioned required a huge investment of both money and manpower. Yes, our armed forces gave back more than what it took in. Our defense industry had heavy industry as its core, with the greatest concentration of modern science and technology anywhere in Korea. Its growth spurred on a great deal of scientific and technological growth throughout every other sector. But that was a long-term benefit. In the immediate term, my decision to build up the military while many starved was an enormously difficult choice. I only hoped that our eventual victory would demonstrate to the people why they had to tighten their belts.

My first steps were to use the KPA to shore up key industries—such as coal-mining, power and rail transport—as well as to further develop agriculture. Fortunately, the KPA was good at everything. They happily built whatever was necessary, from highways and docks to factories and monuments. They went to the power stations to increase electrical generation when it was in short supply; they mined coal when it wasn't supplied in time; they helped peasants in farming so as to solve the food problem. Whenever people died in a train station while waiting for the train to arrive, it was KPA patrol trucks that carted the bodies away. The soldiers' cheerful demeanor kept the Juche spirit alive as the next plagues began to hit Korea.

The loss of electricity wreaked havoc with sanitation: pumps failed, causing waste to flow into the drinking-water systems. Even I don't know how much damage that caused. Malaria was also reported. Then, when the summer came, people weakened by malnourishment fell victim to cholera. The Ministry of Public Health even recorded a handful of cases of polio.

As with the shortage of food, so did we face a shortage of medical supplies. Desperate, I gave orders for the ill to be treated with traditional Koryo medicine instead. We used watermelon and beer to reduce swelling. Animals were hunted for their curative properties. Instead of surgically removing tumors—we had no anesthesia—doctors administered an extract of ginseng and mushrooms. According to tradition, such an extract enhanced a patient's natural healing ability and changed malignant tumors into benign ones. All these procedures worked exactly as well as one might expect.

In the autumn came tidal waves, striking furiously at coastal areas and severely damaged the crops there. Determined to win, I launched a war against the elements themselves. Under my Songun leadership, the military was there to protect the precious grains. All up and down the coast, soldiers carried bags filled with dirt through waist-deep mud. When parts of the embankment gave way, the soldiers held back the water with their own bodies. They kept working even as the nights grew dark, feeling with their hands and fixing any leaks as needed.

It wasn't only physical barriers that were breaking down throughout

Korea: Our walls of order were increasingly turning porous as well. Traitors began to cross the border into China, bringing news of our travails to the outside world. Thankfully, the foreigners scoffed at the famine statistics; the figures sounded too inflated to be possible. It was far easier for them to dismiss the data as yet more hysterical north Korean propaganda.

Then came the thievery. Antirevolutionary elements began to steal from farms or the PDS centers. Highwaymen began to rob Koreans distributing goods from one area to another. In all these cases, the military took care of the offenders. The worst of the thieves were executed publicly, educating hundreds and thousands by striking down one. Such punishments taught an important lesson to those who witnessed them: antisocial behavior was a function of the mind, not of the stomach. These class enemies were choosing to commit crimes against the masses, so the soldiers always aimed for the traitors' corrupt brains.

Not all the developments were bad, however. I learned that small, informal markets had begun to creep up here and there throughout the DPRK. Historically speaking, markets led to the abandonment of a planned national economy and to the disintegration of socialism. But this wasn't history; there was no historical precedent for the Arduous March. I had to admit that the markets seemed like a helpful temporary measure to deal with the food situation. Every so often I had the military make clear that these bazaars were operating under privilege, that they could be shut down at any point. But I also made sure that any repercussions were kept mild.

As the third anniversary of President Kim Il Sung's death approached, I couldn't help but laugh at all the Korean "experts" worldwide. Whether it had been three weeks, three months or three years, their predictions about the DPRK's collapse had all been proven wrong. I decided that that year's memorial services should therefore held in a spirit of triumph. North

Korea had taken the worst of what the world had to throw at us, strife both natural and manmade, and still we walked with our heads held high.

After three years, I felt that I could finally give in to the inevitable without disrespecting the Great Leader. Though I was Chairman of the National Defense Commission and Supreme Commander of the KPA, I didn't yet hold the state leadership position. On October 8, 1997, I accepted the will of the Party members. Resolutions were passed throughout the DPRK acclaiming me as the General Secretary of the Workers' Party of Korea. The leadership succession was official at last.

I received many letters of congratulations, but more important to me were the endless letters of support. It was one particular letter from a North Hwanghae farmer that affected me greatly:

> Dear Leader,
>
> We can survive even if we send two or three months' provisions to the military. Just after liberation, farmer Kim Je Won donated rice to the country in support of the Great Leader Kim Il Sung, and today we will likewise donate rice to the army in support of you.

It wasn't what the farmer wrote that I particularly found to be of interest. I received letters of the sort daily, and though they gave me comfort their contents were virtually identical. Yet

---

THE JUCHE ERA

To further the message that the Great Leader would always be with us, I decided to commemorate his life in the most dramatic way possible. It wasn't enough that his birthday was celebrated as the Sun's Day, the DPRK's greatest national holiday. No, his life needed to be celebrated every single day. There was only one way to achieve such a feat: by changing the calendar itself. Beginning in 1997, our calendar began with the year of the Great Leader's birth, 1912, as Juche 1. 1997 was now Juche 86, 1998 was Juche 87, and so on.

something about this one letter gave me pause, though I couldn't quite understand what it was. I sat there and reread it over and over until I deduced what was unusual: the letter had been written in pencil. I leaned across my desk and grabbed an entire stack of letters that I'd received that day. They'd all been written in pencil, each and every one of them. Not a single one had been written in ink.

I'd been spending the vast majority of my time delivering field guidance to the military, since there was little guidance that I could offer to factories that sat still. It seemed like here in writing was the consequence of my absence. Still unsure as to whether the letters pointed to a shortage or a coincidence, I phoned the pen plant to resolve the matter. "Has there been a problem with production?" I asked the director.

"Yes, comrade," he told me. "But it couldn't be helped. We haven't gotten the metal we need from the steel mill."

So I called the steel mill. "Tell me, why haven't you sent metal to the pen plant?"

"We would be delighted to. But we haven't received any ore."

Next I got the smelter on the phone. "What's been holding up the delivery of ore?"

"Comrade, we can't acquisition any raw iron from the mine."

The more locations I called, the more anxious I became. "The smelter hasn't received any iron ore," I told the mine official.

"I know," he said. "The railway is broken down."

Gritting my teeth, I got in touch with the railways minister. "Why hasn't the railway been repaired?"

"Comrade," he said, "we haven't any railroad ties to replace the ones that were damaged."

Finally I called the forestry minister. "Let me guess: you couldn't produce timber for the railroad because you don't have any gas."

"It is fortunate indeed that our leader is so prescient and informed," he said. "That is indeed our situation."

It was time for industry in Korea to regroup and rebuild, now that the military could provide the proper foundation. To be honest, part of me didn't want to know how badly the factories were doing. After looking over my options, I decided to go revisit the Hwanghae Iron Works first. The mill had been our first automated factory and was a symbol of the DPRK's industrialization. Of all the factories in the northern part of Korea, I knew that it would be the one in the best condition.

As I drove up to the mill with several Party members, I noticed immediately that there weren't any signs of activity within. It wasn't that the iron works were simply idle. Instead, there was a stillness about the mill, as if it had been sitting there untouched for ages. I could practically feel the dust settling in the air. My comrades didn't even attempt to put on an optimistic face. Their scowls told me that they felt exactly the same way that I did.

After we pulled up, I cautiously got out of the car. As I walked to the mill door I saw that it was already half-open. I reached inside, trying to turn on the lights but not expecting them to actually switch on. The lights didn't turn on, of course, but the daylight was enough to show me all I needed to see.

The Hwanghae Iron Works were a gutted corpse. It was obvious at a glance that a majority of the machines had been stripped, dismantled and sold to the highest bidder. As I toured the location near tears, it further became obvious that not one single machine would have been operational even if there had been any electricity.

"We will find out what happened here," said one official, "and the class enemies will be dealt with."

"What happened here is obvious," I said. "The managers sold what they could to the Chinese. Punish them if you want. That still won't make this mill operational again."

That same day, I had warnings issued: those involved in the stripping of the mill would be executed unless all the machinery was returned at once. Sure enough, most of the pieces found their way back to the mill—after which I had nineteen people publicly shot for the crime. But this punishment gained us nothing. Nineteen more dead wasn't just irrelevant; it was statistically insignificant. As a child I could reassemble a car by myself. Now, as an adult, I found myself unable to reassemble a factory even with all of Korea behind me.

A year ago the scene would have filled me with depression. Now it only filled me with resolve. There were those who had made a bad situation better. But there were also those who had made it worse. It made me seethe with rage to compare how the military and the industrial sector had chosen to handle the Arduous March.

No wonder so much had gone wrong when everything I'd done had been right. The extreme pressure Korea faced wasn't enough to explain all the hunger and the death that had occurred. There were still class enemies actively plotting against the people. It was *they* who had made this Arduous March far longer and more painful than it needed to be. It was all the fault of the enemies of Juche Korea, and not mine.

Now I was determined to end lives instead of trying to save them. I needed to figure out who exactly was to blame for all the suffering that the people underwent. I sent out the KPA to interrogate anyone that I suspected of disloyalty. To no surprise, each and every one of them admitted their misdeeds under interrogation.

Of these villains, the worst was our Minister of Agriculture. To my absolute horror, he confessed to providing the country with bad seeds. He also admitted that he'd purposely refrained from introducing high-yields seeds from abroad, and had made sure that any fertilizer that we distributed was ineffective. I immediately made his confession public so that the masses could further see that the Arduous March hadn't been my fault. The minister was of course summarily executed. For good measure, we dug up the body of his predecessor—who was then shot and buried again. I didn't stop until everyone who deserved blame received it.

Now it came time for me to take my place as the leader who saved the masses from certain demise. I launched an international "crybaby operation" to get as much aid as possible. Previously, only our foreign service agents asked for help. Now, I made certain that all our people did so. Guests from abroad were no longer taken to the best places to meet healthy Korean people who insisted that they were living well. Instead, they were presented with the saddest pictures possible to generate the maximum amount of sympathy.

My strategy worked perfectly. Food and money poured in from the Red Cross and the WFP, even from hostile nations—which gave me that much more food and money to send to the military. I knew that there were enemies still conspiring against me. Some in the West and even some in the DPRK thought they could turn my own nation against me, using hunger as a cynical tool. There were many abroad who doubted the validity of my Songun politics. They argued that putting the military first was simply a mechanism for me to maintain my leadership position. They insisted that the money I spent wasn't going for development at all, but for patronage to those loyal to myself. I was determined to prove to all of my opponents, both at home and abroad, that the path of revolution begun by General Kim Il Sung would continue forever—and that it would be continue under my leadership until the day that I died.

The First Session of the Tenth Supreme People's Assembly—the first since the Great Leader's death—would be held in the fall of 1998, with elections held to fill the seats in the interim. Accordingly, on July 14 I registered my candidacy in Constituency No. 666—and unanimously won the seat less than two weeks later. It was a foregone conclusion at home and abroad that the session would end with me being elected to the DPRK Presidency.

I grinned when I heard such reports, especially when they came from the West. All of their prattling about Korea had been consistently proven wrong, again and again, and yet they never seemed to think that, perhaps, they'd made some mistake in their reasoning. Maybe, just maybe, they even had flawed information. But such self-reflection was obviously out of reach for tools of US imperialism. It brought me enormous pleasure to know that I was about to publicly embarrass all these fools—and not once, but twice. It was time to go on the attack again, after the long march of defense.

If one is to defeat the enemy, one must know him well. I fully under- stood America's psychological state. The only difference between who America considered a "rival" and who it called an "enemy" was the strength of that particular nation's military. Russia and China were therefore "rivals"; Cuba and Libya were "enemies." All four condemned and despised the US imperialists. But one pair was relatively strong, and the other much weaker.

I knew that the most effective way of attracting the US to my posi- tion would be in taking a cold attitude—and, if necessary, slapping it across the face. By demonstrating the DPRK's strength, by proving that our weaponry was world-class and that our military was invincible, by showing that I would never change our ways—all these things would make the Americans regard Korea as a rival and not an enemy.

On August 31, 1998 I orchestrated a spectacle that could be seen from everywhere on the planet. On that day, the DPRK became the ninth country to launch a satellite into space. Kwangmyongsong No. 1 flew over the globe, transmitting *The Song of General Kim Il Sung* and *The Song of General Kim Jong Il*, as well as the words "Juche Korea" in Morse code.

My foes were beside themselves. They didn't know what to do or say. Let me quote a foreign newspaper for the reaction, because they put it precisely right: "The DPRK's earth satellite launch drove the Western world into a state of insanity." I could have made no clearer announcement that the rebuilding of a great, prosperous and powerful nation had begun. Weak nations cannot venture into space—nor do "cronies" build satellites due to "patronage."

The international scrambling was immediate. The US imperialists denied the existence of a satellite at all, claiming they detected nothing. The Japs insisted that it hadn't been a satellite launch but a missile of some kind, one that crossed Japanese territory. The outrage from the two nations was as loud as it was incoherent, claiming the DPRK was a fraud or an aggressor or, somehow, both. They both made an enormous commotion about how "unacceptable" it all was—until I forced them to shut their mouths and to, in fact, accept it. They really had no choice. Who knew what else Korea were capable of, now that we'd crossed into space? Once again, peace had been won by struggle—not by begging, compromising or groveling—and guaranteed by arms.

Less than a week later came that Supreme People's Assembly session. The fiftieth anniversary of the DPRK was mere days away, and I couldn't help but notice how proud all those assembled seemed to be. It seemed like every Party member was giving me a subtle nod, an acknowledgment that they knew the worst was over.

The session brought with it my second major surprise. Those of us gathered in the Assembly adopted a new constitution—but we didn't elect a new President. As the introduction to the Kim Il Sung Socialist Constitution put it: "The DPRK and the entire Korean people will uphold the Great Leader Comrade Kim Il Sung as the eternal President of the Republic."

President Kim Il Sung was the only president that the Korean people had ever known. He would *remain* the only president that the Korean people had ever known. Under the new constitution he was the President for infinity even in death. I myself was reelected as Chairman of the National Defense Commission. The constitution now regarded my office as the pivot of the state, enshrining the fact that the military's political authority came first.

I immediately launched a campaign after officially taking over. My picture became posted alongside that of President Kim Il Sung everywhere in the DPRK. Underneath the posters was my official campaign slogan: Do Not Expect Any Change From Me. Nations that were supplying us with food urged reform and an open policy, yet I intended to hold fast to the socialist principle in every possible domain of economics. The fact that capitalist Asia was then experiencing a financial meltdown as our economy was improving was a rude awakening to the would-be reformers. They realized how wise President Kim Il Sung's policy of self-reliance was, and how wise I was for sticking to it.

Holding back my intrinsic sense of modesty, I increasingly had the newspapers report on my extraordinary feats. Over and over, the message was identical: "The Great Leader is precisely the Dear Leader and the Dear Leader is just the Great Leader. He is the same in terms of idea, personality, virtue and so on." The effect was to stop the masses from seeing Kim Jong Il as a "new" leader. Rather, they were to feel was as if President Kim Il Sung had risen from the grave and been born again in me.

The satellite showed my foes that I was strong, and the new constitution showed them that Juche Korea was here to stay. Rather than seeing us as a regime on the verge of collapse, the DPRK's enemies began to respect us as a powerful peer. This new air of mighty determination pervaded my entire administration. During a UN meeting, for example, one of our dialogue partners casually mentioned reform. The DPRK delegates simply stood up and left. My new hardline attitude was noticed worldwide—and most importantly, it was noticed by the US imperialists. My plan worked perfectly, for I understood how the Americans thought as much as they themselves failed to understand the DPRK. The harder a line I took, the closer they tried to get.

As the United States changed its attitude, so did other countries follow suit. As I'd been saying for decades, America's allies were its puppets who did as commanded. Very quickly, all three of the DPRK's biggest enemies—the US, Japan and "South Korea"—contacted me and begged for negotiations. Now, all three tried to calm tensions instead of their usual attempts at escalation. All three came to my capital in my country—to Pyongyang itself—to speak with me on my own terms. The truth of my Songun politics had been blatantly demonstrated for all the world to see. After four years of struggle, the long Arduous March had come to an end.

Victory was finally at hand.

Chapter 19

Delivering Diplomacy

Strategy entails the greatest possible gain at the lowest possible cost. My ultimate strategy in dealing with the US imperialists was to permanently settle the Korean conflict without any gunfire. Songun diplomacy meant compelling the Americans to reach peace by leveraging the threat of Korea's weapons. Of course, I understood that any actual battle would devastate the Korean peninsula—but I still managed to convince the Americans that I wouldn't hesitate to engage in war. It certainly helped my case when the Western media freely described me as "suicidal" and even "possibly psychotic." How "psychotic" that a "suicidal" nation like the DPRK managed to outlive virtually every other socialist state!

The aftermath of our satellite launch announcement was a perfect case in point. I had a meeting in my office with one of my military officials. To my amusement, the man was tremendously stressed by the latest American volley. "Comrade" he said, "we've received word from the Yank bastards. They've changed their story once again. They claim that we didn't launch a satellite at all, but that we fired a missile. Therefore, they're demanding inspection of our underground facilities."

I chuckled, and thought back to my days in the film industry. It was as if the Americans were reciting dialogue that I'd written for them—and they were delivering their lines perfectly. "The Yanks are acting as if these underground facilities are somehow new, correct?"

"This is correct, comrade."

"And are they, in fact, new?" I asked the official.

He bristled. "Of course not!"

"How long has Korea been orchestrating such military actions?"

The officer paused; these were simple facts that every Korean knew. "At least since 1951, when General Kim Il Sung implemented Juche tunnelizing tactics during the battle to defend Height 1211. After the success of the battle, the General spread the experience to all parts of the country. The people build iron-walled, tunnelized defense facilities at the front, along the coast lines and in inland areas. Tunneling is a Juche-oriented, original tactic which cannot be found in the military manuals of any other country."

I was impressed though not surprised that he recalled his Korean history so well. "And how do you learn about these facts?" I said, with a little smirk. "Aren't they military secrets?"

He looked at me like I'd lost my mind. "Comrade, we boast of this reality loudly! We have for decades! We teach it in school. We even put it in all our external propaganda, I believe."

"That's correct. As you know, for decades Korea has been under constant surveillance from US military satellites. Their unmanned spy planes fly over our territory every day. Building underground installations was all that we could do as countermeasures. This is all public knowledge, correct?"

"Yes, comrade."

"So I'm going to issue a response," I assured the official. "Just wait until you see the result!"

I used a formula whenever issuing messages under the auspices of Songun diplomacy. Playing into American expectations, I made certain that my public statements always sounded high and intense. At the same time, I suggested a way out for those who were against me. Time after time, my threats got me precisely what I wanted. It was if I'd been issuing shopping lists instead of warning of complete annihilation! In this case, the blast of intensity came first: "The inspection clamor is an outrageous infringement upon the sovereignty of our Republic and the security of the state, so it will never be tolerated." Then came the way out for the Americans: "If they want to dispel their doubt, they should offer substantial political and economic compensations for bringing disgrace to the image of our Republic by means of despicable slander and profanity." Meaning, Korea was horribly, terribly, mortally offended—but if the Americans wanted to compensate me for hurting our feelings, then I'd be willing to consider it.

In this case, the strategy worked. The strategy *always* worked. The United States was 78 times larger than Korea, with ten times the population. But I had the Americans like an elephant in an anthill. The ants could never devour the elephant—but they could still lead it in the direction that they wanted. The ants could get their way, especially when they came together as one.

After much grandstanding and hyperbole, the American and Korean negotiators reached a compromise. The Americans claimed that they were neither rewarding me nor condoning my violent rhetoric. That is absolutely true. They didn't "reward" me or "condone" my rhetoric. On the other hand, they did financially compensate me because of my aggression.

On March 22, 1999, the United States announced that it would be supplying the DPRK with two hundred thousand tons of food, including one hundred thousand tons of potatoes. Instead of being funneled through the UN's WFP, these goods would be offered directly—a first. This didn't contradict the Juche principle of self-reliance one bit. I didn't look at the package as aid so much as the repayment of a debt. The US imperialists had been threatening Korea for decades. It was entirely their fault that I'd had to expend such enormous sums on the military.

In exchange for the food, I agreed to give the Americans a tour of our underground facilities. I even managed to force the Yanks to change their terminology—officially referring to a "visit" but never an "inspection." If they wanted to give us hundreds of millions of dollars' worth of food to have a look around, I was glad to oblige. Our tourist package usually went for far less.

Before the Americans arrived for their visit, I called my diplomats together to discuss how best to approach the situation. "In a capitalist society," I explained, "customers are catered to. Their pockets are picked clean in every possible way. Unfortunately, the socialist system is sometimes ice-cold and indifferent to the customer. Store workers don't care if the customers buy anything or not. Instead of trying to sell something or even offering pleasant service, they'd rather no one show up so they won't have to do anything. Please, treat these Yank bastards as they are used to be treating at home. Provide them with every amenity possible."

> ### THE POTATO REVOLUTION
>
> The New Year's joint editorial of 1999 called for making a revolution in potato farming. Potatoes aren't particular about soil conditions, growing well even on dry and sterile land. They require less fertilizer than corn does and have a faster growth period than both rice and wheat. The potato is therefore uniquely qualified to play the role of a famine-relief crop. Time and time again, many countries escaped famine by increasing potato production—and in 1999, Korea added herself to that list.

Per my instructions, the Americans were treated very well. After they left, they swiftly announced that they'd found nothing out of order in the facilities that they'd been shown and delivered the food that they promised. I couldn't help but smile at how easy it had been for me to play them for fools. Such was the difference between being a "rival" nation and being an "enemy." Such was the difference of a powerful military presence.

Like any good general, I further pressed my advantage in the subsequent negotiations. The Americans couldn't agree to my demands fast enough. The crippling economic sanctions were strongly reduced. The US would reexamine our official designation as a "state sponsor of terrorism" (a holdover from the 1987 Korean Air bombing). Finally, talks would be held to establish full and official diplomatic relations between the two countries. This last item was what most excited me; the Great Leader had been fighting for such relations until his last breath. The talks were so successful on my part that President Clinton's opponents described them as "a surrender of the White House to the pressure of north Korea."

Yet the most important thing that the Yanks gave me was never discussed publicly. For the first time, the US backed away from opposing direct talks between north and south Korea. I always claimed that such talks would occur immediately as soon as the US imperialists got out of the way. Now the truth of my contention was proven. In early 2000, I elaborated a plan for a summit between the north and the south. South Korean President Kim Dae Jung agreed to come to Pyongyang on June 13, the first southern leader to ever do so. It was by far the biggest step toward reconciliation and reunification since Korea's division after World War II.

Kim Dae Jung had taken over south Korea in 1998. In a complete break with his dictator predecessors, he called for a "Sunshine Policy" with north Korea. He advocated ignoring past hostilities for the sake of better relations in the immediate future. When I heard a common acquaintance describe Kim Dae Jung as "peasant-like," I grew extremely hopeful about our future relations. It seemed like he was exactly my favorite type of person to deal with.

THE CASE FOR REUNIFICATION

It's difficult for some Westerners to understand how I could have possibly hoped for reunification at such a late date. For them, the goal was no longer a realistic one—but that was because it had never been *their* goal to begin with. Korea's fate had always been the sole concern of the Korean people themselves. When Korea had been colonized and enslaved, international inquiries only came from foreign nations worried about threats to their own vested interests. They never cared about Korea or the Korean people themselves, not for a moment. That's something that never changed.

There were many concrete reasons that I held out hope for reunification. Only one other country was divided due to World War II: Germany. Despite the political, social and even physical barriers, Germany was very successfully reunited in 1990. Yes there had been difficulties, but the Germans came together and overcame them. Reunification worked even though "Germany" had only existed as a country for less than two centuries. Korea, of course, had been a nation for far longer, for millennia.

There was another, even more recent case that filled me with hope: the May 22, 1998 peace-proposal referendum between Northern Ireland and the Republic of Ireland. In that case, all sides concerned voted overwhelmingly in favor of the agreement. Yes, violence from hardliners ensued as a consequence. But the radicals soon had no choice but to declare a complete ceasefire, due to the almost complete lack of support from the people.

There were undoubtedly obstacles to Korean reunification, the biggest of which was considered to be the financial cost. During the Arduous March, the south had provided a great amount of temporary assistance to the north. But viewing this exchange strictly from a financial perspective was a very capitalistic, very flawed approach. No matter how much money the south might have had at a given time, there were things that only the north could provide to them. South Korea was a region characterized by the prevalence of immoral acts such as sexual flirtation, rape and a high rate of divorce. The deplorable misery of wives being beaten, of husbands being killed in retaliation, was a daily occurrence there. By its own data, the south had the most suicides and most plastic surgeries per capita on earth. The south was nothing less than a land devoid of true love—and there was no place in the world where the virtue of loving others was realized as it was in the north. What we offered the south was far greater than anything they could send us in return.

As Kim Dae Jung's visit approaches, I too had to deal with doubters. It's no secret that most of the DPRK's political leadership would be considered "hardliners" and "radicals" outside of Korea. It was a natural consequence of a nation formed by violent revolution and led under the direction of my Songun politics. In fact, one prominent Korean whose name I won't mention came to speak with me about the forthcoming summit. There was no doubt that he considered it a waste of time at best. "The United States will never withdraw its troops from the south," he insisted. "This is yet another trick!"

"What about China?" I said.

"What do you mean?"

"The Americans reconciled with China in 1972, didn't they? Do you remember what happened?"

"I do," he replied. "They issued the Shanghai Joint Communique."

"And did they stick to those terms?"

Now he lowered his head. "Yes, they did."

"What happened then?"

"The American soldiers withdrew from Taiwan and the military bases there were closed."

"That's right," I said. "The two countries established diplomatic relations in 1979, with the US severing diplomatic relations with Taiwan at the same time. It's my hope that the conflict between Korea and the United States can come to a similar peaceful resolution, and soon. This summit might very well go down in history as the first step toward that all-important goal."

I knew there were worries in the south about how Kim Dae Jung would be received. I'd been so demonized in their media that it sounded like I was capable of every depravity imaginable. I was dumb and ridiculous and ugly, an alcoholic and a sex-maniac. Their articles were more interested in explaining that I enjoyed Hennessey Paradis than in explaining my economic policies. Amazingly, there were even southern fears that Kim Dae Jung would be arrested and held hostage! Of all the comments against my character, it was those from my fellow countrymen hurt most. Korea had long been known as a country of good manners. There wasn't the slightest question that I'd receive Kim Dae Jung with every possible display of respect, in line with traditional Korean etiquette.

Because Kim Dae Jung was my elder, I made it a point to go to him with a personal greeting at the Pyongyang Airport. As he got off the plane I walked up and shook his hand warmly, even sharing a hug with my brother from the south. Though I was in my usual people's clothes and he was in a conservative suit, still we were of one blood. Our only separation had been geographical.

All throughout the airport, cheers emerged as people burst into tears. The masses had been waiting for reunification their entire lives, and here in front of their very eyes were the men who had the power to make it happen. I made it a point to deferentially walk behind Kim Dae Jung as we went to the arranged car. As the two of us drove to the capital, hundreds of thousands of Pyongyangites stood on the road alongside our route, waving Korean flags and cheering "Manse!"

At the guest house, I let Kim Dae Jung be the first one to speak to the assembled journalists. After he was done I said a few words myself. Then I felt what seemed like hundreds of cameras going off at once. The photographers called out for us to pose with our hands lifted up together. "What, you want us to be actors for the cameras?" I quipped, as we got into position. Everyone in the room burst out into laughter, even those skeptics in Kim Dae Jung's entourage. It wasn't that I had said something particularly funny. Rather, it was the fact I obviously wasn't some humorless monster with horns growing out of my head. The pictures done, I looked around and smiled. "Well, now you have to pay for our acting! How much did I earn for my performance?"

Since Kim Dae Jung would only be in Pyongyang for two days, I made sure that his itinerary covered all the sights that the city had to offer. Seeing the capital for himself would tell him far more about the state of the DPRK than anything that I could possibly say. Being Korean, it would obviously be of enormous curiosity to him on a personal level as well. Together with his party, he ended up visiting the Mangyongdae Schoolchildren's Palace, the Pyongyang Maternity Hospital and the Grand People's Study House. He also paid a courtesy call to the Supreme People's Assembly.

The schedule had four hours blocked out for the two of us to speak by ourselves. At first we made typical small talk, both of us trying to establish commonalities and trust. But the conversation soon took off in every direction possible, both of us extremely interested in the other one's thinking. Obviously we focused heavily on politics, but we also talked about films and even popular south Korean celebrities. If Kim Dae Jung was surprised that I could discuss such matters at length, he didn't show it. If anything, he was amused by how much I knew. Regardless of the subject under consideration, there was no tension or awkwardness between the two of us whatsoever.

It was one of the worst conversations of my life.

I thought that Kim Dae Jung was mumbling when we first began our discussion. Then it seemed like he was speaking too quickly from excitement. Finally, there was even a moment where I feared that something was amiss with my hearing. Understanding that none of these possibilities were actually the case, I still couldn't figure out why I was having such a difficult time following him. Eventually I deduced what was happening: We were speaking different languages. Or, to be more precise, we were speaking one language in the process of becoming two.

Kim Dae Jung hadn't been trying to stress the differences between us. Quite the opposite: his every sentence was designed to bring us together and create a sense of unity. But I could only understand approximately 80% of what he was saying. The rest was filled with terms I didn't know—probably borrowed from Western languages—and pronunciations completely foreign to my native Korean. I even felt slightly self-conscious, knowing that southerners regard the northern accent as "guttural." But the northern version of Korean could no longer be described an "accent." No, it was a *dialect*. There wasn't any clearer illustration of how the two Koreas had been growing apart.

I had looked at Kim Dae Jung as a brother when we first met. A long-lost brother, and one raised by a family terribly different from my own, yet a brother all the same. But I was naive. He didn't look at me as a brother. I was a cousin to him at best, and a backwards one at that. I wondered how long would it take before those in the DPRK were regarded by southerners as distant relatives. Twenty years? Thirty? After that, we'd just be neighbors. The five-millennia history of Korea would become a thing of the past, really and truly—and irrevocably.

That conversation was the first time in my life when I suspected that reunification might not happen. After the Arduous March, I expected Korea to emerge victorious on the other side just as with the original Arduous March. It is well known that one can lose a battle and still win the war. It terrified me to see that apparently the reverse could be true as well. One could win a battle, but the war for a unified Korea seemed to be slipping away.

Soon it came time for the two of us to attend a banquet at Mokran House, where all visiting foreign dignitaries are hosted. I've often said that "time is something very easy to spend but very difficult to spare," so I was aware of how urgent things had become. I made a decision to switch priorities and focus on the short-term during the rest of the summit. The first such thing on my agenda would be the release of all the unconverted long-term prisoners still held captive in the south, men like Ri In Mo who had never lost faith in the Juche idea despite years of incarceration. This went hand in hand with all the families who'd been separated since the 1950s. I quickly thought about how best to broach these admittedly very sensitive subjects.

I saw my opportunity as we sat down at the banquet. Per custom, Kim Dae Jung's wife was seated apart from us. Seeing this, I stood up in front of the packed room. Instantly it grew silent, as if I were making a toast. Instead I turned and addressed the south's first lady. "We meet to address the issue of separated families, and yet here we are making another separated family. Please, come sit by me!"

With a smile and a chuckle she got up and sat down by her husband

and myself. When I glanced over at Kim Dae Jung, he gave a very brief nod as acknowledgment. He was a shrewd man; he understood what I was getting at and why I chose to broach the subject in such a manner. He didn't say another word about the issue at dinner, but when we left and got into the car it was he who brought the issue up. "I couldn't help but catch your reference to separated families," he told me. "This is something, I think, that we can come to a quick, easy agreement on. It would be proof of the summit's success. The truth of my Sunshine Policy would be blatantly demonstrated for all the world to see."

I grinned. "What I'd personally like to see happen is the return of the remaining unconverted long-term prisoners."

Kim Dae Jung winced and looked away. "I expected you to bring that up."

"Look, these men are all aged. None of them will cause you any problems when released. In the south, they're just taking up space. Here, they'll be awarded the highest honors and provided with the finest living conditions. All they want at this point is to be able to die in their homeland, and to be buried in the north. Please, consider it a personal favor."

He paused, carefully considering his words. "This can't be played as some sort of surrender on my part."

"No, of course not. It will be presented as an agreement, not a defeat. There are 63 men in total. I don't see why they can't all be released."

Now he turned back, and I saw the strength behind the sunshine. "Then you'll let families come to visit Seoul."

"63 prisoners, and 63 families."

"No," he insisted. "100 families for 63 prisoners."

"Fine," I said right away. "How about for August 15th? It would be a superb element to add to Liberation Day celebrations."

"Perfect. We'll let the prisoners out immediately following that."

So he still didn't completely trust me, and wanted to make sure that I could be held to our agreement. I didn't blame him, and didn't begrudge him that either. To give him confidence, I vowed to put my promise in writing. On the day Kim Dae Jung left, June 15, the two of us signed the North-South Joint Declaration pledging further cooperation between the two sides. Also included in the declaration was an invitation for me to come visit Seoul at an appropriate time in the future. Later that day, I saw him off at the airport, shaking his hand firmly and vowing to pay him a return visit.

Just as we agreed, the separated families were reunited in August to great worldwide applause. A month after that, all of the south's remaining prisoners were released to the north with great fanfare. I kept my promise to Kim Dae Jung, checking to make sure that all of our newspaper articles treated his decision respectfully. I sincerely hoped that we could build on these small steps in the future—and, frankly, I was interested in going to see Seoul for myself.

Soon word got to me that Kim Dae Jung and myself were under consideration to share the Nobel Peace Prize. There had been recent precedent for sharing the award. The men who'd negotiated the Irish ceasefire agreements had won, as had Arafat, Peres and Rabin for their Middle East work. In the end, the committee blatantly snubbed me and awarded the Prize to Kim Dae Jung alone. This was how toxic the perception of me had become in the Western world. I was less palatable to them than even Arafat was.

I didn't dwell too much on this slight. I was focused on winning peace, not winning Peace Prizes. Mere months after Kim Dae Jung's visit, an American Secretary of State was going to visit Pyongyang for the first time. Even though President Clinton's term of office was about to conclude, my summit with Madeline Albright still retained had enormous potential. If it went well, a presidential visit would follow—and diplomatic relations with it. It would be the highlight of my career as leader, a fulfillment of President Kim Il Sung's lifelong goal.

Establishing diplomatic relations with the United States would bring immediate and profound consequences to the DPRK. We'd be able to radically reduce military expenditures and instead focus on building the economy, agriculture and infrastructure. It would also mean an elimination of the American sanctions, which would lead to a great deal of foreign investment into resource-rich Korea. I was especially eager to lose the "state sponsor of terrorism" designation, a legal classification with many harmful implications.

This time around, I was the one who spent time worrying about the summit. Albright wouldn't be coming as a peer; she knew perfectly well that she represented vast power. There wouldn't be a sense of kinship, as there had been with Kim Dae Jung. The only thing the United States and Korea had in common was a shared history of animosity and war, a history of hatred that went back to the 1860s. Just as I did since I'd been a child, I read as much as I could about the subject in preparation—and was surprised by what I uncovered about Madeline Albright.

The first female Secretary of State, Albright had a reputation for delivering political messages through the brooches that she wore. She carried a large array of them everywhere that she went, with each brooch being a subtle indicator of what she was feeling that particular day. When she met President Putin, for example, she wore a brooch of monkeys covering their eyes to protest his position on Chechnya. I was very pleased to learn of this information. It would allow me to ascertain her thoughts—especially if I played dumb about her jewelry's meaning.

I left very explicit instructions to receive a phone call as soon as Albright landed on October 22, 2000. I could barely work, silently urging the phone to ring. Finally, the call came through. "Comrade," the official said, "the Americans have landed. There are about two hundred of them in total."

"And Mrs. Albright, what is she wearing?" I said.

"Uh...she has on a jacket in the Western style—"

"No, not the jacket!" I snapped. "Her brooch! What kind of brooch does she have pinned to her lapel?"

Fortunately DPRK diplomatic training encourages our staff to pay extraordinary attention to detail. "It's a large one with the design of the Stars and Stripes, the emblem of the American flag."

"Large? How large?"

"It's the boldest brooch that I've ever seen, about the size of a playing card."

"I understand. Good work." I hung up the phone and considered what this first brooch meant. There was little to deduce, since the message that Albright was sending wasn't very subtle. It's well-known that everyone in the DPRK always wears a lapel pin with a picture of either the Great Leader, myself or both. Albright's first brooch was a symbol of defiance, that America would not be submitting to Korean ways even for the sake of diplomatic pleasantries. When I finally briefly met her later that day, I saw that the brooch was even larger than I'd envisioned, almost to the point of obnoxiousness.

The next day Albright and I were due for our first real diplomatic meeting. I knew that she'd gone in the morning to pay her respects to the Great Leader at the Kumsusan Memorial Palace. After her gratuitous first brooch, a tiny part of me was worried that she wouldn't be as deferential as I would have liked. Thankfully, by all accounts she showed every possible courtesy to the eternal image. This, too, told me a great deal. Albright could have easily refused to tour the temple of Juche. Or worse, she could have gone but refused to act in a dignified manner. Instead she chose to act respectfully. That meant she was turning her back on the usual American high-handedness and dominationism—or at least, pretending to.

Then it finally came time for me to meet with Secretary Albright. She smiled brightly when she saw me entering the meeting room. As I walked in, I cursed myself for not wearing my sunglasses. I had made eye contact with her right when I'd arrived! Now I couldn't glance down at her lapel, for then she'd realize that I knew about her jewelry code. I knew I needed a distraction, so I went with something that would certainly throw her off guard: a joke.

"Well, here I am!" I announced. "The last of the communist devils!" I waited as the translator repeated what I said, and then Albright burst out laughing despite herself. Quickly I cast a glance at her brooch. To my consternation, she was wearing not one but two different symbols of American arrogance! The first was an American eagle, and above it was Uncle Sam's top hat. I wasn't sure what she meant by these. Did it symbolize one piece of jewelry broken into two, as Korea herself was divided? I realized her brooch code was far more complex than I'd given the woman credit for.

"I've brought you a present," Albright said. She gestured to one of her entourage and he brought over a basketball. "This has been signed to you by Michael Jordan."

I was flattered. I of course often received gifts from prominent personalities from all over the world. There were so many, in fact, that I put them on display in our International Friendship Exhibition for the appreciation of all the people. But this was the first basketball that I'd ever been given—and from such an acclaimed international athlete! "Do you want me to go outside and bounce it around?" I asked her.

She smiled again. "No, I think I'd rather talk."

"Me too."

So we sat and discussed all sorts of issues. I made it a point to give her concise, clear-cut answers so that she would encourage President Clinton to make a visit in the brief time he had left in office. The most important thing for both of us was to find agreement on the issue of terrorism—and very quickly such agreement was found. Our two nations had issued a joint statement on the subject earlier that month. It was good for both of us to validate and confirm what had been said. "I would greatly like it," urged Albright, "if we could count on the DPRK's cooperation regarding the issue of terrorism, per our statement."

I bit my tongue, not pointing out to her that we ourselves had been the victims of American terrorism. In that moment, I vividly recalled seeing that downed Yankee soldier when I was a young boy—but I put it out of my mind immediately. That was a lifetime ago, I decided. "As we said in the statement," I told her, "the DPRK opposes all forms of terrorism against any country or individual. It is an unacceptable threat to global security and peace, and should be opposed in all its forms."

Albright nodded, listening with intense concentration. "This sort of cooperation will go far toward removing the DPRK from the list of state sponsors of terrorism."

"All I want," I told her, "was peace."

Albright and I so genuinely enjoyed one another's company that we ran far over our scheduled time together. Just as with Kim Dae Jung, she saw for herself that I wasn't the madman that many people portrayed me as. She recognized that I was practical and thoughtful, just like a real live human being. At one point Albright seemed to forget that we were having formal talks and openly expressed admiration. "You know," she said, "some of the things you say are really quite fascinating."

"Well," I replied, "we have much to learn from one another." For an

American Secretary of State to praise me, even in a quasi-private setting, was without precedent. Yet I still wasn't sure if she was speaking the truth or if she was simply using flattery and her womanly wiles to further her goals.

The next time I saw Albright was at the banquet we had scheduled that evening. Immediately my eyes went to her brooch. To my profound delight, it was in the shape of a heart. There could have been no clearer icon of respect and friendship. Seeing that, I greeted her warmly and looked forward to having a wonderful dinner with the Secretary.

At one point during dinner, Albright turned to everyone at the table and issued a challenge. "There's a puzzle I know back in America," she said. "How can you get to sixteen, just using your ten fingers?"

I knew the answer immediately. I looked up and down the table to see if anyone else would be able to solve the riddle. The Secretary grinned to herself, thinking she had gotten us all with her trick question. "I have it," I said. "It's quite easy." I extended both my hands with the thumbs overlapping to form a multiplication sign, thereby indicating "4x4."

"That's right!" she said with delight, leading the room into applause.

The summit could not have gone better. When Albright left for the airport, I once again had an official call to tell me what she was wearing. "Comrade," he said, "her brooch was in the shape of a cowboy."

"A cowboy!" I said. "Are you sure?"

"I am absolutely certain. I checked twice to make sure I was seeing the right thing. Does that mean something?"

"If it does," I said coyly, "then you'd have to ask Mrs. Albright. Thank you, that will be all."

I was an admirer of the cinema. I knew what that cowboy brooch meant. It was the emblem of a person who settled hostilities in a far-off, seemingly inhospitable land. It was a symbol of peace. That day, Secretary

Albright was the hero riding off into the sunset, living her American happy ending.

I, on the other hand, was left behind, not knowing how much danger loomed on the horizon.

Chapter 20

Korea is Two

Life is neither a Hollywood fairy tale nor even a Korean one. Cowboys aren't always heroes who come to bring peace. Sometimes they come to bring war, consciously and gleefully, and woe to anyone who gets in their way. In American imagery, the heroic lawman isn't the only who comes in on a white horse. That's also the steed ridden by death himself.

On November 7, 2000 Al Gore overwhelmed the cowboy George W. Bush in the presidential election by a margin of 337,000 votes. Despite this, Bush spent an enormous sum of money and manipulated the incoherent election system to his own advantage. The following January, Bush was sworn into the White House.

It was very obvious to me from early on that President Bush and I would have very little in common. But what was shocking to me and to the world public was how little he had in common with his very own predecessors. From the first day of his inauguration, Bush launched an offensive against any and every international treaty that had been signed by those in power before him.

We're not isolationists in Korea, but we want to keep the status quo. Part of that means honoring international agreements that we've committed ourselves to. It's both the right thing to do and the strategic thing to do. I regarded such forthrightness as a very basic principle to follow in seeking a peaceful world, a world free of imperialism and dominationism. Yet not everyone sought such a world. For some people, war itself was the goal—and those people were now in charge of the most powerful army on earth.

Bush's philosophy was rooted in the ideological confrontation of the Cold War days, based on the belief that strength meant justice. If another country had been as dismissive and contemptuous of the international order as President Bush was, he'd regard them as a "rogue nation." But since America had so many soldiers and so much weaponry, such classifications apparently didn't apply.

The Bush administration quickly began beating

> **INTERNATIONAL AGREEMENTS REPUDIATED BY BUSH**
>
> The ABM Treaty
> The Biological Weapons Convention
> The Chemical Weapons Convention
> The Comprehensive Test Ban Treaty
> The Ottawa Convention
> The Rome Statute
> The Kyoto Protocol

the war drums. Every area in the world was under consideration for American strikes. It was as if Bush and his team sat down with a globe and wondered where they should next unleash destruction. The fact that such talk was so open and so public only added to the horror and disgust felt by most other countries—with the DPRK certainly foremost among those. Any hopes I had that the summit with Secretary Albright would lead to a presidential visit to Korea were crushed completely.

All this put me in a very difficult position. There were two possible ways to further Korea's goals on the world stage: either calming tensions with our enemies or bolstering them with our friends. Seeing that the former wasn't an option under Bush, I turned to the latter. Russian president Putin had visited the DPRK in July of 2000. When I saw how quickly US-Korea relations were deteriorating, I returned the favor in the summer of 2001. Immediately afterward, I hosted Jiang Zemin, the first Chinese president to visit north Korea in almost twenty years. But though our talks were warm, even cordial, they weren't what they could have been. Putin was no Premier Stalin and Jiang was no Chairman Mao. The relations between Korea and Russia, and Korea and China, would never again be what they'd once been.

Just one week after the visit from the Chinese president came the events of September 11th, Juche 90 (2001). The facts of that day are well-known: Using Japanese-style kamikaze tactics, nineteen mostly-Saudi men hijacked several planes and flew them into the World Trade Center and the Pentagon. My heart went out to the American people as I, like billions of others, watched the events unfold.

It was a tragic day not just for the United States but for the world. I say that as a humanitarian, but I also say it as a tactician. President Bush now had the pretext he'd been seeking to launch any war that he desired. I often said that we in Korea do not want war, but we are not afraid of it. This didn't mean that I had any misconceptions about how truly devastating war could be. I'd lived through two wars myself. I knew that they needed to be avoided at all costs. But they didn't seem to share my concerns in Washington. In the days that followed the 9/11 attacks, the sadism emanating from the White House was like something out of a horror story. They wanted blood. They wanted vengeance. Someone had to die. The only question was *who*.

Bush addressed a joint session of Congress on September 20. "We will pursue nations that provide aid or safe haven to terrorists," he said. "Every nation, in every region, now has a decision to make. Either you are with the US, or you are with the terrorists." In other words, the US imperialists were demanding a blank check to do as they wished with impunity and to disagree with them was to side with the terroristic murderers of 9/11. This was, simply put, obscene. One nation's suffering didn't give it the right to violate another's sovereignty.

North Korea became an explicit target for Bush in January of 2002.

He blustered that the DPRK, Iran and Iraq "constitute an axis of evil, arming to threaten the peace of the world. By seeking weapons of mass destruction, these regimes pose a grave and growing danger. They could provide these arms to terrorists, giving them the means to match their hatred." My reaction to his speech was one of disgust but not surprise. I knew exactly who Bush was and how he thought. I'd been fighting the US imperialists since I'd been a little boy.

It's difficult for me to convey how much his speech poisoned relations between the DPRK and the United States. Besides the hostility, the entire speech was grounded in dishonesty. To begin with, the very expression "Axis of Evil" was an act of double plagiarism. The evil came from "evil empire," used by President Reagan to denounce the USSR during the Cold War—the same long-gone Cold War which the US imperialists cite to justify remaining in south Korea in perpetuity.

Second, the word "axis" was stolen from the "Axis Powers" during the Second World War. As such, the term had strong rhetorical power and with good reason. The Axis Powers were perhaps the most despicable force that the world had ever seen. To compare the DPRK to Imperial Japan was the worst insult imaginable to my country's dignity. It was to dismiss the suffering, the brutality and the torture that the Korean people had to suffer under the control of the wicked Japs—the same Japs who were now such close friends with the United States, not Korea.

But the concept of an "axis" didn't make any sense either. Anyone with a basic knowledge of mathematics knows that an axis requires an intersection between two lines. Yet Iran and Iraq had spent practically the entire 1980s at war. The former was an Islamic state populated by Persians; the latter a secular state populated by Arabs. Where was this "evil" intersection between Iran and Iraq? And between either of them and the DPRK? There was none, of course.

It was apparent to commentators around the world that this "axis of evil" was a kill list, nothing more and nothing less. We three were the nations that President Bush and his team of fascists were seeking to invade. I'd been warning for decades that this was the ultimate intention of the US imperialists. Bush's speech, televised worldwide, proved the validity of my warnings.

The worst part was that Bush wasn't all talk. He very much meant what he was saying, to a terrifying degree, and backed up his rhetoric with action. The Anti-Ballistic Missile (ABM) Treaty had been in force since 1972, a compromise between the Soviet Union and the United States. It was universally regarded as a cornerstone of world stability, since it limited both nations to one and only one ABM deployment area. This treaty formed the basis of thirty-two subsequent arms-control and -reduction agreements, including such landmarks as SALT I, SALT II and the NPT which had been such an issue for Korea. In June of 2002, thirty years and six presidents after its inception, President Bush declared that the ABM Treaty would no longer apply to the United States. These were not the actions of a friend of international peace and democracy. These were the actions of a high-handed war maniac who did not want any limits on his ability to murder.

I saw that I needed to fortify the DPRK as much as possible and as quickly as I could. Unfortunately, the options that I had were extremely limited. I could request little more from Russia and China. And despite overtures of friendship, the south Korean puppets would at best remain neutral in a conflict between the DPRK and the United States. Any other nation in the region wouldn't be strong enough to make a difference. All the remaining countries in other parts of the world were either under the thrall of America, trying to maintain their own defenses or even simply indifferent to our plight. I was left with one and only one option, and it was the most unlikely one of all: Japan.

Many visitors to the DPRK are surprised by how much anti-Japanese information we present. Some even go so far as to claim that this animus proves that north Korea is "stuck in the past." What they don't appreciate is that the pain that the Japanese caused Korea still lingers in the present. The injuries never healed, let alone scarred over. After all, what is the DMZ but a giant gaping wound originally drawn by the Japs?

I wanted to make amends with Japan—but making amends requires the wrongdoer to acknowledge, apologize and pay restitution for what he's done. It wasn't as if Japan couldn't afford to pay for our past suffering. The Japanese are good at saving, and are very frugal (probably because they live on islands). But most essential to their wealth was their industry, and this too they owed to Korea.

Historically speaking, the Japanese devils were never creative. Rather, they were good at copying other people's inventions and then modifying them. Every product they had, they borrowed or stole from other people. Rice-farming, Buddhism, writing, steelmaking, ceramics, pharmaceuticals, paper manufacturing and architecture were all things that Japan imported from Korea a long time ago. It's no exaggeration to say that virtually all the historic relics unearthed in several regions of Japan, almost everything that had been handed down from ancient times, bore Korean characteristics. In fact, Japan's foremost symbol received its name from Korean. In ancient times, the Koreans who found an active volcano in Japan called it "*Punsan*" (fire mountain). A slight phonetic modification changed it to the present "Mt. Fuji."

But simply because they could and should afford to make amends didn't mean that the Japs would. Germany came to recognize Nazism as a crime and resolutely broke away from it. The acts of Hitler and his fascists are still a source of great shame for the German people, who denounce his barbarism at every opportunity. Many Westerners assume that the Japanese have the same attitude toward their own past villainy—but unfortunately, this is not the case.

To this day, the sons of samurai haven't easily abandoned their dream of conquering Asia. For every Jap politician who speaks of reflection or apology, there are ten who make remarks downplaying or even justifying their past atrocities: "Japanese colonial rule greatly benefited the modernization of Korea." "The state cannot apologize or compensate for the 'comfort women' because those were the affairs of the army." "The Pacific War was a war for self-defense." By and large, Japanese politicians are hooligans without any conscience.

It might have been silly on my part to expect such insolent and inhuman people to have the slightest sense of morality. But Japan was the only option I had, and it was Japan that most had America's ear. Candidly, Japan had a vested interest in ensuring that a second Korean war wouldn't break out. I would be loathe to fire missiles into Seoul, but I would have no compunction about striking Tokyo—which was effectively striking America. I knew it and, more importantly, the Japanese knew it too.

Given all this, I understood that I needed to extend myself greatly to normalize relations with Japan and to receive any restitution. Fortunately, Japanese Prime Minister Koizumi agreed to visit Pyongyang in September 2002. We had a great deal of work to do to establish any trust. Napoleon once said, "You believe me, and I also believe you." But my strategy with Koizumi was to say, "I believe you. Believe me, you, too."

When we finally met, Koizumi quickly turned to a subject that I'd been preparing for: the kidnapping of Japanese citizens by north Korean agents. The issues had been absolutely taboo in prior talks between our nations, with my side denying it completely. "It has been proven that the persons identified by Japanese sources do not exist within our territories and have never entered nor resided in the country in the past," we insisted. During one meeting, our diplomats had slammed the table—literally— and walked out at the mere mention of the subject. When it was later brought up again, we cancelled the talks on the spot and didn't resume them for eight years.

But this wasn't a meeting between diplomats. This was the Prime Minister of Japan meeting with the Chairman of the DPRK National Defense Commission. So when Koizumi brought the matter up, I was prepared. "I know that there have been difficult issues between our nations in the past," I said. "The subject of these alleged kidnappings is certainly an important one. I realize that the DPRK has insisted for years that such things have never happened. Well, it's come to my attention that these abductions have, in fact, happened. Further, I can acknowledge that they were undertaken by persons affiliated with north Korea. These people have been punished most severely. I apologize sincerely for what has transpired, and I regret it tremendously." It was the first time that any representative of the DPRK had apologized for anything.

The Japs, like most liars, have a well-earned reputation for being slick-tongued. One might not believe what they're saying, but they always did have something to say. In fact, more often than not, such people often knew the exact right thing to say at any given moment. This is what made them such effective liars—and being a successful politician on top of that meant that Koizumi must have been one of the smoothest talkers in the world. But in that moment Koizumi was speechless.

Koizumi had surely played out this scenario a million times in his mind, with different outcomes each time. I'm sure he had responses for each possibility, ranging from an outright denial on my part to some sort of tacit admission—the typical range of options for a politician. But Koizumi forgot that he wasn't dealing with just some politician. He was dealing with Kim Jong Il, the Genuine People's Leader.

Koizumi gestured to his staff to hand him the names of the missing persons. He was trying to act like nothing had happened, as if I would somehow recant what I'd just said in front of a roomful of witnesses. But I myself had also come prepared with a list of names, so I pulled out my notes for comparison. "There are thirteen of them," I said. "Five of which are still alive."

"We have seventeen names," he insisted, "at the very least."

"Let's go through them," I said. "Together."

To Koizumi's amazement, some of the names I put forward were completely unfamiliar to him; Japan hadn't even suspected the DPRK. Similarly, there were a couple of names that he mentioned that weren't our doing. "These people shall be returned at once!" he finally snapped. He so easily switched to an aggressive demeanor that I knew he'd be presenting this as some sort of personal triumph once back in Japan, even though I'd freely confessed to the matter. If he needed to do that for the Japanese public to accept assisting the DPRK, I was more than glad to let Koizumi have his charade.

"Of course," I told him. As if I would have brought the names up otherwise!

"Let me thank you for your cooperation in this most sensitive matter," he said. "I'm very glad that this summit is off to such a productive start. Perhaps there are things that Japan can apologize for as well. These admissions can go a great way toward establishing relations between our two countries, who share such a complex and interrelated history."

At the end of Koizumi's visit, the two of us signed and released the Pyongyang Declaration. In it, he "expressed deep remorse and heartfelt apology" for Japan's past actions and agreed to give the DPRK billions of dollars in reparation funds and food aid. It went against everything I knew, but for that day I believed that I could do business with the Japs and that Korea could finally put the most hurtful episode of her past to rest.

Then Koizumi returned to Tokyo.

The Japanese Prime Minister didn't have to be two-faced to back-pedal on our agreement. No, the Japs—whipped up into a fury by their media—broke the deal for him. Rather than accepting my apology, the vitriol directed at the DPRK in general and me in particular reached heights unheard of since the Pacific War. Some were so enraged by my admission that they called for armed conflict.

I hoped that the furor would subside once the remaining abductees returned to Japan. But still the Jap devils reneged despite my magnanimity. There was no restitution, no aid, nothing further to discuss. At the time, Japan had so much food—millions of tons of surplus rice—that they ran out of storage space. By their own admission and in complete disregard for any international humanitarian principles, they chose to destroy it rather than deliver it to the DPRK. They were happy to have the Korean people go hungry or even starve in order to punish some subordinates of mine who got carried away. The Japs got their wish, all right. The Korean people went hungry. Once again, I learned that the DPRK would have to stand alone.

In the following month came the last straw. In October 2002 the Bush administration once again raised nuclear suspicions, accusing north Korea of seeking to enrich uranium. An American diplomat even claimed that the DPRK had secretly admitted during negotiations to having a hidden nuclear weapon program. This was a very clever move on the part of the Yanks. I denied it, of course, but it seemed highly plausible on the heels of my public apology to Japan.

Bush then went further, openly imagining north Korea selling nuclear bombs to terrorist agents in other nations. It was absurd even given his own premises. After all, the past allegations of DPRK "terrorism"—Korean Air Flight 858—had supposedly been committed by Korean agents under Korean training with Korean equipment. Based on Bush's absurd claims, the Americans cut off the heavy fuel oil shipments promised under the Framework Agreement of 1994. In one move, Bush broke the promises of three past presidents, the agreement having been worked out between President Kim Il Sung and President Carter and signed by President Clinton.

It was absolutely true that the DPRK made missiles to sell to foreign countries. This was our right as a sovereign nation. It was also America's right—one which it engaged in on a daily basis, being the largest arms dealer in the world. But regarding nuclear materials, Korea's past, present and future policy was that we would never allow such transfers to any terrorist group. The American ego and hubris were downright staggering. The only nation that had ever used nuclear weapons was the United States. Every single American president had proclaimed that "all options are on the table" against whichever nation was their target that day. The indisputable meaning of this phrase is "we might strike you with nuclear weapons if we see fit."

But President Bush didn't need anyone to believe him, since his suspicions were a mere pretext. At this precise time, the same exact thing was happening regarding Iraq and Bush's claims of invisible "weapons of mass destruction." In complete disregard of international law, he declared that this gave the US the right to invade and conquer Iraq, a nation on the other side of the world that had nothing to do with the United States and had never threatened it.

Virtually every nation on earth has a military. Every military on earth has weaponry. If "suspecting"—which clearly includes "imagining"—the presence of some weapons is grounds for invasion, then literally no other country in the world was safe from US aggression, by America's own explicitly stated terms. And since the United States had no problem going to war without UN sanction, smaller nations had nowhere to appeal and were at America's mercy. This was the Bush Doctrine truly meant.

The rest of the scenario played out as expected. The IAEA convened a special session of its Board of Governors in January of 2003, adopting that resolution that the DPRK would be hit with even more sanctions if inspectors weren't allowed in. This time, the inspectors demanded to have a permanent presence on our soil. It was the same drama, played out over and over again. The plot hadn't changed—and it never would, unless I did something about it.

The Americans, the Japanese, the south Korean puppets: even during the Arduous March, none of them had ever really tried to help us. They had *never* been trying to help us. *They were trying to break us.* Everything that General Kim Il Sung had said nearly a century ago was right, and every warning he had given was now being proven true beyond dispute. The revolution had to be carried out on one's own responsibility and with one's own conviction, without asking for approval or directives from others. To suit the Korean situation, the Korean revolution needed to be carried out by Koreans themselves at all times.

It had been my lifelong conviction that the Korean nation was unique. By 2002, everyone else agreed. There was no denying the fact that the DPRK was unlike every other nation on the face of the earth. China and Russia couldn't be counted on at all. We were utterly alone in every way imaginable. It had always been that way and it would always be that way. The only true reliance was the self-reliance of the Juche idea.

I knew that Bush intended to invade Iran or the DPRK after he was done with Iraq. He'd said as much in his "Axis of Evil" speech. Never had the threat from the United States been so imminent and so palpable.

During those darkest of days, I thought back to 1991's "nuclear crisis." President Kim Il Sung had called in all his top military commanders, including myself, to an important meeting. "If the Yanks start a war against us," he asked, "will we be able to defeat them?"

The commanders' answers were unanimous if predictable: "We shall win!" "We have never lost a war!" "Every battle shall be a Korean victory!" "We will drive out the US imperialists from the peninsula, and unify Korea once and for all!" "No force on earth can defeat the glorious Korean People's Army, following the brilliant Juche tactics of the Great Leader Kim Il Sung!"

The General let out a deep breath. "But what if we do lose? What shall we do then?"

A Korean loss was unspeakable; discussing it in front of the Great Leader himself was unthinkable. So, wordless and thoughtless, the military men stood there completely unable to communicate anything.

That's when I stood up and clenched my fist. "What good is this world without Korea? Without the DPRK, there can be no Earth. If north Korea is going to disappear, I will smash the Earth to pieces!"

The Great Leader looked at me and smiled. "Those are words suitable for a Supreme Commander," he said. "That is the answer."

A decade on, it was still the answer. After World War II, south Korea had become a mad dog with the backing of the American lion and the Japanese monkey. The DPRK had sought an alliance with the Russian bear and the Chinese dragon—only to find those animals far too dangerous in their own right. I knew what I had to do in 2003: I had to turn Korea into a hedgehog.

A hedgehog's body is covered with sharp spines. Just as no ferocious animal can attack a hedgehog, so too would no one dare attack a similarly fortified country. The Korean hedgehog would have the sharpest and most powerful spines of all: nuclear missiles. If the DPRK was going to be constantly attacked, condemned and punished for a nuclear program, if we were going to suffer the consequences for it, then it made sense for us to reap the benefits of such a program as well.

So on January 10, 2003 I had the DPRK officially withdraw from the Treaty on the Non-Proliferation of Nuclear Weapons once and for all. I publicly declared that I felt obliged to possess a war deterrent—and everyone knew what I meant by a "war deterrent." I'd warned the US imperialists that I wouldn't tolerate the slightest violation of DPRK sovereignty. Now, I was demonstrating to the United States and its followers that my warning wasn't just empty talk.

The course of acquiring gaining nuclear technology wasn't smooth for north Korea. Foreign forces introduced obstructive maneuvers. Technological bottlenecks had to be overcome, with great difficulty. Yet none of these things stopped us. Soon, nothing on earth would ever be able to defeat the Korean people. Not hunger, not war, not the Jap devils—and most certainly not the US imperialists.

Throughout my life, all my decisions were characterized by attack: attacking the foes of the Great Leader; attacking the arts and remaking them; attacking the problems of construction; attacking the enemy when confronted. I always responded to an enemy's knife with a sword, and to his rifle with a cannon. It usually didn't need to come to violence; an enemy will inevitably back down if you simply yell louder than him. And never in history did anyone yell as loudly as I did on October 9, 2006, when the world heard the sound of north Korea's successful underground nuclear test.

Early in the twentieth century, Theodore Roosevelt had said that the Korean people were incapable of lifting a finger to defend their country. One hundred years later, no one could deny our military power as a nuclear state. As soon as the DPRK acquired atomic weapons, the discussion in America switched subjects. Talk went from "Should we invade Korea?" to "What should we do about Korea?"

Lest there be any confusion, I confirmed that America's worst fears had been realized. "If the US imperialists infringe even one inch upon the DPRK's territory," I announced, "if they threaten our right to exist in the slightest, we will wipe them out with a single blow." It might seem hyperbolic to believe that such a mighty force could be felled by one attack. Even as I said it, I myself was a bit skeptical that such a thing could be possible.

But then it happened to me.

In Korea we say that "your life flashes before your eyes" when you are about to die. I didn't have such an experience. All that happened to me one day was a great deal of pain, and then waking up to be told that I'd suffered a stroke. Of the event itself I remembered nothing. Fortunately, my superb memory spared me those details. All I remembered was lying in bed, feeling the weakest that I'd ever felt in my entire life.

No, my life never flashed before my eyes during my long recovery—but I took time to think back upon it with great care instead. I desperately wanted to be sure that I still remembered every event that mattered: My birth on Mt. Paektu. General Kim Il Sung's victory over imperialism, and his triumphant homecoming. The loss of my mother. My school years. Recreating and reviving the Korean arts. Bringing worldwide glory to the name of the Great Leader—and grieving when he passed. Leading the people through the Arduous March and coming out all the stronger for it.

As I looked back upon my life, I allowed myself to feel a most unsocialist emotion, one utterly at odds with the basis of my character: pride. My claims of military accomplishment are dismissed as propaganda by foreigners, since they tend to measure military success by the amount of blood that had been spilled. But I believe differently. True, it's difficult to win a victory with bullets flying by. Yet it is far more difficult to win a victory without any shots being fired and without any casualties—precisely what I'd done.

I realized that there were times when my choices had results that were less than ideal. If the outcomes seemed undesirable, I was confident that the alternatives would have been far worse. Despite decades of attack from every angle, despite hundreds of claims of collapse, Korea was still essentially what it has been for decades. It was still essentially the same nation that President Kim Il Sung had led, populated exclusively by the same people that had lived on the same land since the beginning of mankind.

Of course, I regretted many things that had occurred throughout my life. But when it came to my actions, my only regret was that I had but one life to give for my country.

For Korea.

Chapter 21

My Three Sons

I always lived my life on behalf of Korea, never believing that my personal affairs mattered to anyone in the slightest. I was never like the Western celebrities, obsessed with attention of any kind and willing to pay for it at the cost of my dignity. For me, the only important thing on any given day was whatever I happened to be doing for the masses, and the DPRK's newspapers and television programs accordingly reported on such issues alone. My personal life was never the subject of journalism. Because I was so hard-working, so skilled and so dedicated, it was difficult for many to perceive me as a real man. Yet a real man I certainly am. I catch cold, I get hungry, I go to the bathroom—and I fall in love.

I'd first crossed paths with her in 1956, when I was just a schoolboy. At the time, Hye Rim was engaged to my close friend's older brother. I was five years her junior, but at that age I might as well have been five generations younger. I had to indulge in my crush from afar because she was on her way to getting married. I wasn't the only one who thought about Hye Rim in that way, either. Everyone had eyes for her, but she only had eyes for her betrothed.

She was just nineteen then, a theatre student, but Hye Rim was well on her way to becoming a prominent actress. Though I'd already developed a sense for that sort of thing, it was still pretty obvious. I never met anyone who exuded grace like she did, from her sly smile and the demure way she walked to how her eyelashes fluttered when she spoke.

One of Hye Rim's first roles was in the enormously successful film *A Village by the Demarcation Line*. The Great Leader himself saw it and praised it, especially the character she played and her interpretation of the part. After that her career was unstoppable. In the subsequent years, Hye Rim blossomed into one of Korea's best known and most beloved actresses. It was no surprise, then, that I ran into her again in 1968 when I was working in the cinema.

I saw her on a film set, and from afar I noticed how everyone was in awe of her. I only rarely observed such behavior in the DPRK. In fact, I really only witnessed it with regard to General Kim Il Sung himself. I wanted to go speak with Hye Rim, very much so, but in fact I was nervous. At first I worried that she'd remember me as the awkward youngster I'd been and not register me as the fine sophisticated man that I'd become. Then I worried that she wouldn't remember me at all.

Get it together, I told myself. *You're a director. Direct this conversation to a successful conclusion!* I walked up to Hye Rim and was about to tap her on the shoulder when I had another embarrassing realization. I didn't know whether to call her by her professional name (which would imply that I'd never met her) or by her married name (which would tell her that I knew about her personal life). Not knowing what to do, I caught her attention by waving. "Hello! I'm Kim Jong Il."

She smiled that dazzling movie-star smile at me. "Are you Kim Jong Il the producer, or the Kim Jong Il who I knew years ago? Or do you not remember me?"

"Of course I remember you!" I blurted out, a bit too defensively. "The last time I saw you, you were about to get married."

She rolled her eyes. "I was young and foolish. I can't say that it was a mistake, for without him I would never have become a mother. But I can say that it's over, and I'm the better for it."

"You don't say..."

After that we were inseparable. It was easy for us to play out our relationship in plain sight, for she was an actress and I was shaping the film industry. She'd read over scripts with me, giving me useful advice based on her years of experience. I'd ask her opinion when I was casting different films. The two of us often went to scout potential shooting locations: a remote beach, a secluded resort, a charming forest. Once we even took a helicopter to Mt. Paektu, and when I looked at Hye Rim I understood what the Great Leader felt when he looked at my mother.

At the same time, we very much did have to hide what was going on. To begin with, Hye Rim's father was from the south, and her entire family had once lived there. Worse, he had been a landlord. In other words, her *songbun* wasn't up to the expected standards for a girlfriend of mine. If General Kim Il Sung found out—or worse, one of my personal enemies—then the consequences would be dire. The fact that she'd already been married and bore a child didn't help matters either. Nor that she was five years older than me.

Hye Rim had as much to lose from our relationship as I did. Her power in film meant that there were many jealous people seeking any opportunity they could to undermine her. Her career as an actress was heavily based on her image as the idealized young Korean wife. Any evidence to the contrary might destroy her, and actresses rarely received second chances to revive their careers.

It's easy for outsiders to claim that I was playing favorites with her when I cast her in my films, or that she was using me to help her career along. But neither was the case. We truly loved one another, and when you love someone who's a performer you see them at their most vulnerable—and therefore know just how powerful they can be on the screen. I put her in many roles and negotiated her membership into the Party. It wasn't very difficult to get such a prominent celebrity admitted, even considering her poor *songbun*.

Hye Rim and I moved in together about a year after getting reacquainted. I considered her to be my wife but of course we could never get married legally. The paper trail would be too damning, and the possibility of us keeping something like that a secret in Korea was nil. All that mattered was that I regarded her as the woman with whom I wanted to spend the rest of my life.

One thing led to another and nature inevitably took its course. One day I came home from another exhausting day at work and Hye Rim ran into me. She almost knocked me over, squeezing me as tightly as she could. I hugged her back, not knowing what was the matter. "Have you been crying?" I asked her.

"I have, I have," she said.

"Then why are you smiling like that? What happened?"

Without another word, she took my hand, kissed it and then placed it against her stomach. "Life happened," Hye Rim said.

It was the best news that I ever could have received, so I wanted to be absolutely certain that I wasn't misunderstanding her. "Are you pregnant?"

She nodded. "And it's going to be a boy."

I snickered. "You can't possibly know that."

"I can. I do. Mothers know these things. Just as your mother must have known."

She was right. Nine months later, on May 10, 1971, Kim Jong Nam was born at Pyongyang's Ponghwa Clinic. The entire hospital staff was sworn to the utmost secrecy. Given that the clinic was reserved for the Party leadership, I knew that I could count on their discretion. I was so elated that night that I honked my horn all the way home. My cheers of joy were so loud that I'm sure they could hear me all the way down at the DMZ. If I made some US imperialists anxious that night, so much the better!

I doted over Jong Nam almost as much as Hye Rim did. She had a large staff to assist her when I left for work every day. Though it was a far quieter life than she'd been used to, there was no doubt that motherhood suited her. She also had her family to keep her company if she got lonely, for we had to keep Jong Nam a secret too. Life was good.

In fact, life was too good. One day in early 1972 I was on an inspection tour with the Great Leader, attending to a radish farm. The sun was warm on my face and I thought everything was perfect. I was living the Korean dream that General Kim Il Sung had worked so hard to construct. "You look like you're glowing," he told me.

"Of course. I'm in the company of the sun!" I joked.

"It makes me happy to see you doing so well," he said. "But there's something you can do to make me even happier."

Instantly my grin faded. "What is it? I'll attend to it at once."

"You're thirty-one years old. It is far past time for you to get married."

"We've discussed this. My priority is to the Juche idea and to my work."

The Great Leader shook his head. "The most important thing you can do for the revolution is to give me a grandson so that our bloodline can continue."

It killed me to lie to him, but it could have *actually* killed me if I told him the truth. "I haven't met the right person. Soon."

"When?"

"Soon."

I kept putting him off as much as I could. Then, after about a year, the Great Leader brought me to his home. "Sit down," he told me. "I've been quite cross with you, but I've struck upon a solution."

I sat down, anxious. "What have I done?"

"Nothing," he told me. "That's the problem. You've not found a wife. You haven't even come close. So I found one for you."

"What? Where?"

"Her name is Kim Young Suk. She works in the Party office, and comes from a very good background. You've met her, I believe, and you've met her father."

"Yes," I said, "I know who she is. And I know her father."

"Splendid," he said. "Then it's settled."

"Of course."

Reader, I married her. Young Suk was perfectly sweet and nice, even pretty. I liked her as a person and she certainly did everything she could to win my heart—but that heart belonged to someone else. Unfortunately, now I had to tell that someone else what I'd done before she found out for herself. There was no easy way for me to do it.

One day I took Hye Rim to a beach we'd frequented when we first started seeing each another. We sat on a blanket and watched the water on the lake. After a while, I realized there was no good segue. No matter how many times I'd practiced telling her, it was going to be an excruciating conversation. "You know I love you," I said, "and you know that our family means everything to me. But you also know that I'm in a unique position in a country unlike any other."

She scowled. "Of course I know that."

"There's even talk of me officially being named successor, but I don't know if the Great Leader is completely comfortable with the idea. Since I'm his son, it would appear highly irregular even to our allies. That isn't the only issue between he and I, either. It's also been bothering him that I'd never married."

"Oh! This is wonderful! We can finally tell him about us and about Jong Nam. We won't have to hide anymore!"

"No, I can't. He'd realize that I've been less than truthful with him. Then there's absolutely no way that he'd name me to be his successor."

"Is it that important to you?" Hye Rim said. She had an edge to her voice that I rarely heard from anyone anymore.

"I can't afford to get in trouble."

"Nonsense. No one is going to harm the President's son!"

"But they might harm his wife. Or her family."

Hye Rim wiped a tear away from her cheek. She knew how things worked in the DPRK. "So what does this mean?"

I told her about what had transpired with the Great Leader and I told her about Kim Young Suk. I expected her to be angry, and I expected her to cry, and I expected her to—eventually—understand. But I didn't expect her to have virtually no reaction at all. Her face was as still as the lake's surface. "So the man that I think of as my husband—the man who refers to me as his wife—is married to another woman?"

"I'm sorry it had to be this way," I said, preparing to console her. But Hye Rim didn't need any consoling at all.

"I knew something was wrong and spent nights wondering what it could have been," she said. "Maybe something was going on with the Americans, I thought. Maybe there was a problem with the harvest this year, or with steel production. I even worried that you were sick and scared to tell me about it. I'm—no, I *was* an actress. Every conceivable drama ran through my head as a possibility. But this? This I never imagined."

"I'll still be home very frequently," I said, weakly.

"Did you hear what I said? I was an actress. Then I was your wife. And now I'm *nothing*. It's like I'm not even a person anymore. Can we go home now?"

"But we just got here."

"I want to go home. I'm tired. I've been tired for a while now. And now I finally know why. So thank you for that, my *husband*. At least I know what's the matter."

So I took her home. I knew things would change after I told her, but I didn't expect how they would change. It wasn't just that Hye Rim grew cold toward me. She grew cold toward everyone and everything. Actually, it wasn't that she was cold. It's as if she wasn't even there. The woman who had made a name for herself by portraying strength and intensity seemed as if she had no emotion left within her.

Raising Jong Nam increasingly fell on the staff and myself, and half the time I wasn't even there. The older my son grew, the trickier hiding him became. I was a bit obsessive about his health and always worried over every little scratch he acquired. If he had a fever, I'd be so unable to concentrate on anything else that my work suffered. Of course this meant that I made sure that he was regularly taken to see his doctoress.

One day when Jong Nam was about three years old, I cleared my schedule so that I could go with him to the doctoress. I was sitting in the room holding his hand as she listened to his heartbeat with the stethoscope. I paused for a moment, hearing some people walking down the hall. Listening closer, I was certain that I recognized one of the voices. "Who's coming down the hallway?" I asked the doctoress.

"I think there's an inspection tour," she said off-handedly. Then the doctoress realized that there was no reason for me to be in the hospital, especially with a young boy who looked a great deal like me. She must have thought I was going to kill her, because all the color trained out of her face.

As scared as the doctoress was, I was even more terrified. The inspection tour was being led by a prominent Party member, one with whom I'd had strong disagreements. Though we'd smoothed over the matter, I still didn't trust him. Nor could I liquidate him, because of his influence with the Great Leader. "Stall them!" I snapped at the doctoress, wondering what to do.

She nodded. "Right away." The doctoress got up and walked into the hall, shutting the door tightly behind her.

I kneeled down and smiled at my son. "Jong Nam, do you remember last week when you were hiding from Mother?"

He giggled. "Uh huh."

"It took her over an hour to find you, because you were being so quiet and you were such a good hider. Well, I need you to be even quieter and an even better hider now. Will you do that for me?"

He flashed me a sneaky little smile. "Can I get candy?" It was an unfortunate way to discover that my son had inherited the family's strategic thinking.

Now I could clearly hear the doctoress speaking with the tour; the enemy had reached the doorway. "You can have all the candy you want," I told Jong Nam. "You can eat candy until you get such a stomachache that I'll have to bring you back here to the hospital, all right?"

"All right!"

I picked him up and handed him to my secretary. "Quick, out the window!"

The man grabbed my son and was gone instantly. I stood there by myself for a second until I heard the door very very slowly creak open. "Of course you can take a look in here!" the doctoress said from the hallway, making sure that I could hear her.

The members of the tour poured into the room, one by one registering the fact that I was there and then staring at me with confusion. Acting nonchalant, I took the stethoscope in my hands and put it up against my heart, listening very carefully. Finally the Party member entered the room. "Comrade Jong Il!" he said, startled. "I didn't expect to see you here."

"There's no reason we can't both conduct an inspection!" I snapped, trying to sound offended.

"No," he agreed, "of course not."

"Well, everything seems to be in order in this room," I told the group.

The staff ushered everyone out as I exhaled a sigh of relief. When we returned home that afternoon, I got Jong Nam all the candy he could possibly eat and then I got him some more. To be honest, I didn't just give him the candy because he'd listened to me. I was happy to do it because I desperately wanted his upbringing to be different than mine had been, huddled hungry in the snows of Mt. Paektu. Yes, the kinship I'd felt with the guerrillas had been irreplaceable, but it had still been a extraordinarily difficult experience. As an adult, I worked as hard as possible to ensure that the Korean people could live a comfortable life, eating rice and meat soup every day and dwelling in tile-roofed houses. If I wanted this for the sons and daughters of Korea, of course I wanted the same for my own son.

I made it a point to have dinner with Jong Nam and Hye Rim as much as possible. The food really did taste better that way, I felt. I also tried to spent as much time with my son as I could because I sympathized with him. Due to our family's secret circumstances, he had to grow up alone. Yes, he had the staff, but he never interacted with any other children lest they run their mouths as children are prone to do. Not only was Hye Rim a target for my opponents, but so too was my heir. The thought of something happening to him sometimes kept me up at night.

One day in April of 1974, I sat Jong Nam on my lap. "Son, do you know what May 10 is?" I asked him.

"My birthday?"

"That's right!" I said. "Do you know what you want for your birthday? You can have anything you want, just ask for it."

He put his finger to his lips and thought. I couldn't blame him for not knowing what to say. Jong Nam had more toys than he could count, literally. I even let him watch as much television as he desired on any of his three sets. "I know!" he said. "I want to see the man on the TV!"

I thought he must have seen a film and wanted to meet the star. Of course that would be very easy to accomplish. "Which man? Will you show me, son?"

He took me by the hand and walked me over to a television. He turned it on and went through all the channels before giving up. "He's not there," Jong Nam said.

I sat down knee to knee with him on the floor. "You keep watching. The next time he's on the TV, you tell one of the staff. They'll tell me the man's name, and you'll get to meet him for your birthday."

"OK!" Jong Nam said, giving me a big hug.

Three days later, I came home and was called over by one of the cooks. "Comrade," he said, "I feel embarrassed to bother you with this, but Jong Nam was most insistent that I speak with you."

"Oh! Has he found the actor that he wants to meet?"

The poor cook didn't look at me, and spoke quietly. "Um, yes. Yes, he did."

"So? Who is it?"

"I'm not sure."

"You're not sure?" I rattled off some of the more prominent actors of the era, but the cook merely shook his head. "Well, what film was he in?"

"He wasn't in a film."

"So what program was he on? Was he a reporter of some kind?"

"No, comrade. I don't know his name because it wasn't given. He was playing a character."

I rolled my eyes. "So what was the character's name?"

"I can't tell. With all due respect, I turned away from the set as soon as I heard them speak. The program seemed to come from the village below."

"You mean south Korea."

The chef nodded. "I will discuss this in my criticism session this week."

"Very well," I said, dismissing the man. Against my better judgment, I permitted Jong Nam to watch foreign cartoons and children's shows. Now he was taken with some south Korean celebrity and wanted to meet him for his birthday. I'd promised my son anything he wanted—but this even I couldn't deliver. I was at a loss as to what to do, so I did what most fathers would in my situation: I ignored it and hoped that the kid would forget.

It was an unfortunate way to also discover that my son had inherited my prodigious memory. From that point on, it was the same thing every time I came home: "Have you spoken to him yet?" "Is he coming to my birthday?" "Should I get him a present too?"

I was Kim Jong Il, the incarnation of love and morality. Surely I could think of some way to solve this dilemma! I rejected the first option I thought of: kidnapping the performer and bringing him to the north. It would be too public and lead to too many questions, defeating the whole purpose of secrecy.

There were no good solutions, only poor ones. I was being defeated by a child—one who hadn't even tried to pit himself against me. Finally, I came up with a plan. It wasn't up to my usual standards, but it was pretty much the only plausible choice that I had. I acquired a stack of south Korean children's publications and had the chef pick out the performer for me. Then I called a meeting with my most trusted agent in our intelligence division. The man had done great work for me in the past, and intuitively knew to keep his mouth shut under any circumstances.

Late one night, he met me in my office. I sat down across from him at my desk and slid him the picture from the magazine. "This is a very popular children's entertainer in the south. We need to find someone who looks just like him in the north. Someone who looks so much like him that his own mother wouldn't be able to spot the difference."

The agent held up the picture and chuckled. "A brilliant plan, comrade. You've outdone yourself."

"But I haven't told you the plan yet."

He scowled. "Pardon?"

"What do you think the plan is?"

"I'm assuming that we abduct this performer and replace him with one of our own, making sure he encourages the children to see the north in a more positive light. A long-term project, perhaps, but the youngsters will be adults soon enough."

I paused. That actually *was* a brilliant plan, but I was focusing on my son at the moment. "I of course had been thinking along those lines, but we need something more immediate for now. Sort of a test run."

"Very well. What timeframe am I operating under?"

"He'll be putting on a show on May 10th."

"I'm assuming this will be televised?" asked the agent.

"No. It's for a party."

"A party?"

"Why does it matter what it's for?" I barked.

"My apologies, comrade. I ask because I need to understand what sort of scrutiny this performer will be under. That will affect how, say, we alter his appearance and how much we need to work on his dialect. Things like that."

"Very well. The audience will be one boy."

The agent blinked. "A boy?"

"Yes, there's a boy who is a member of my family and meeting this performer is his birthday wish."

"I...see. I'll make sure this task is accomplished right away."

The agent scoured the Korean countryside until he found a farmer who looked reasonably similar to the TV performer. Then he took him to a private studio to watch the show and practice mimicking it. The man was happy to do it, because I made sure that his family was very well taken care of.

As promised, Jong Nam had his birthday party on May 10. He unwrapped toy after toy, but I could tell that he was getting antsy for the big surprise that I'd promised him. Finally, a staff member gathered everyone's attention and introduced the "performer." I applauded heartily, watching Jong Nam's reaction out of the corner of my eye. Minutes after the man began his act, my son stood up and went to leave.

Calling for a pause in the show, I went after Jong Nam and caught up to him in the hall. "Where are you going? He came all the way from Seoul to be here with you on your birthday."

"That's not him."

"Of course it is. Just look!" I glanced back at the performer. Now *he*, I'm sure, really did see his whole life flash before his eyes in that moment. He didn't knew what the consequences would be if his fraud were exposed, but they surely wouldn't be pleasant.

Jong Nam stared me down. It was the same stare I'd seen his grandfather deliver to men who'd failed him. "You're a liar," my son said. "You make up stories and everyone in the house acts like they're true. Even Mother. Well, they're not true." Then he shrugged my hand off and walked to his room.

I turned around; everyone was waiting for me to tell them what to do. "Let's clean up," I muttered. "I'm going to go do some work in my office."

It was apparent that the secrecy regarding Jong Nam was untenable and would only get worse as he got older. It would be harder and harder to explain to him why he couldn't play with other children or go to school. Yet I didn't know what to do or even who I could speak to. In circumstances like this I always looked to the Great Leader for advice, but he was the main individual that I was keeping Jong Nam from.

There was only one person in all of the DPRK who'd appreciate the situation that I'd gotten myself in, only one person who I could trust and who knew the Great Leader almost as well as I did: my sister. Kim Kyong Hui was no longer the little girl I'd comforted when Mother had died. As befitting the daughter of two Mt. Paektu revolutionaries, she'd grown into a strong, opinionated woman in her own right. She held an important position in the Korean Democratic Women's Union where she had a reputation for being downright gruff. I arranged to have dinner with her in a restaurant in Pyongyang shortly after Jong Nam's birthday debacle.

Kyong Hui sat there chain-smoking cigarettes as I told her everything, not omitting a single important detail. Letting me get the story out, her reactions alternated between rolling her eyes and grunting with amusement. "So how do you think I should handle this?" I finally asked her.

"Look," she said, "Hye Rim is older than you. She's been married before, and has an older daughter. Do you understand that there is absolutely no possibility she would be acceptable as your wife, regardless of your position or whatever the circumstances might be?"

It sounded so much harsher when she said it, but of course it was all true. "Yes, I do understand that. That's why I've kept all this a secret."

"So get rid of her."

"Get rid of her? What do you mean?"

Kyong Hui shrugged, stamping out her cigarette. "Send her abroad. Moscow, Beijing. You can send her to New York, it doesn't matter. Just get rid of her."

"I can't ask her to leave!"

"From everything that you've told me, it sounds like she wants to leave. You said that she complains about being trapped in that house.

Fine. If she doesn't want to be trapped, she can go wherever she wants on the entire planet. Just make sure that she's provided for and then she won't be so miserable."

"But what about Jong Nam?"

"I'll raise him," Kyong Hui said.

"Really?"

"Of course. We'll have to get tutors and the like, but it'll be fine. I grew up without a mother. So did you, and we both turned out very well. It was difficult, but there wasn't anything that we could do about it."

I thought about what Kyong Hui was suggesting. It did seem like the best plan for all concerned. The more I mulled it over in my head, the more it seemed like a new life for Hye Rim was exactly what she needed to regain her vigor. But still, it was a lot to demand from her. "I can't do it," I finally said. "I can't bring myself to ask her to leave a household that we've both built together."

"Fine," Kyong Hui said. "I'll talk to her."

"You will?"

"Of course. This woman is nothing to me. And if you really want to know my opinion, she was never that good of an actress anyway."

My sister and I fixed a date for her to approach Hye Rim. I made it a point to work very late that night so that I could avoid any awkwardness. As the minutes passed by, I kept glancing at the phone in anticipation of Kyong Hui calling to tell me how the talk went. I truthfully had no way of predicting how Hye Rim would react. By this point, I couldn't predict anything Hye Rim did anymore. Finally, the call came through. "How did it go?" I asked my sister.

"Not all that well."

"Really?"

"Really," Kyong Hui said. "She absolutely refused. She said that she was Jong Nam's mother and that she was going to raise her own son. She insisted that she would never abandon him."

I winced. "I see."

"She also said something very curious."

"What? What else did she say?"

"She said that if you try something like this again, then she will personally bring Jong Nam to see President Kim Il Sung."

"Well, that's that," I told my sister. "Thank you very much."

"Wait, there's one more thing I need to tell you. It's just a feeling I have, but I know that there's truth behind it. Listen to me carefully: there's something not right with her."

"What do you mean, 'not right'?"

"I don't know. Like I said, it's just have an impression that she gave me. It was more how she spoke than anything that she said. It made me... uneasy."

On some level I knew what Kyong Hui meant, but I confess that I quickly put the thought out of my mind. That night I went to my other home to sleep, not wanting to deal with Hye Rim. It took a few days before I returned to my primary household. There I found Hye Rim in bed, even though it was late afternoon. "Are you sleeping?" I asked her.

"I've been tired lately," she said casually, as if her conversation with Kyong Hui had never happened. "I don't feel well."

I sat down on the bed beside her. She looked awful, like she was in the midst of some sickness. "How long has this been going on?"

"I don't know. Please, let me rest."

"All right," I said, leaving her be.

As the weeks went on, Hye Rim didn't seem to get any better. At the time I didn't register how ill she seemed or how long she'd been sick. I was too busy focusing on officially being named as successor. Once that happened, I breathed a little easier. In 1975, I knew it was finally time to let the Great Leader know about Hye Rim and Jong Nam. Though this was a deception of several years' standing, I actually wasn't worried in the slightest. On my side of the conversation I had the very thing that President Kim Il Sung wanted most: a grandson.

I went over to his villa one evening when I knew that his plans had been cancelled. I didn't even bother explaining why I was paying him a visit. "There's someone here I want you to meet," I told him. "Jong Nam, come in here!"

In walked little Jong Nam, wearing his best military-style uniform. The boy went up to the Great Leader and gave him the solemnest of salutes—just as we'd practiced at home. "It's a honor to meet you, General."

The General laughed at the scene. "It's an honor to meet you as well. What's your name?"

"I'm Kim Jong Nam."

The General looked up at me, wondering what this was about. "He's very cute. Do you remember when you were a little boy, and you kept General Shtykov waiting because I was sleeping?"

"I do," I said. "I must have looked quite like this."

He turned back to Jong Nam. "You did look like this when you were his age..."

"That's because this is my son," I told him. "Your grandson."

It was as I'd told him that I'd been born in Russia or that he'd been the one to start the Korean War. The statement was so absurd that President Kim Il Sung didn't know how to respond. Finally he came up with a plausible explanation. "You've adopted a boy?" he whispered under his breath.

"No. Jong Nam, why don't you have a seat on your grandfather's lap while I have a little talk with him."

"OK!" He quickly clambered right up, much to the Great Leader's amusement.

I then proceeded to tell President Kim Il Sung everything that had happened. He was livid at various points, and with good reason. But he was also a human being. Here was his very own flesh and blood, just as he'd been asking for for years. I'm not sure whether Jong Nam was doing it intentionally, but he was masterful at mollifying the Great Leader's anger. Anytime President Kim Il Sung seemed to start getting upset, Jong Nam would interrupt with a question: "What's your favorite candy?" "Why are some of your hairs gray?" "Can I see your glasses?" It was absolutely impossible for the Great Leader to remain annoyed under such circumstances.

From that day on, President Kim Il Sung doted over Jong Nam even more than I did. His anger with me was over within days—and with that, the biggest source of stress in my life was gone. It was a wonderful time for everyone in the family, but for one glaring exception: Hye Rim. She was always sick or tired or some combination of the two. She never truly complained about it, either. It was more the fact that she always seemed to be in bed whenever I came home. Unprompted, the staff confided to me that she spent virtually all her time in her room. She was clearly losing weight, and they were all quite worried about her.

The only I could do was make sure that she went to the doctor. Hye Rim was examined by the best medical minds that Korea had to offer. I even flew in a specialist from abroad, without disclosing to him who this woman was. Every physician said the same thing, virtually verbatim: "There is nothing physically wrong with her. She is suffering from depression and needs treatment immediately."

I wanted Hye Rim to get the greatest care for her condition that she could, so I sent her to a psychiatrist. But it didn't seem to make much of a difference. The face that had once lit up movie screens throughout the

DPRK was now fading away before my eyes. I was so concerned that I spoke to her therapist after he'd met with her a few times. "What's your professional opinion as to the best course of action?"

The man couldn't look at me directly. He played around with the papers on his desk and strumming his fingers awkwardly. "It's an atypical situation, Dear Leader."

"In what sense?"

"In terms of the patient's...preferred...treatment."

"Please be frank with me. Nothing you say will leave this room. You have my word."

He nodded, acknowledging that he believed my promise. "Understand that I wouldn't say this for another patient, and that I've never said anything like this before."

"Understood, understood. What is it?"

"It's my belief that the patient would be better treated...elsewhere."

"You don't mean another doctor or another hospital, do you?"

"No."

I clenched my jaw. "You mean abroad."

"I would never say such a thing! The Juche idea—"

I rolled my eyes as I interrupted him. "Where, then? Moscow?"

"...Yes."

"Will you tell her this?"

"With your permission I will."

"Actually, let me tell her." I wanted to face Hye Rim, so that she could see for herself how genuinely concerned I was. I drove straight home from the hospital, and of course found her in bed when I got back.

Hye Rim whimpered as I turned on the light in her bedroom. "Jong Il? Is that you? I was just resting a bit."

"I spoke to your doctor," I told her from the doorway.

She didn't move. "And? Obviously you want to tell me something."

"He feels that you would be better treated abroad. In Moscow, specifically."

"Of course he does."

"What?"

Hye Rim turned onto her side and leaned on her elbow. "This is what you wanted, isn't it? Me out of the country? Let me guess: I'll have a wonderful apartment. I'll be taken care of, and I'll never have anything to worry about."

"That doesn't sound so bad."

"It didn't sound so bad when your sister suggested it to me months ago, either."

"Hye Rim—"

She turned back around as she began to cry. "I'll go, I'll go. Living abroad can only be better than this. Because *this* isn't living."

And so she went, and I never saw her again. It was hard for Jong Nam to watch his mother leave, but even he could tell that she wasn't well. The circumstances of his birth still required keeping him a secret from Korean society, but now I allowed myself a bit more leeway. He couldn't go to school but I still found him some tutors that he enjoyed studying under. And sometimes, when things were quiet, I brought him into one of my offices. One such visit I picked him up and sat him at my desk, smiling with pride. "How does that feel?" I asked him.

"OK."

"That will be your desk when you grow up," I said.

As Jong Nam got older, the Great Leader grew increasingly enamored with the idea of grooming him to take my place one day. Then, one evening when we were having dinner, he let me know that he'd made an important decision. "Building an independent, self-reliant national economy," he recited, "does not mean building an economy in isolation. Yes, we are opposed to foreign economic domination, but we need not rule out international economic cooperation."

I paused. "That's from *On the Juche Idea*."

"Yes," he told me. "A great work. I'm well-acquainted with the author, you know."

At another time I might have laughed, but I wasn't in the mood for jokes. Clearly President Kim Il Sung was building up to something unpalatable. "And why do you bring it up?"

"The world Jong Nam grows up in will be very different than the one that you grew up in—let alone myself. Now that we've established the monolithic ideological system in Korea, we are increasingly engaging with the outside world. It would be good to have agents that we can completely trust, ones who know about foreign cultures."

"I agree..."

"So I think that Jong Nam should go to school abroad."

As a father I couldn't bear what the Great Leader was saying. But as an advocate of the Juche idea, and as a military genius, I knew that he was speaking the truth. He always was. Even during the Fatherland Liberation War, as the son of the Supreme Commander, I had still managed to have a childhood surrounded by friends of my age growing up in the same environment. Jong Nam, on the other hand, was growing up completely isolated. If he stayed in Korea, that was how he would have to remain. If his family background were uncovered, his upbringing would forestall him from following me into the leadership position. Better to keep his background a mystery than to have to deal with gossip as Jong Nam grew up in Pyongyang.

I was devastated when I eventually watched Jong Nam fly off to school in Geneva. Unfortunately, coming home to Kim Young Suk only made it worse. The two of us had nothing in common whatsoever. Our attempts to engage in conversation only ended up in awkwardness and tension. It wasn't her fault and it wasn't mine, but it was more than clear to both of us that our marriage existed in name only. Nothing of value was ever going to come out of it.

That's when I fell in love for the last time.

I was at a party for some army functionary when a very attractive woman sidled up to me. "Do you remember me, Dear Leader?" she smiled.

"Of course," I told her. "You're Ko Young Hee."

Her eyes opened wide with amazement. "How did you remember that?"

"Oh, it's simple. I remember the name and birthday of everyone that I've ever met."

She folded her arms, skeptical. "What's my birthday, then?"

"June 16. And out of deference to you being a beautiful lady, I won't mention the year." The reason I remembered her birthday was because it was exactly four months after my own. And the reason I remembered her at all was because she'd been a dancer with the Mansudae Art Troupe. She had stood out even among all those gorgeous women.

Unlike with Kim Young Suk, I had an enormous amount in common with Young Hee. We started spending many nights together watching movies—and then many mornings together discussing them. She reminded me of Hye Rim, but the Hye Rim that I'd first fallen in love with: vibrant and witty, someone with an enthusiasm that she brought to every conversation.

Any idea of us being an official couple was of course absolutely impossible. Forgetting my other two wives, Young Hee hadn't even been born in Korea. Though of Korean blood, she had grown up in Osaka, Japan.

When she was a girl, she'd moved back to the DPRK alongside many other Japanese-born Koreans. Her background was too tainted to ever put her forward publicly.

As the years passed, Young Hee gave me two more wonderful sons: Kim Jong Chul in 1981 and Kim Jong Un in 1983. But there still was never any doubt that Jong Nam would be my heir. The eldest son is always the successor.

Eventually Jong Nam graduated from school and returned to Korea. I'd worried when he had been away, yet I remained worried when he returned. He often spoke at length about all the "international" friends that he'd made while abroad. This made me highly suspicious. If he regarded these foreigners as useful contacts, if they were insights into possible allied countries, then it was wonderful. But if he regarded friendship with outsiders as some sort of exciting pursuit, then I had a big problem on my hands. I did my best to try and put such concerns aside. I told myself that I was just being a perfectionist since I cared so much about Korea's future. When all was said and done, Jong Nam was still heir to the bloodline of Mt. Paektu.

There were many positive characteristics my son displayed as he became a young man. He was very bright and very sociable, far more like his grandfather in this regard than like myself. And, like his father and both of his paternal grandparents, Jong Nam loved guns. On more than one occasion I heard talk of him getting drunk and shooting up the ceiling at either the Koryo Hotel bar or Pyongyang's other nightspot. No one ever got hurt, so I let it slide. After all, I didn't *want* a son who was afraid to pull a trigger. He was going to be inheriting my Songun politics!

Jong Nam soon got married and had children as well, which delighted me. His political career, meanwhile, following a similar path to my own. I got him a position in the Party's Propaganda and Agitation Bureau, where he excelled. Still, I knew he longed to work on the international scene, so this is where I eventually put him. In many ways, Korea is a unique nation. But, like every other country in the world, the DPRK sometimes engages in activities that are "unsavory" and best not discussed. It is with these types of matters that I entrusted Jong Nam, fulfilling the Great Leader's purpose of sending him to school abroad.

In early May 2001 I received word from my contacts in Tokyo that something had gone terribly wrong with one of Jong Nam's trips to Japan. I was receiving all the information as soon as it was occurring—but so was the international media. The debacle had immediately turned very public, which made it that much more embarrassing.

Jong Nam and his family had been intercepted by Japanese immigration authorities on suspicion of their fake Dominican Republic passports. His was under the name "Pang Xiong," Chinese for "fat bear"—a too-clever reference to his portly carriage. The Japs had asked him questions for an hour before he admitted to being my son. Thankfully, he lied to them about the purpose of his trip and said he was there to visit Tokyo Disneyland. In fact, I knew he'd been there to collect money for a covert weapons shipment.

I suspected that the Japanese knew why he was in Japan and I further suspected that someone had tipped them off. But thankfully they took his reasoning at face value, possibly to protect their sources. Or maybe they thought his public humiliation would be punishment enough. In either case, it surely made him aware that they were on to him and would be watching him in the future.

Behind the scenes, I was told, the Japs were feverishly arguing over how to handle the situation. The police wanted a long, full interrogation, as police are wont to do. The diplomats wanted to merely expel him from the country and avoid an international incident, as diplomats are wont to do. Thankfully, the diplomats carried the day. On May 4, Jong Nam and his family were expelled to Beijing with no charges, explicitly so as to prevent conflict with the DPRK.

It was when they got to China that I finally managed to get my son on the phone. "How are you?" I asked. "How is everyone?"

"We're fine," he said. "Don't worry, they took very good care of us. We were treated with the utmost respect."

"I don't trust those Jap bastards for a second."

"It's not like it was back in the day."

"It's exactly like it was back in the day!" I yelled. "They didn't get any information out of you, did they?"

"No," he said, "they didn't."

"So why did you tell them that you were going to Disneyland?"

Jong Nam sighed. I could tell he was tired and exasperated. He'd always had a short fuse, even as a boy. "I had to tell them something!"

"Yes, I understand. But why Disneyland?"

"It was a joke."

"A joke? Going to Disneyland is a joke?"

"Yes. Like in the commercials. You know, 'What are you going to do now? I'm going to Disneyland!' The Americans say it."

"I see." And I did see. The fact that Western journalists took his Disneyland joke at face value spoke to how little they understood the supposedly humorless DPRK. It also showed how quick they were to repeat what they are told, verbatim, by those in power. Neither of these things surprised nor concerned me. What did bother me was this: My own son was making jokes about America to the Japanese devils, when he should have been making jokes about America and Japan to the Korean people. It seemed as if his entire frame of reference was foreign. This time, I too gave him the benefit of the doubt. Again.

It was only after the DPRK's successful nuclear test in 2006 that I understood the truth of the situation. Everyone in the Party was in a celebratory mood. My Songun politics had been vindicated beyond dispute. No longer would Korea have to live under threat of nuclear blackmail, wondering if one night the US imperialists would decide that they'd had enough and choose to rain death upon us once again. Our nuclear capacity was the greatest possible impediment to a military strike, an urgently needed step toward ensuring that war would never again break out on the Korean peninsula.

Yet the only one who seemed to be less than enthusiastic was Jong Nam. He applauded at the meetings like everyone else, but he seemed to be upset by the whole thing. The evening of the announcement I spoke to him at my home, assuming that something else had to be the matter. "What's wrong?" I asked him. "This is a wonderful day for Korea!"

He shook his head. "It's not. We need to abolish nuclear weapons, all nuclear weapons, lest we destroy mankind."

"...What?"

Jong Nam looked right at me, and I realized I didn't know this man who was peering at me from behind foreign designer glasses. "I know you don't agree," he said.

"As a matter of fact, I don't!"

"But how do you think all this is going to end?"

"It's going to end in an independent Korea whose sovereignty is respected!" I said, trying not to raise my voice—and trying to remember the last time that someone had spoken to me like that.

"I've talked with you before about how we need to make changes."

"I thought you meant changes in allocation between heavy and light industry. I didn't realize you meant throwing our whole system away!"

"I'm not speaking of throwing our system away," he insisted. "You yourself always cite how much the weather contributed to the famine. Doesn't that imply protecting the environment, in order to lessen the impact of natural disasters? Doesn't that imply a need to take action to protect the ecosystem?"

"The *ecosystem?*" I laughed a bit. I'd never heard the word spoken in Korea before.

"Look," he said, "I've traveled with you to Beijing on more than one occasion, many years apart. You've seen what happened there. You've seen the growth, the progress. We can follow their lead."

"Yes," I said, "I've seen what happened there. I've seen the complete collapse of the moral order! I've seen Chairman Mao become regarded as an embarrassment instead of the liberator of the Chinese people. We could never implement the Chinese reforms. We do not have a large agricultural sector in Korea, as the Chinese did. But regardless of that, *we are not China*. We are Korea! Any 'change' needs to be change in our way, in line with the Juche idea put forth by the Great Leader."

"We need more openness," he asserted.

"If you want openness, open a window!"

That's when it hit me: My own son had been infected with flunkey-ism. He wanted to put other foreign powers and their methods above that of Korea and Korean principles. He wanted to disregard what President Kim Il Sung had established and what I'd upheld. Jong Nam didn't want to succeed me. He wanted to *oppose* me, but he was going to wait until I'd died to do so. This wasn't simply him disagreeing with me. No, this was him taunting me with what would happen after I was gone.

He forgot one thing: I wasn't gone yet.

It wasn't inevitable that the eldest son be the next leader, just as it hadn't been inevitable with me. The fact that I was the Great Leader's son had been an important factor, to be sure. Who else would be as loyal and supportive? Who else could be trusted to carry forth a father's vision than his own son? But I hadn't been the only one carrying the blood of President Kim Il Sung. My uncle had been under consideration at one point, and others were a possibility. It was my loyalty and my skill which had carried the day, not merely the circumstances of my birth. It was precisely *loyalty* that Jong Nam was lacking: loyalty to me, loyalty to Korea and, most importantly, loyalty to the Great Leader and the Juche idea. Naming some other successor than Jong Nam would prove that I too had earned the leadership role and didn't simply "inherit" it.

My other choices for succession were very limited. My second son, Kim Jong Chul, was an impossible option. I suspected he had some sort of hormonal imbalance, for he was so effeminate that he was like a girl. I couldn't very well leave a military-first society in the hands of a sissy.

That left my youngest son, Kim Jong Un. And he was young, very young. At first I thought that meant he too would be unacceptable. But the more I thought about it, the more I warmed to the idea. My own youth had been used against me when I'd been named successor. And as General, Kim Il Sung had been so young that many in the south claimed that he must've been an impostor who merely adopted the actual Kim Il Sung's name.

Jong Un wouldn't be alone when he took over. Kim Kyong Hui would make sure to advise Jong Un and help in the transition of power after I was gone. My sister had seen everything I had, shared the exact same bloodline and was even more loyal to the Juche idea than I—if such a thing were possible. When her own daughter insisted on having a boyfriend with an unsuitable *songbun*, Kyong Hui had driven the poor girl to suicide. She would certainly make sure that my youngest son stayed the course.

But there would be more than simply Kyong Hui supporting Kim Jong Un. The entire DPRK leadership was there for one reason. They weren't there because they were the most experienced; many had worked for far longer. They weren't there because they were the most intelligent; many of our foes were admittedly extremely crafty. The one attribute that maintained them in their positions was their loyalty, both to myself personally and to my Songun politics.

Not being Korean, some in the West are unable to comprehend the ineffable beauty of the Juche idea. They assume that our Party officials simply repeat things that they don't believe for the sake of retaining power. They forget that the leaders of the WPK are constantly watching one another for signs of faithlessness. Faking allegiance under such scrutiny for such extended lengths of time would be absolutely impossible even for the best of actors. These men and women aren't cynical power-seekers. No, they are true believers. I knew that they would never be agents of change.

I considered the worst of scenarios. I supposed that, for whatever reason, some Party official changed his point of view. He no longer regarded the Juche idea as the most impressive concept ever put forward by the greatest leader of our time or any other. How would this play out? If he voiced such concerns publicly, then he would immediately be removed from any position of power.

Then I took things one step further. What if he was discreet and quietly persuaded some of his comrades to join with him? There was no need to speculate as to what would happen then. This sort of thing has occurred in Korea before. A group of Party members who were opposed to the current leadership had gathered together—the definition of a faction. Everyone in the DPRK knows how we handle factions: we liquidate them. The Party officials know it particularly well, as they'd all taken part in such purges themselves. For any Party member to join a faction is to endanger every single one of their family members, friends and associates. All would put under suspicion, and there's little room for suspicious activity in a nation dedicated to a monolithic ideological system. *Those who can effect change never would, and those who would effect change never could.*

The Great Leader said that we must "desiccate the seedlings of counterrevolution and pull them out by their roots," that "class enemies must be actively exterminated to three generations." So when we punish wrongdoers, we don't simply punish the individual. We do not believe in individualism. We agree with those US politicians who say that "the family is the basic unit of society." But unlike the hypocritical Americans, we apply this idea thoroughly, sincerely and consistently. Our punishment comes via *yongoje*, the "family purge." When someone is identified as a hostile element, it is three generations of his family that are punished. This is why the Korean people say, "Misspeak once, kill thrice."

As we have construction "in our way" and books "in our way," so too do we have justice "in our way." There are no "show trials," where the criminal is publicly paraded, accused and denounced in front of his entire country. Nor is there "sentencing" or "charges" or "time served"; these are all bourgeois ideas. We don't tell class enemies what they've done wrong, giving them an opportunity to feign innocence. Instead, we take the class enemy and his family in the middle of the night and send them to our "enlightenment centers." No one else knows what has happened to them—and no one ever asks. As far as they're concerned, a social problem has miraculously vanished overnight.

At any given time, there are well over one hundred thousand class enemies in these enlightenment centers. We never refer to the inhabitants as "political prisoners"; therefore, we don't have any "political prison camps" or "concentration camps." What we have are villages under the control of armed guards, surrounded by barbed-wire and/or electrified fences.

In the DPRK, we believe that labor is the best mechanism for rehabilitation and for instilling Juche consciousness. Our class enemies are encouraged to work as much as possible to achieve enlightenment in the shortest time possible. They work in mines, they farm, they manufacture. There is no shortage of possibilities for them to give back to the nation that they've betrayed. We provide them with food—a handful of corn or so per day—and with shelter, an undeserved kindness that must be also repaid in labor. Except for the national holidays, they work for at least twelve hours every day until they work off their debt to society. Should one commit suicide, then their family members must fulfill their work quota. Again: the family is the basic unit of society.

THE REEDUCATED
Class enemies
Collaborators
Anti-revolutionaries
State opponents
Defectors

Increasingly, these enlightenment centers are being used as a pretext to label the DPRK as a "human rights abuser." We do believe in human rights in Korea—but only "in our way." Our enlightenment centers are, as the Great Leader put it, "a legitimate measure to protect the country from impure elements who have attempted to destroy our socialist system." Juche human rights do not include the "right" to oppose socialism or to violate the interests of the people. No nation, even the United States, recognizes a "right" to treason. Rights are not granted irrespective of the state and society, but are rather guaranteed by the state and society. Imprisoning hostile elements without trial in isolated locations means that we are *protecting* human rights, not violating them.

Since any rights are only guaranteed by sovereign states, any talk of "human rights" must begin with national sovereignty. For a nation to interfere in another's internal affairs, to infringe on its sovereignty, to impose its will and not respect the other's system, is itself a violation of human rights. The US constitution enshrines the "right" to bear arms. The

DPRK constitution protects the right to housing and health care—two rights that American bourgeois politics do not recognize. That doesn't give DPRK the right to impose our values on the United States. Nor does America have the right to impose its values on Korea simply because it's stronger. Might doesn't make rights.

Our philosophy is clear and explicit in north Korea. Our beliefs are no secret. We discuss them so constantly and openly that the West dismisses them as propaganda. I have personally and repeatedly put into writing our perspective that the most valuable thing for a man's survival as a social being, his sociopolitical life, is conferred to him by the Leader—and what is given by the Leader can also be taken away.

Anyone who sets himself against his nation, his mother Party, or his Leader has thereby rendered his sociopolitical life worthless. Such an abnormal, inferior man lives counter to his intrinsic nature and is no better than an animal. This is why any disagreement over "human rights" is irrelevant when it comes to class enemies. *Class enemies, the enemies of the Leader, are not human beings.*

This is not simply a philosophical perspective. This has been the reaction of anyone who has ever seen one of our enlightenment centers. Once they've been removed from the broader society, our class enemies reveal their true beastly nature. They eat anything they can get their hands on: weeds, leaves or rats. They dress in filthy rags, even in winter, and fail to bathe for months or even years at a time.

After years of work, the class enemies physically transform into animals. Their backs grow hunched. They lose toes and fingers, or even hands and limbs, just like lizards. If a work-unit misses its quota, they leap upon one another like wild dogs. They inform on their neighbors—delivering them to certain public execution—simply for the reward of one additional meal. (Though this, of course, is something even an animal wouldn't do.) This is the life that their choices have brought them, in the glorious Juche paradise of the DPRK.

It is true that my criticism of the US imperialists is unremitting, and it might be easy to reject my perspective as biased and inaccurate. But facts are much harder to dismiss. In the relationship between the United States and the DPRK, nowhere are the facts more damning than with regard to human rights. All the American presidents knew what was happening in Korea, and none of them ever did anything—and none of them ever will.

Harry Truman said nothing when his mentor FDR brought concentration camps to American soil, something now regarded more as a historical footnote than as a source of horror.

Dwight Eisenhower personally oversaw the liberation of the Nazi camps, ordering them to be documented as much as possible so that history would never forget. But about the Korean camps he said not a word.

John F. Kennedy stared down the Soviet Union and brought the world to the brink of nuclear war over what was happening in Cuba. But over the Korean incarcerations he challenged no one.

Lyndon Johnson was prepared to fight the DPRK for the sake of one ship, *Pueblo*, and her crew of eighty-two Americans. But about hundreds of thousands of Koreans he did nothing.

Richard Nixon established relations with Chairman Mao, guiding China into a more liberal direction. But he never engaged with the far-weaker President Kim Il Sung, and never asked Mao to engage either.

Gerald Ford almost went to war with Korea because of a tree. Because of a tree! He made sure that it was struck down, while doing nothing about dismantling hundreds of yards of barbed wire.

Jimmy Carter personally visited Pyongyang several times, and based his entire post-Presidential career on advocating for human rights. But when it came to the DPRK, he kept silent.

Ronald Reagan told Gorbachev to tear down the Berlin Wall, and wore a bulletproof vest as he visited the Bergen-Belsen camp. But he never spoke of tearing down the DMZ, or freeing those on the other side.

George H. W. Bush had been director of the CIA, privy to more intelligence than any other President before or since. But he never made any of his information public, nor did he act on it in private.

Bill Clinton sent his Secretary of State to Pyongyang. As a child, the Jewish-born Albright fled the Nazi occupation of her native Czechoslovakia. But rather than helping the children in the Korean camps, she raised a glass of wine in my honor.

George W. Bush included north Korea in his imaginary axis of evil and publicly said that he loathed me. But his primary concern was that we were seeking nuclear weapons, not interning hundreds of thousands of our people.

Barack Obama won a Nobel Peace Prize after a campaign touting the audacity of hope. Yet for the prisoners in our camps, there is no hope possible. Should north Korea ever be invaded, all of them will be immediately executed before the camps are razed to the ground. The hostile elements know this with every fiber of their being, because the guards constantly and explicitly remind them of this fact.

There's a Western expression that "all it takes for evil to triumph is for good men to do nothing." What an absurdity! A "good man" will always at least *attempt* to do something, by definition. It can't be said that the American people themselves don't care. They do care—so much so that the DPRK is constantly discussed in the news. No other foreign leader is as much the subject of American curiosity as myself. By contrast, how many in the United States can name the current President of south Korea? How many can name *any* President of south Korea? Yes, the Americans care—but they care about the spectacle, and not about the people.

Dear reader, while students in your schools wring their hands, wondering how the Nazi camps could have been allowed to happen, children in our enlightenment centers are being clubbed to death in front of their peers for stealing grains of corn. While ladies in your stores complain about the fit of their clothes, women in our enlightenment centers are having their legs amputated for submitting to rape—and then using tires to push themselves to report to work. While men in your offices stress over their workload, men in our enlightenment centers are sent to mines that they will knowingly die in, literally never seeing sunlight again. There's nothing you can do about it, and there's nothing that your leaders—or *any* world leaders—*will* do about it.

Let me be perfectly clear: North Korea is no joke, and I am no buffoon. While you've been reading this book, laughing and rolling your eyes, twenty-four million people have been living their lives with every moment of their day accounted for and accountable to the government for every action they take. They will never be granted any sort of "human rights"—*and they know it.* They know that no one is coming to their aid. They understand that the only people with the power to help them are the very ones guaranteed to never do so.

Such is the greatness of the Juche idea.

Our philosophy is a source of pride, not shame. We advocate it constantly and explicitly. In fact, nothing fills me with as much glee as recalling what I've done with the DPRK and its people. So take a second and glance at this book's cover once again. Look at my beaming face, the same face that everyone in my country sees on their wall every single day. I smile whenever I think of north Korea.

Do you?

KIM JONG IL'S
OFFICIAL ENEMIES LIST

Justin Esch	Adrian Hong
Ed Berlen	Harjit Jaiswal
George W. Bush	Justin Kazmark
Dave Cirilli	Nikita Khrushchev
Molly Crabapple	Kickstarter
John Durant	Kim Young Sam
Michael Fazio	Anne Krechmer
FEE	Casey Lartigue
Jesse Forgione	Maddox
Simon Franek	Allison Oldak
John Girgus	Mary Pilon
Mikhail Gorbachev	Stephie Russell
Chuck Grimmett	Todd Seavey
Michael Harriot	Cole Stryker
Ryan Holiday	The Trollboard

Made in United States
Orlando, FL
24 April 2023

32408725R00232